NEWSREEL:
Documentary Filmmaking on the American Left

This is a volume in the Arno Press Collection

DISSERTATIONS ON FILM 1980

Advisory Editor
Garth S. Jowett

*See last pages of this volume
for a complete list of titles*

NEWSREEL:
Documentary Filmmaking on the American Left

Bill Nichols

ARNO PRESS
A New York Times Company
New York • 1980

Editorial Supervision: Steve Bedney

First publication in book form 1980 by Arno Press Inc.

Copyright © 1977 by Bill Nichols

Reproduced by permission of Bill Nichols

DISSERTATIONS ON FILM 1980
ISBN for complete set: 0-405-12900-9
See last pages of this volume for titles.

Publisher's Note: The text in this book has been reproduced from the best available copy.

Manufactured in the United States of America

Library of Congress Cataloging in Publication Data

Nichols, Bill.
  Newsreel.

  (Dissertations on film 1980)
  Originally presented as the author's thesis, University of California at Los Angeles, 1975.
  Bibliography: p.
  1. Newsreel (Firm) 2. Moving-pictures, Documentary--United States--History and criticism.
I. Title. II. Series.
PN1999.N4N5   791.43'53   79-6681
ISBN 0-405-12914-9

NEWSREEL: DOCUMENTARY FILMMAKING

ON THE AMERICAN LEFT

Bill Nichols

© 1977 Bill Nichols

TABLE OF CONTENTS

CHAPTER

I. TERMS AND METHODS 1

II. TRANSITION: FROM NEW YORK NEWSREEL TO
    THIRD WORLD NEWSREEL 20

III. THIRD WORLD NEWSREEL'S FILMS 41

IV. SAN FRANCISCO NEWSREEL 183

V. SAN FRANCISCO NEWSREEL'S FILMS 224

VI. CONCLUSION 251

SOURCES CONSULTED 308

ABSTRACT OF THE DISSERTATION

Newsreel: Documentary Filmmaking

on the American Left (1971-1975)

by

William James Nichols

Doctor of Philosophy in Theatre Arts

University of California, Los Angeles, 1978

Professor Frank LaTourette, Chairman

The inner dynamics of the New Left and its contemporary successor --an amalgam of political groups centering around Third World peoples and their struggles--have been ill-examined. The political strategies and tactics for the use of the film medium in revolutionary struggle have been long debated but remain open to considerable disagreement. The theoretical foundations for rigorous scrutiny of the formal qualities of the documentary film form (and, their political implications) have been scarcely examined at all. This study attempts to probe aspects of these three areas by means of an intensive examination of the work of the political filmmaking collective, Newsreel, during the years 1971-1975.

Information was gathered through standard library research and also through interviews with present and former members of Newsreel in New York and San Francisco. (Other individuals, in other locations, were also interviewed but the study is restricted to these two centers, the only ones where both filmmaking and film distribution were consistently carried out.) In addition, all available films made or distributed by Newsreel during the period 1971-1975 were screened and, in many instances, the sound tracks recorded.

The analysis is based upon marxism, semiology, systems theory, and aspects of structuralism. It attempts to examine the internal structure and political practice of Newsreel in relation to its historical context (the American left in its post-New Left period). The study also examines Newsreel's films both in terms of their political analysis and in their use as organizing tools, and in terms of their formal structure and its relationship to a broader, politically motivated, theory of documentary film.

The study finds that Newsreel has retained a barometric relationship to the Left, most obviously in its current emphasis upon Third World membership and orientation, but also in the nature of the films made or distributed by Newsreel. It finds that Newsreel continues to be a major source of political films otherwise unattainable which are distributed in a manner that promotes their use in Third World communities and among working class people. These films address many crucial political questions, especially institutional oppression and national liberation, and provide valuable information while also revealing complex problems about the political implications of various formal and stylistic strategies. The study attempts to inaugurate a more rigorous examination of the theoretical aspects of political filmmaking and the documentary form, and concludes that such work will need to be an essential component of the development of those political filmmaking groups that assume a leadership role within the cultural dimension of the American Left.

Addendum: 1980

Certain problems remain embedded in the dissertation which cannot be corrected within Arno Press' publication deadlines. These are in addition to possible errors of fact or circumstance of which I remain unaware but that others may note. They are problems of approach, adequacy and context, large problems about which I would like to make a few comments.

First, I should stress that the importance of work in the general area of politics and film remains as vital now as when I first undertook to chronicle the history of Newsreel in 1970 for my M. A. degree at U. C. L. A. The history of the left struggle is all too frequently a forgotten history, when it is not a repressed one. Works like Richard O. Boyer and Herbert M. Morais' Labor's Untold Story bring alive tales of conflict, struggle, victory and defeat which more mainstream works ignore or underemphasize or denature into the timid mythologies of parliamentary democracy. And what has been true of the working class struggle has also been true of the women's movement, black liberation, gay liberation, and third world struggles everywhere. These and all other struggles to overcome exploitation and the systematic oppression that inevitably accompanies it deserve as full and rich a documentation as that accorded the lives of the heroes of bourgeois ideology--presidents, generals, inventors and the titans of commerce. There remains much to be done along these lines in the narrow realm of film alone and hopefully others will find the effort recorded here a modest but instructive example of both the importance of this work in general and the pitfalls that lie along the way.

These pitfalls partly derive from the lack of a highly developed body of previous work and partly from the contemporaneousness of this particular study. One must often begin from scratch, with few guides and many misleading signs. The letter printed in <u>Screen</u>, 17, 1 (Spring 1976) indicates some of the problems I encountered in being the first person to write about the Film and Photo League after a period of some twenty years: the relative importance of the printed sources I found, and their reliability, could not be readily ascertained, nor did I have adequate resources to conduct the more prolonged research actually required. This problem reappears in studying Newsreel. The members published few descriptions of their work or statements of their positions. And those that were published seldom represented the thoughts of all; they may not have even represented the thoughts of the majority.

Choosing for one's approach the study of a contemporary leftist filmmaking group creates specific problems. An essential aid in overcoming these problems is the oral history. Much of the material presented here depends heavily upon interviews with members and ex-members of Newsreel. (At the time I conducted them, Newsreel members sought annonymity; hence they are identified only by first name.) And yet this is also an area of deficiency. I lacked the financial support necessary to conduct extensive interviews so that the adequacy with which a comprehensive perspective on Newsreel has been achieved remains moot. There is certainly room for additional work. Those who use this study as a basis for their research are strongly cautioned against taking it as gospel; it can more profitably be considered a preliminary report from which more definitive studies can benefit. (I have tried to compensate for the inadequacies I had to accept in this area by arranging to see all the films distributed by Newsreel during the period of research (1970-74): hopefully the comments made regarding documentary form and political effect benefit from this thoroughness.)

Finally, there remains the problem of context. In terms of content, it was simply not possible within the financial and temporal constraints established by the U. C. L. A. doctorate program to carry out background research on all the other left filmmakers or left filmmaking groups during the 1960s and early 1970s. These groups, like New Day, Kartemquin or Cine Manifest, stand in need of historical study as well, as do groups in other countries. Likewise, it has not always proved possible to place Newsreel's films in relation to the work of other left filmmakers in the United States and elsewhere. These are contextual limitations that are part of choosing a specific focus; they, too, suggest numerous areas for further research.

In terms of form, the context of writing a dissertation, as a graduate student, for professors and an institutional system that can be loosely described as non-political, poses problems of its own. An enormous pressure exists, even when not consciously admitted, to write what others want to hear, to take no unnecessary risks, to demonstrate competence but not commitment. This is an enormous problem and I feel it has proven one I have not successfully overcome here. The text often displays a vacillatory tone, passive constructions and a judgmentalness toward weaknesses in Newsreel's work unbalanced by a solid defense of its achievements. Perhaps one useful recourse is to show drafts of material like this to politically engaged individuals, groups or publications and not exclusively to one's academic supervisors. Such feedback can prove invaluable and provide a necessary, galvanizing, reminder of for whom such work should be primarily dedicated. I regret that I did not do this to a greater degree. The feedback and criticism I have received from Newsreel members and Jump Cut editors, for example, has been of enormous value and I only wish the timing had been such that this interaction could have played a more active role in the final shape of the dissertation.

These problems can all be overcome. Hopefully this account of them will be helpful to others. Certainly, they are not problems of sufficient magnitude to act as a serious deterrent, not in the face of the urgent necessity to continue the struggle for liberation from all exploitation and oppression, and to record the history of that struggle whenever and wherever we have the opportunity to do so.

Chapter One

TERMS AND METHODS

From 1971 until Spring, 1972, New York Newsreel was located at 322 Seventh Avenue. The address was in the Garment District, the office a slot in a ramshackle, seven-story building whose granite facade retained traces of its original gray only above the fifth floor. At one time the building had been subdivided into garment makers' sweatshops. The sweatshops were gone now, replaced by a smattering of businesses for whom appearances were not essential.

Newsreel occupied an entire floor but even after two years it did not look as if the occupation were going well. The small, hard-to-open windows proudly wore their year-round coat of foggy gray soot. Three flourescent light fixtures hung down from the ceiling casting a harshly pure white light through the middle of the office. The floor was done in hard wood that had lost its elegance: it not only creaked and groaned but gave--dryly, threateningly--when walked upon. Near the rear of the large open core of the office was a bathroom whose frosted glass window looked out on a ten foot wide air shaft. A constant gurgle of running water came from the toilet's reservoir. Newsreel's rent included utilities.

The large central area was used as a meeting space and screening room. A dozen folding chairs had been set across the floor in front of a large, slightly damaged silver screen. Against the make-shift partition at the far end stood racks of films in no particular order. Some were upright; others were stacked like piles of loose change along the floor and bottom shelf. Behind the partition was a narrow storage area where projectors, editing, and some filmmaking equipment were kept. Latticed across the bulkier, more expensive equipment were leftover pieces of wood, panelling, and sections of old partitions and fixtures whose fate had not been determined. Robert, my guide, said they planned to convert this area into an editing room eventually.

The Newsreel office was a quiet place in the early spring of 1973. No films were currently under production. The group had already divided into white and Third World caucuses. Many individuals had left in the previous two years. The external appearance of the office seemed to confirm an inner loss of direction or purpose. It was my first visit to New York Newsreel in two years, since the completion of my previous study <u>Newsreel: Film and Revolution</u>. I would not return for another 2 years. During that time many changes were to take place.

In September, 1972, after a brief stay of eight or nine months at an office on 6th Avenue, Newsreel moved to a new location on 20th Street.[1] The group's name was also changed from New York Newsreel to Third World Newsreel. The group also reached its low-point in terms of numbers: the total membership of three individuals did all the moving themselves.[2]

West 20th Street is still in the garment district, but it lies on a quiet side street bracketed at one end by a reddish-brown stoned Episcopal Church and at the other by a store selling imported Italian shoes. After office hours the street is virtually deserted; there are very few residential units although business space is shared by garment shops, a couple of printing presses, and some import-export concerns. There are sandwich shops on the block. All open by seven in the morning. None are open after five at night.

Business activity spills out across the street during the day. Delivery trucks jockey for openings to the unbarricaded loading platforms of the cottage-industry sized businesses. At night they will be doubly and triply locked and the street vacant. Now they gape open, passive, as the scores of manual laborers attend to inventories and orders. Most of the workers are Third World men and when there is a lull in the coming and going of the delivery trucks, they knot up on the sidewalk, talking easily, watching the occasional female passerby with surgical precision. Women do not like to walk to the Newsreel office alone.

There is no lobby in the Newsreel's building, only an all-gray hallway with a small foot-square directory on which three groups are listed. One of the others is a pseudonym for Newsreel. Newsreel's office is on the third floor and can be reached by stairs or by the single elevator; it's about as large as a homeowner's deep freezer and as intimidating to enter. On my first visit I opt for the staircase.

Most New Yorkers are well accustomed to rickety elevators in run-down buildings. The Newsreelers have barricaded the stairway entrance with a padlocked, steel-coated door. It takes them the equivalent of two elevator trips to let me in.

The interior of the office belies its external surroundings.

The floor has been divided by self-made partitions into a number of different work areas. The walls are painted in lively colors that bring the space alive. The wall facing the street is composed of three large windows, each a single pane stretching from a low bench top to the ceiling. The windows rotate open on the horizontal axis that bisects them. Each is clean, its frame painted a shade of bright red. It isn't possible to swing them fully open, though. Several potted plants hang from the ceiling nearby, restricting their rotation.

The main office area is adjacent to these windows. The file cabinets have been painted in tasteful combinations of yellow and blue. The shelves above the work desks are painted red. The booking records are handy, carefully organized, and very active. One or two of the eight Newsreel members are kept constantly busy answering the phone and updating the rental information.

The remainder of the space is divided into a graphics design area, a screening and a projection room, a darkroom, a film storage area and editing space. The partitions have been made as soundproof as possible so that several activities can go on at once without interfering with one another. The films have been organized into neat rows and carefully labelled. They include many of the early Newsreels no longer distributed, outakes, material from television news reports, and other media sources catalogued according to subject-matter, and a videotape library from various community projects Newsreel has been involved in. The film material is organized to the point where Newsreel can now state in a recent pamphlet,

> We have recently completed the cataloguing and
> preservation of historical and recent film footage
> pertaining to the history, culture and political
> development of Third World people. These materials
> will form the basis of a resource for filmmakers,
> researchers, instructors and other individuals for
> viewing and/or purchase.[3]

The only office I had seen in the Movement that was comparably well organized and orderly was an anti-draft or-anization run by ex-soldiers. And even that one did not have potted plants.

On an average day there will be around a dozen visitors. Some arrive simply to pick up films or return them. Others come to discuss projects in which Newsreel is an ongoing participant. Still others are visiting leftists from other parts of the country or from other countries, stopping by to exchange information. This form of contact is a continuation of Newsreel's long-standing relationship with other radical filmmaking groups, a relationship in which Newsreel often performed a catalytic role in the late sixties. As Leonard Henny recently wrote, "... Newsreel served as a model for groups in England, Holland, Sweden, and Germany; while some of the alternative cinema groups in Europe (e.g., "The Angry Arts" in London and "Cineclub" in Amsterdam) became regional distribution centers for Newsreel films overseas."[4]

An example of this continuing contact is a member of Cinema Action from London who is travelling around North America seeking a way to distribute some of their films here. On the day he arrives he brings with him four films made by Cinema Action, three of which he is re-screening that night for Impact Films. Newsreel members drift in and out of the screening room as phone calls and other visitors impose their varying demands.

The first three films—<u>Arise Ye Workers</u>, <u>Fighting the Bill</u>, and <u>The UCS Struggle</u>—are between 20 and 30 minutes long and describe specific examples of trade union militancy in England. They are impressive records of the particular struggles but some Newsreelers wonder about their more general relevance. The last film is a 105 minute sprawling chronicle of several months in the duel for power in the north of Ireland. With little overview or analysis and accents difficult to follow most of the audience dwindles away before the film's conclusion. It is after five and the street is deserted when the Cinema Action representative leaves with the four films for his evening screening.

On another day, two young white filmmakers come in with a film they have done on Watergate to see if Newsreel is interested in distributing it. Called <u>Nixon: Fact or Fiction</u> it surveys a D.C. protest rally, incorporates a series of interviews with people "on the street," and uses a montage of headlines to summarize much of the history of Watergate. There are problems with the film though. It is slack without a firm overview or tight analysis. A young leftist speaking about the development of a general movement against governmental policy while he stands alone, leaning against a fence, sums up the lax tone. Allen, Newsreel's only white member, encourages them to try again, next time with "more analysis." Later, Robert, whom I had seen at the 7th Avenue office, and I go out to dinner with the filmmakers. They are not discouraged. Already they speak enthusiastically about their next project: a film on the labor movement in the '30's.

One other significant difference in Newsreel's office now in contrast to a few years ago is the predominance of women. The men who remain do not assume they are in control or should assume the role of spokesman. They have no qualms about helping attend to the babies and children who sometimes share the office space. Nor is there any paternalistic tolerance while the women try to say or do what the men could do better, and faster. Quite the contrary. Newsreel women have as many skills as the men, as much political consciousness, and as great a facility for articulation. Newsreel's internal relationships give the notion of <u>fraternite</u> a new dimension.

Entire books could be written in this vein. But description, a mode of empirical impressionism, will not suffice. It does, however, illustrate the problem. We begin with surface structure, material facts, phenomena that are recorded and perhaps reordered. From this beginning we hope to arrive at deep structure, at determining principles that are necessary and sufficient explanations for the phenomena we record. How, though, is the transition made? Where is it made? Starting from everyday reality, how do we arrive at a conceptual whole? If the one is simply an answer key slapped across the other, excluding incorrect data, highlighting those events or responses that are judged "correct," then the sense of arbitrariness, of a mechanistic determinism, will be apparent.

The only possible recourse would seem to be in the direction of deriving deep structure from the phenomena themselves, or more precisely, from our relationship to phenomena which we are often tempted to think exist apart from our own intervention. If, in bringing together a series of events, a chronicle of impressions, a larger configuration appears in the mosaic which orders, explains or reconstitutes that which is initially observed, then we can say that we have derived a deep structure. The topographical model is out of joint with most of its synonyms, however. What we are calling here deep structure is in fact a more abstract, more conceptual or theoretical model within which we can locate discrete phenomena rather than something buried inside them like a golden essence. Deep structure is of a higher logical type than surface phenomena. It is in the same relation to surface phenomena as a class is to its members. It cannot be reduced to the latter. It does not inhere within them although it arises from them. Deep structure is a product of our intentionality, our intervention, and signals a conceptual understanding of the rules of relation between phenomena. It breaks with all forms of empiricism in denying that the thing itself is all we can know or speak about. Above sensory impressions lies deep structure, an awkwardly mixed topographical model, perhaps, but an indispensable tool of analysis. Roland Barthes summarizes the distinction somewhat more axiomatically as, "Any process presupposes a system: thus there has been elaborated an opposition between event and structure which has become accepted and whose fruitfulness in history is well known."[5]

***

Going beyond events to explanatory models is an obvious problem in a discussion of a political filmmaking group. Some of the questions we would want to answer would include: what are the forms of political action in a period of relative quiescence? Does Newsreel continue to play a barometric role vis a vis the left in America as I argued in Newsreel: Film and Revolution?[6] Can Newsreel function as a multinational organization when political struggle in white and Third World communities continues to follow largely separate paths? To what extent has Newsreel or the Left in general succeeded in overcoming the problem of generations--the transmission of values from one age-group to the next, the creation of ongoing institutions to ensure such transmission? For whom is propaganda made and what are the political reasons for this decision? How is propaganda distributed and used? How large a role should a filmmaking unit play in distribution and the organizing that takes place around it? What general drift is apparent in American politics? Will there be a phase of legal Marxism or will leftists be driven underground by increasing fascism?

These are crucial questions and indications of possible answers to some of them will be given in the course of this study. A full accounting of these questions would lead, however, to a primarily political-historical study, one of great importance but one which I am less equipped to carry out than others. There are other questions, though, that also command considerable attention. These are questions surrounding the nature of documentary film, its propagandistic role and its general attributes. In examining the films we see that they present the same problems for viewer/critic and the filmmaker as the observational or empirical mode does for the historian. Documentaries begin with phenomena recorded on strips of film. (The transfer of phenomena to film marks the pro-filmic event.) These strips or shots are then rearranged, organized, coupled and recoupled with strips of sound recording and other visual strips. The end result is a finished film, what I will refer to as a textual system: distinctive in the manner of an ideolect (by the specific operations of style and formal structure), and indicative in the manner of a deep structure (by dint of its conceptual pattern which shapes its assemblage of sound and image strips into a whole).

But we expect even more of a documentary film's deep structure, its explanatory model. It will not only inform the parts constituting it, but also the referents of those parts: the operation of a realist aesthetic to which almost all documentary subscribes minimizes the distance between pro-filmic event and surface structure, between sound and image strips and the phenomena in the material world to which they refer. A documentary film's deep structure is thereby understood to be an explanatory model of phenomena as they occur in the social world, in history, and it is quite easy to lose sight of its more immediate referent--the textual system and the part/whole relationships within it.

To overlook this necessary obliquity is frequently to overlook the importance of formal organization in the documentary. Style and structure are of crucial importance in making the experience of the film viewing reality as conceptually rigorous as the experience of that *other* reality to which the film's deep structure also refers (the surface phenomena of everyday reality). Documentaries begin at an empirical level but need to move to a higher logical type--the deep structure that governs and explains the phenomena at first recorded. How this transition is effected becomes of crucial importance and it will be one of my basic theses that it must arise from style and structure, from the overall configuration of the film, and not from an answer key (one aspect of style) imposed upon an otherwise inert and unimportant series of illustrations. If one aspect of style--most commonly a voice-over narration--is consistently promoted to a higher logical type than other aspects, it creates the impression that deep structure exists "out there," apart from our own intervention with surface phenomena. Deep structure comes ready-made, a beam of light in a colloidal murk. It is no longer a product of our interaction with the style itself, the overall pattern into which surface phenomena have been arranged. It has become embedded in the film, objectified into a tangible quantity that no longer calls for our participation, only acquiescence. This form of the reification of deep structure is also known as dogma.

Film is a form of production incomplete at the point of production insofar as a primary function of film is the production of meaning and/or ideology. A film's meaning cannot be packaged. It produces new meaning at the point of consumption through its participation in systems of use and exchange value. Film participates in an exchange of value at an ideological level (though this is never wholly separate from production of economic value). This exchange is conditioned by internal and external factors. These I will call the textual and extra-textual systems, respectively. Together, they located the production of meaning within the realm of ideology--the generation of an imaginary relationship to real conditions of existence. Alternatively the production of meaning may be within the realm of theory--the generation of a symbolic relationship to real conditions of existence.[7] In neither case does a film actually present the real conditions of existence insofar as it only represents them through a system of signs, a map by which to know an otherwise inaccessible territory. Film is not a mirror of social conditions, repeating them in a point-for-point determinism, but a message, a message-in-circuit between viewer and screen: film is social conditions in practice, the practice of (ideologically or theoretically) knowing them.

By textual system I mean the particular confluence of codes found in a single film or text. Together these make up the style and formal structure of the film. The extra-textual system involves all those codes impinging upon the text. They make up the context and as such do not so much exist as an autonomous system but as one overlapping between film and other categories of social practice. Whereas the textual system is unique in the manner of an ideolect, the extra-textual system is common to an entire culture, or at least sub-culture. Together they constitute the meaning of a film as a system of presences and absences, a system whose meaning ultimately depends not only on what is said but also upon what is left unsaid. For this reason this study of films requires formal and contextual moments: neither on its own is adequate. This point is well made in Garnham's critique of Thierry Kuntzel's analysis of M:

> (Kuntzel's) critical method is based upon a misapprehension that it is possible to study a non-arbitrary sign system as a "system that knows only its own order." (I leave open the question of whether this is possible in linguistics.) Sign systems are social structures. We can never derive meaning from the study of the filmic fact in isolation.[8]

There are two moments of particular importance in the production of meaning in the documentary film: the pro-filmic event and the filmic event. By pro-filmic event I mean the interaction between camera and phenomena. What gets into the camera is not reality in any sense although there is a strong tendency to think so in one way or another.

That which is recorded is itself a product of an interaction between the camera and those using it and the event which is recorded, no matter how neutral or unbiased the recording may seem to be. Codes contributing to textual systems are at work from the very first moment of encounter and include camera speed, lens length, lens perspective, framing, focus, depth of focus, exposure, aspect ratio, film speed, camera angle, camera movement, point of view, etc.[9] Although certain choices among these systems may seem more natural or realistic than others, this is basically a function of aesthetic codes of realism, themselves a function of ideology. An analysis of the pro-filmic event is therefore primarily a consideration of how surface phenomena are encoded within textual systems (the arena of style) from the very first instance.

The filmic event is the moment of viewing, the point of consumption at which new meanings are produced. As such it recapitulates all those further alterations of the pro-filmic event effected by cinematic codes: montage above all, including relationships between images, between sounds, and between sound-image tracks. The filmic event is the viewer's point of entry to the textual system and marks the film/viewer interface just as the pro-filmic event marks the film/reality interface.

Like capital, film cannot be reified into a thing. It is primarily a system of relationships between things. These two moments (the filmic and pro-filmic events) establish relationships that are on the one hand subject to empirical observation and description and on the other the starting points for a realization of deep structure. It is in the patterns that we first experience but subsequently incorporate into meta-communication, into critical practice, that we discover a film's relationship to theory and ideology.

In focusing upon these two moments it is important to consider both the textual and extra-textual systems. To concentrate upon the textual systems is to concentrate upon style and structure in its formal aspects or upon the mood or affect generated by style. If such study is grounded in a phenomenology of the filmic event, as it is for Metz, for example,[10] it will lead to an idealist formalism. Although we seek to begin with phenomena, with what is empirically observed, this level does not provide the foundation for our methodology. It is the object of study for a methodology whose foundations lie elsewhere, i.e., in materialist theory. Such theory does not seek to explain textual systems by their compatability with experiential reality (as is so often the case with defenses of various modes of realism) but by their function at the level of deep structure to organize and control experiential reality. Such theory therefore does not simply provide access to understanding but also offers a tool for effecting change.

To concentrate upon the film's textual system in relation to the extra-textual systems impinging upon it is to concentrate upon style in its ideological aspects or upon the epistemological assumptions rooted in the style. Such considerations will form an important part of this study of Newsreel. All textual systems function at an ideological level whether our methodology is equipped to respond at this level or not. A given form of ideological relationship need not imply a particular textual system, however. Textual systems are themselves overdetermined, and ideology, being manifest in a variety of textual systems (different film texts being only one variety), is likewise overdetermined and not subject to immediate, one-to-one correlation with a given style. The relation between textual system and ideology is mediated--by the filmic event, by extra-textual systems impinging upon it --and it is the function of a film theory to understand these mediations as a first step to changing them and the ideology thereby constituted.

A self-reflexive example of the interaction between textual system and the extra-textual systems impinging upon it is the choice in this study to focus more intensively upon the films Newsreel distributes than on the political questions surrounding Newsreel as a group. There is not only the question of writing a dissertation for the Theater Arts Department rather than the History or Political Science Department (a very real example of the academic system of exchange impinging upon the text, to be sure, but not perhaps altogether determining), but also the question of the state of the left at this point in time (1975). Defining Newsreel's relationship to a movement that is no longer moving with any sense of immediate clarity, with any sense of specific direction is particularly difficult. (This very lack, however, does in fact generate special characteristics which we will discuss to some degree.) There are few standards or political lines of proposed action by which to measure Newsreel's intent and achievements. There are few poles around which political consciousness can coalesce and mobilize as it did with S.D.S., the Black Panthers, S.N.C.C., the Young Lords, or Weathermen. Without those poles it is difficult to locate Newsreel's practice within a larger areana of political practice precisely. There seems to be more activity around the entrance gates than in the once so clearly defined arena of political action itself. As a result, reading only the presences in this study (the concentration upon Newsreel and Newsreel's films in relative political isolation), might lead to the erroneous conclusion that filmmaking groups and films enjoy considerable autonomy from their historical situation. Coupling the presences with the absences, however, suggests that this autonomy can also be regarded as an arbitrary (but defended) priority established by the author, that political quiescence frees space for theoretical investigations less possible in times of intense activism. The principal concerns of this study can then be seen as symptomatic of a particular historical moment rather than a timeless assumption about the relationship of art, or film, to social conditions.

As a final introductory remark, Newsreel's films tend to be either agit-prop or educational, concerned with immediate or long-range issues that have primary reference to extra-textual systems. Seldom do the films address themselves to a formal level of political interrogation, to a concern with the ideological significance of the textual systems themselves. This kind of concern need not be incompatible with a strong commitment to mobilization or education around particular aspects of the struggle to change the real conditions of existence. It is, however, a form of filmmaking largely foreign to Newsreel and hence a great deal of the discussion of the films Newsreel distributes will center around their political use value. That the question of the films' ideological implications is not addressed directly nor their textual systems arranged to bracket or interrogate the dominant bourgeois ideology's impingement upon documentary filmmaking, does not mean, however, that these questions will not be addressed by this study. In fact, one goal of this study will be to arrive at a preliminary understanding of these larger questions through careful scrutiny of the formal organization of Newsreel's films. As a prelude to such considerations it will be useful to turn to a brief discussion of Third World Newsreel's recent history.

FOOTNOTES

Chapter One

[1] Interview with Chris, *Third World Newsreel*, New York, December, 1974.

[2] Ibid.

[3] *Third World Newsreel* (a film catalogue), (Fall, 1974), n.p.

[4] Leonard M. Henny, "Film Technology and Revolutionary Social Change," a paper delivered at The International Conference on Alternative Media, Montreal, June, 1974, n.p.

[5] Roland Barthes, *Elements of Semiology*, trans. by Annette Lavers and Colin Smith (London: Jonathan Cape, 1967), p. 24.

[6] William J. Nichols, *Newsreel: Film and Revolution* (unpublished M.A. Thesis, U.C.L.A., 1972).

[7] Theory and ideology are mediated relationships between ourselves and the real conditions of existence, the economic base. There is no more immediate relationship possible apart from intuition, gut response. For intuition to be elevated to a discourse, a pattern of exchange, however, it must become theory or ideology. An ideological or imaginary relationship is primarily unconscious or natural. It is a specular relationship constituted by an image we take to be ourselves, an image we "buy" as our true relation to the real conditions of existence. But it is the image of an other, an image that makes the subject the deceptive center of a false pride or egoism for its true locus is outside itself--in the extra-textual systems determined, ultimately, by the economic base, that is, in capitalist ideology. A symbolic relationship establishes the subject as a locus in a nexus of relationships. Its nature is not externally, specularly determined but actively established by interaction. A symbolic relationship also admits of meta-communication, discourse about the communication itself, a necessary condition for breaking out of the self-other identity bind created at

the ideological level. Without being able to talk about a pattern of communication it may be impossible to move to a higher logical type, to the level of deep structure.

8
Nicholas Garnham, "Reply to Thierry Kuntzel's 'The Treatment of Ideology in the Textual Analysis of Film'," Screen, vol. 14, no. 3 (Autumn, 1973), p. 58.

9
Based on elaboration of a list in "Documentary, Realism and Women's Cinema" by Eileen McGarry, Women & Film, vol. 2, no. 7 (Summer, 1975), p. 52.

10
See Brian Henderson, "Metz: Essais I and Film Theory," Film Quarterly, vol. 28, no. 3 (Spring, 1975), pp. 18-33 for a comprehensive analysis of Metz's phenomenological base.

Chapter Two

TRANSITION: FROM NEW YORK NEWSREEL

TO THIRD WORLD NEWSREEL

    Present both in the "street action"--with its coupling of exhilaration and paranoia--and in the backstage rooms where, to the extent things were planned at all, the theater was plotted, Chicago and its aftermath compacted and distilled essential elements present both in the Movement and in American society. The romantic militancy of the street mobs, the mindlessness of mass psychology, the willingness of the Movement leaders to utilize the same media fakery as "the enemy" crystallized no less than did the police-state behaviour of the ruling class.

> Jan Jost, "Afterimages: Notes from Practice" (Jump Cut, no. 5).

    On the left, the baleful influence of Newsreel with its ultra-left disdain for quality (the-larger-the-grain-the better-the-politics) and its anxiety to strangle reality with the correct line, created a group of films which, with a few notable exceptions, will take their place with the other graffiti of the '60's.

> Peter Biskind, "Radical American Film? A Questionnaire" (Cineaste, vol. 5, no. 4)

If the New Left is considered as more or less co-terminous with the amalgam of forces that revolved around S.D.S., then it is clearly dead.[1] In fact, we can say that the New Left only truly existed as a national force from 1965 to 1969. If we expand our definition to take in the other groups formed to promote and organize the civil rights movement at one end and the anti-war effort at the other, the New Left's existence can be extended from four years to ten: from 1962 to 1972, roughly. In either case a new form of political left has to be defined for the time since 1970-72 and lessons learned from the one which has passed away.

The moral tone of the two epitaphs regarding the New Left's demise which head this chapter are by no means coincidental. The course of the New Left is a virtual morality play between Good (young, white, middle-class, college educated) and Evil (governmental, military, imperialist, capitalist) forces in which Evil finally triumphs by redirecting and redisguising its terrible ways faster than Good can work itself to the proper moralistic pitch. Members of the New Left were frequently radicalized by shock, by the sudden recognition of cruelty beneath banality, of violence beneath stability, of racism beneath benevolence. It was a form of radicalization that was perhaps peculiar to a generation raised on Cold War and grey-flannel pap, an interwar generation that floated through the political limbo between the Korean War and the Vietnam War in a stream of consciousness from which the working-class, political activism of the previous generation in the Thirties and early Forties was systematically excluded. The voices of protest that were raised in the early Sixties shared a common tone whether they were Black or White: "The tone was marked on the one hand by a distinct caution about political judgments, and on the other by a sense of a need to make a personal moral witness against things which seemed so far out of line with our ideals as to be unambiguously evil."[2]

Beginning with the Civil Rights movement where the link between Black leaders and the church, the absence of a well-defined Communist presence among blacks, and the persistent allusion to the melting-pot goal of assimilation and equality all helped support a clearly moral argument against discrimination and continuing into the Vietnamese conflict where issues of racism, genocide, and gross injustice were heatedly argued, the New Left was supplied with a set of situations to which a moralistic, personal expression of outraged seemed both necessary and sufficient. Necessary because for most New Left members these issues only indirectly affected their own lives yet cried out for response; sufficient because the belief persisted that no social system could willfully continue such outrages once their inherent evil was exposed. The New Left may have been unclear about its own social vision but it was certain that racism and imperialism were outright evils: "No social movement never better expressed the principal of Negative Unity, the progressive transformation of a force through continual shedding of outward forms, than the New Left."[3]

Even if there were a chameleon-esque quality to the New Left, what led it from a changing of colors to a final demise? Its demise seems to have been built into its beginning insofar as its growth, peak, and decline all centered very heavily around the college campus, primarily a number of private, prestigious universities, larger state universities, and small, high-quality colleges where a large percentage of the student body came from solid middle-class backgrounds and were enrolled in liberal-arts programs. Institutions where trade and vocational programs predominated or where working class students attended were generally outside the core of the New Left constituency.[4] Radicalization usually involved exposure to the Vietnamese War, to the Civil Rights struggle and later the idea of Black Power, to the youth or counter-culture, to the oppressive alienation of middle-class life in America, and to the rise of Third World liberation struggles as a phenomenon reaching far beyond Vietnam. Seldom did radicalization involve any direct exposure to what it means to labor in a capitalist system or to the repression reserved for working class militancy.

The vicarious relationship between the student-radicals and most of the sources of their radicalization set the stage for instability as a political force. This was further heightened by a more gradually emergent form of radicalization that initially affected only a portion of the New Left: feminism. Once the critique of the male chauvinist ideology and practice visible within most of the New Left's (male) leadership and many of its policies had been initiated, however, there was no turning back. The moralistic and personalistic base of the New Left only served as additional fuel for the feminist arguments and, in fact, it was the feminist position that made these stances take on an immediate, political relevance. A moral tone was no longer reserved for evil forces "out there" in a society one chooses to denounce, it had to be also applied to the evil forces, as it were, internalized within the individual, even if he declared himself a radical. The woman's question turned the movement in upon itself where it discovered the same diseases it thought it had isolated in the social body from which it had cut itself loose.

The lack of a broad social base, the minimal contact with those directly engaged by the forces of production, the self-doubt and splintering precipitated by the woman's question became crystalized in the

S.D.S. convention of 1969. Three factions struggled to regain the organization's consensus: Progressive Labor, advocating integration into the working-class and opposition to all forms of nationalism such as those proposed by the Black Panthers, Young Lords, etc.; the Weathermen, advocating guerrilla insurrection with whites as shock troops for a lumpen-proletarian black vanguard; and RYM II (Revolutionary Youth Movement), advocating multi-national support of Third World liberation struggles, far closer ties to the blue-collar working class and a loosely Stalinist form of disciplined political organization. The latter two groups joined together to oust Progressive Labor but then divided between themselves as well. As O'Brien describes it, "At the end of the spring, the organization (S.D.S.) had immense prestige and tens of thousands of local members; at the end of the summer it had three sets of national 'spokesmen' trying to inflate a punctured balloon."[5]

A deceptive "Indian summer" through the 1969-70 academic year of short-range events and issues including Nixon's adamant disregard of protest against the war, Agnew's attack on the media and radicals, the sensational police attacks against the Black Panthers, the outrageous seriocomic trial of the Chicago Eight, the invasion of Cambodia, and the killings at Kent and Jackson State colleges put a healthy color on a movement already beginning to come apart from the inside.

Before passing away, however, the New Left bequeathed several lessons to its Seventies inheritors: it demonstrated the inherent instability of a political opposition without a clear political analysis or a solid foothold within the forces of production; it legitimated moral and personal outrage as a political act while also demonstrating the inadequacy of this expression as a political tool; it broadened the concept of what is political to include the personal especially through the influence of the women's movement; it saw the crucial role played by higher education in post-World War II America in contrast to its previously marginal relationship to the means of production; and it identified imperialism and Third World liberation struggles as the principle contradiction but without being able to resolve the relation of this contradiction to that between workers and owners. Unlike the forms of political left that centered around the point of production and the economic demands that exploitation provokes, the New Left centered around the nexus of consumption and invested choices of lifestyle, states of consciousness, and personal relationships with political relevance. Although the forms which these choices took in the late sixties were often politically questionable, it seems that new political formations in the seventies can no longer separate the personal from the political, consumption from production, the definition of the private self from the definition of the public worker.

Ironically, though, the major threads of continuity in the development of the American left through the sixties and seventies may not be found in the rise and fall of the New Left but in the unbroken growth of Third World consciousness and struggle, both within and beyond the borders of the imperialist countries. In this context the lessons about the integration of the personal and the political may continue to have major significance, but the broader outlines of a political movement with a firm base of support and realistic chances of emerging from a potentially revolutionary confrontation victorious may well lie elsewhere. The final dissolution of S.D.S. is symptomatic of such a possibility for the choices argued at the 1969 convention involved a radical shift of identity in any case: S.D.S. would either have to subordinate itself to a working class and/or Third World movement (P.L. and RYM II) or become the adventuristic cohorts of such a movement (Weathermen). In either case S.D.S.'s own base of student activists was excluded from center stage. At this point it is not possible to do more than suggest the possibility that a study of the American left in the sixties will find its main line of development in the movement from the Civil Rights demonstrations through SNCC and the Black Panthers to the Black Workers Congress and the Congress of Afrikan People. If this is the case, however, it may also mean that recording the history of Newsreel since 1971 is not the writing of a epitaph but the recognition of the Third World people's struggle to gain mastery of forms of communication previously denied them.

The impetus behind the New Left was not so much to understand the conditions shaping their own lives as to react to conditions affecting the lives of others. The nature of the war in Vietnam and the possibility of fighting in it was ample fuel for reaction; it did not need to be grounded in a critique of capitalism since theory would be a form of mediacy diluting the call to immediate response. But when the conditions to which others respond are also the conditions under which they live, there is less inclination to react (from what base can they without the most serious of risks?) than to understand. The history of Third World struggle throughout the last decade and a half can be seen as attempt to reach such understanding. As the New Left's own rhethoric repeatedly emphasized, those who were directly exploited and oppressed were in a better position to determine what was to be done than concerned but less affected onlookers. Actually putting this recognition in practice, though, was another story, one which formed a major part of the history of Newsreel since 1971.

In 1971, New York Newsreel was located at the Seventh Avenue office described above. In the early part of that year a decision was made to place a priority upon recruiting Third World members. This was a logical choice since most of Newsreel's films were concerned with Third World struggle: "The change from middle-class leadership was necessary because few middle-class people grew up in the neighborhoods or near the places about which Newsreel films are needed."[6] It was a choice which, like those posed at the S.D.S. convention in 1969, carried within it a self-destruct mechanism against Newsreel's previous mode of organization.

Third World people entered an organization that had developed a certain sense of purpose and direction and had institutionalized that sense in a well-defined training program lasting several months. New members had to attend political education (P.E.) classes and struggle sessions devoted to critical analysis of each member's family and social background, work and personal relationships, etc.[7] They found, however, that their political education was heavily oriented toward Marx, Engels, etc. with little attention to Black history or Third World writers in general. They also found that the struggle sessions were led by white members who were not equipped to deal with the differences between white and Third World experience or the articulation of that experience.[8]

A need for a Third World caucus or section was increasingly felt and finally realized in the fall of 1971.[9]

At the same time, New York Newsreel was organized on the principles of democratic centralism involving a central committee of four and workteams revolving around it. There were no Third World members on the central committee. That too became a demand. In June, 1971 a Third World member was added to the central committee but even this posed problems. As Ernie described it, "We had one Third World person among 4 or 5 whites. Our voice was minimal. It was like having a Black Congressman shoved in with 400 white ones."[10] As the numbers of Third World members increased rapidly toward the end of 1971 until there were 12, roughly half the total membership, pressure mounted for even greater autonomy. A national conference of Third World Newsreel members in the late summer of 1971 brought together the 4 Third World members from across the country at which it was decided to press for even greater emphasis on Third World recruiting.[11] By the time the membership in New York had reached 12, it was also decided that the Third World representative should resign from the central committee since representation was only tokenistic at best. After the winter of 1971-72, New York Newsreel was effectively divided into white and Third World sections, each virtually autonomous.[12]

These political struggles carried over into Newsreel's filmmaking work. There were examples of radically different attitudes toward filmmaking and the means of production between Third World people with little technical training and lower-class backgrounds and whites with skills and middle-class background. When Third World members moved to a new office in 1972 they found supplies and equipment no one knew existed, much of it damaged by careless use and storage.[13] And when Third World members attempted to put into practice their theoretical priorities, difficulties only multiplied.

In September, 1971 the Attica rebellion took place and Newsreel decided to do a film about prisoners. The central committee, acknowledging that most prisoners at Attica and elsewhere were Third World agreed that the film crew should be made up of white and Third World Newsreel members. A crew of six was formed, three of whom were Third World. Of the three, only one had any skills at all; the other two were selected because of their lumpen-proletarian background on the assumption that it would afford them greater access to the prison population.[14]

The crew began to splinter almost immediately. There was little dialogue between white and Third World members. One white member left due to a feeling of inadequacy in terms of filmmaking and relating to the Third World members, another left due to inconsistent work habits, a Third World member left out of frustration.[15] The remaining three were all women but personal misunderstandings arose and the white woman left the crew as well. That left two Third World crew members, the two who had no filmmaking skill at all when the project began.[16]

The result of these two women's efforts was the film Teach Our Children. The struggle around its production is reminiscent of the struggle in San Francisco Newsreel by Third World members to have an active voice in the production of Revolution Until Victory (whose title was later changed to We The Palestinian People), discussed in chapter 5 below. In New York, however, the Third World members completed the film and acquired the essential filmmaking skills. In San Francisco the white Newsreel members completed the film and passed on relatively few skills to Third World members. This difference seems central to the later development of the two Newsreel centers.

The early part of 1972 was a period of dramatic change in Newsreel. Divisions were apparent between white and Third World members, between men and women, between "haves and have-nots"--those from middle-class backgrounds and those from working class and lumpen backgrounds. The same person would often be found straddling different sides of these divisions: a Third World member was considered a "have," for example, because she had earned a Master's Degree.[17] Some of the whites came from working class families and were in closer touch with the working class constituencies Newsreel sought to work with than other whites. At the same time the central committee attempted to hold things together by meting out discipline in accordance with its own evaluation of these divisions. When a white male and white female both resigned from the group, the male was required to write a long letter of self-criticism and participate in a session where his practice was criticized.[18] The female left with no letter and little explanation.

But it was an arbitrary discipline. The central committee could not arrive at a coherent position nor impose unity from the top down on a group so deeply divided. By February, 1972 the central committee had decided to disband and reorganize Newsreel around two caucuses--one white, one Third World--each responsible for its own direction and discipline.[19] The Third World caucus immediately organized itself around the areas of finance, distribution, and production (Teach Our Children was still in progress). The white caucus limited itself to distribution and began a period of intensive political education.[20] After several months of study and debate, with no clear notion of what films a white caucus could make, the white members decided to disband. In April, 1972 New York Newsreel became Third World Newsreel.[21]

Third World Newsreel went through a year-long period of consolidation and reorientation, an extremely difficult period which the group almost did not survive, before emerging in 1973 as a relatively stable group that has undergone minimal change since that time. With the drastic decrease in numbers, the loss of experience and expertise, and the increased concern for sheer survival both as a group and for individuals who could not rely on family support or income earned from skills, Newsreel wavered in its priorities. Individuals demanded salaries in order to survive. The burden of paying salaries taxed the distribution system to its limit; there was no money left to put out new catalogues and by the time the group moved to a new office in the spring of 1972 many of their previously regular customers could no longer locate them.[22] As distribution declined and with no money for new production as well as conflicting ideas of what films to make, the workload tapered off:

> New people have no work to do, get bored, mainly get bored. They sat in the office doing a little distribution. In terms of work experience, it really diminished; there was nothing there. People started ripping each other off, demanding more of each other. Then people left, several people left. It was a genuine crisis and three of us decided we had to reorganize the group from scratch, with people getting jobs to support themselves and putting all our efforts into reviving distribution.[23]

These three individuals--Chris, Sue, and Robert--constituted the entire membership by summer, 1972. They moved to a new office on their own. Chris and Sue completed <u>Teach Our Children</u>. Gradually, as money came in, they were able to rebuild the distribution and bring in other Third World members. In fall, 1972 they moved to their current address on West 20th St., gradually increased their membership to eight, put out a new catalogue, and initiated new filmmaking projects. Currently, the group is in the process of making films tentatively titled, <u>Women in Prison</u>, <u>Day Care from a Child's Perspective</u>, and <u>Energy Crisis</u>, plus a film on the recent political struggles of the Mohawk Indians in upstate New York.[24]

In 1974, Third World Newsreel had roughly 2,000 bookings and an audience of at least 20,000 people.[25] Approximately 60 percent of the bookings were to college groups--from which the greatest income derives although the political priority for this kind of screening is lower-- while the remainder is split evenly, 20 percent each, among community groups and political organizations.[26] Among their most popular films are <u>Salt of the Earth</u>, <u>El Pueblo Se Levanta</u> (<u>The People Are Rising</u>), <u>Rompiendo Puertas</u> (<u>Break and Enter</u>), <u>La Luta Continua</u>, <u>We The Palestinian People</u>, <u>Viva Frelimo</u>, and other films dealing with Third World liberation struggles in America and around the world.[27] Distribution provides 99 percent of the group's income and has now reached a level where members can draw a monthly stipend although most members take part-time, working-class jobs in order to channel more Newsreel money into production and acquisition of new films.[28]

Newsreel now sees itself in a barometric role to the movement at large. This was the relationship I argued existed in Newsreel: Film and Revolution but up until 1971 Newsreel saw itself providing leadership as part of a New Left vanguard.[29] As Chris explains,

> We constantly run into situations where Newsreel doesn't have any clearly defined political line. What's happening is our political direction is based on the mass movement outside, the propaganda network around it, and I personally don't think that's bad. We cannot give political direction to the masses in an isolated situation. We have to learn from them and then put that knowledge into broader circulation.[30]

Newsreel has chosen to remain apart from the current debate among multi-national but largely white political organizations regarding the formation of a new communist party in the United States.[31] To Third World Newsreel it suggests a form of decision from the top down that does not have strong impetus in working class and Third World organizations where much more emphasis is going into community, point of production, and common-interest group organizing. Third World Newsreel does, however, feel quite strongly about who should be making films for working-class and Third World people: "It's not people who have a vocation to make films. Technique for us is secondary. The people themselves have a rich life experience, a knowledge of history and their culture and community organization. And these people are far more qualified to make films than people who have learned their skills in a school."[32] The struggle for Third World people to acquire the skills to carry out this filmmaking work continues to be one of Third World Newsreel's highest priorities, and the continuing distrust of intensive scrutiny of film aesthetics and theory as petty-bourgeois one of the nagging consequences.

Third World Newsreel remains strongly linked to its New York City environment. The vast majority of workers in New York are in service industries: "If you want to speak to workers in New York City, you can't talk about point of production."[33] As a consequence, Newsreel's films tend to be about situations or experiences that are systematically oppressive but not directly related to the work place: inadequate housing, lack of day care, prisons, etc.. Simultaneously, there is less concern with following events and recording major, but ephemeral, demonstrations, rallies, and protests. The persistent conditions of day-to-day existence exert a greater influence upon filmmaking decisions now than they did up through 1970 or 1971. This may be a direct result of the shift in Newsreel to a basically Third World organization. Symbolic protest and street violence may have had a stronger appeal for individuals for whom these events represented a movement that was rebelling, in part, against an everyday life of middle-class conformity. The New Left sought escape from the everyday, from its own past, from the world it was being groomed to run. Third World people find that their fight starts within the everyday, in the fight for housing, day care, food, day-to-day survival. These conditions become a crucial part of the struggle rather than representations of the mainstream conformity from which they seek to disinherit themselves. And for similar reasons, more recent films are less concerned with leaders and flashy rhetoric than with the common people and the forms of expression that come out of everyday experience.

From that level of concern, though, the films seem to jump to a much broader one of self-determination for minorities and Third World liberation, an emphasis that derives in part from the continuing influence of the Young Lords, Black Panthers, and lumpen-proletarian ideologies emphasizing aspects of the national question and racism over multi-national revolution and working-class solidarity.[34] It's a matter of emphasis and not of political line, however, for once queried Newsreel members state, "There is great confusion on the national question and national identity. That's brought into the whole question of party building. National identities are very different from the national question, and that's not being analyzed very critically. It's easier to say that every minority should have its own nation."[35] Or, as Ernie put it,

> We change with the times. Whatever the times are, they'll show up in Newsreel. It seems to me the national question shall be whether we will continue to be oppressed by Chrysler, General Motors, Nixon, and the rest of them. That's more important to me than worrying about those who call themselves revolutionaries and fight over the national question while the White House blows up black, brown, Latin, yellow people all over the world. They'll resolve the national question and all the actual conditions will remain the same.[36]

Films such as the one currently under production on the Mohawk Nation and Iroquois Confederacy may give a clearer indication of how Newsreel's combination of united front and Third World emphasis will actually relate to more precise arguments about the role of the national question, but for now Newsreel's point of view is open-ended. Several films are distributed, including Black Power, in which a specific political line is advanced with which Newsreel does not fully agree. They are more concerned with seeing people learn from the history of Third World struggle, however, than in carrying only films that embody what they now consider the best line: "We distribute it (Black Power) so that people can learn from what he (Stokely Carmichael) said. They can discuss it and decide what is correct and what is incorrect."[37] "Some of the things he said may have been wrong, but black people can look at that and say, 'That was wrong'. We have an important historical background and have gone in many directions since then (1969 when Stokely Carmichael addressed the Black Panthers). What was said was important at the time and should be looked at."[38]

Another indication of Newsreel's current direction is offered by the printed material, newspapers and magazines, that they make available at their office. These include: Guatamala Report, a socio-economic study by the American Friends of Guatamala; Midnight Special, paper of the National Lawyers Guild with heavy emphasis on prison issues from a Third World perspective; Attica News, devoted largely to prison issues involving Third World people (one article features the history of Martin Sostre's struggle for his rights inside New York State prisons); Unity and Struggle, paper of the Congress of Afrikan People led by Amiri Baraka (formerly Leroi Jones) whose comments about some of the "sectarian" organizations on the left that engage in "academic struggles characterized by verbal overkill,"[39] strikes a similar note to Newsreel's own feeling about the debate about the national question and party building; NACLA newsletters (North American Congress on Latin America); and White Lightning, a Bronx, N.Y. newspaper from "A Revolutionary Organization Dedicated to Serving the People," White Lightning features stories on Martin Sostre, Muhammed Ali, Carlos Felliciano (a Puerto Rican leader in New York City), Lincoln Hospital's Detoxification

Program for methadone users, Cambodia and Puerto Rico. Its lay-out is reminiscent of the New Left's underground newspapers with psychedelic colors and appreciable graphic work although its orientation is clearly directed toward Third World struggle.

In summary, it is clear that Third World Newsreel's present orientation centers around serving Third World people with special attention to the particular needs and experiences of Third World people in New York City. As the group has stabilized since the early part of 1973, securing a strong financial base in a widespread distribution system, adequate membership to handle the workload without constant strain and without more people than work, and a sense of collective identity--they have also radically reshaped the nature and purpose of Newsreel. Newsreel seeks to raise Third World and working people's consciousness about everyday oppression in the home, the community, institutions ostensibly "serving" people's needs, and the work-place, to ultimately connect these forms of oppression with economic exploitation resulting from the dynamics of monopoly capitalism, or imperialism, and to link these issues to the yet larger, revolutionary question of the right to self-determination as a race, as a nation, and as members of a working-class. In what order, at what rate, and in what form remain questions for which Newsreel, like the rest of the present-day movement, continues to seek solutions.

FOOTNOTES

Chapter Two

1
This brief account of the New Left is based primarily upon personal experience and reflection. In addition, the following sources were consulted: Todd Gittlin, "Toward a New New Left," Partisan Review, vol. 39, no. 3 (Summer, 1972), pp. 454-461; Paul Buhle, "The Eclipse of the New Left: Some Notes," Radical America, vol. 6, no. 4 (July-August, 1972), pp. 1-9; James O'Brien, "Beyond Reminiscence: The New Left in History," Radical America, vol. 6, no. 4 (July-August, 1972), pp. 11-48; Elinor Langer, "Notes for Next Time: A Memoir of the 1960s," Working Papers (Fall, 1973), pp. 48-83; Alan Adelson, SDS: A Profile (New York: Charles Scribner's Sons, 1972); Stephen Goode, Affluent Revolutionaries: A Portrait of the New Left (New York: Franklin Watts, Inc., 1974); Kirkpatrick Sale, SDS (New York: Vintage Books of Random House, 1973); Irwin Unger, The Movement: A History of the American New Left 1959-1972, (New York: Dodd, Mead & Company, 1974).

2
O'Brien, "Beyond Reminiscence," p. 18.

3
Buhle, "Eclipse of the New Left," pp. 5-6.

4
O'Brien, "Beyond Reminiscence," p. 18.

5
Ibid., p. 38.

6
Rebecca Pulliam, "Newsreel," The Velvet Light Trap, no. 4 (Spring, 1972), p. 9.

7
Interview with Chris, Third World Newsreel, New York, December, 1974.

8
Interview with Ernie, Third World Newsreel, New York, December, 1974.

9
Ibid.

10
Interview with Ernie, December, 1974.

11
Interview with Chris, December, 1974.

12
Interview with Robert, former member of Third World Newsreel, New York, July, 1974.

13
Ibid.

14
Interview with Chris, Third World Newsreel, New York, July, 1974.

15
Ibid.

16
Ibid.

17
Ibid.

18
Ibid.

19
Interview with Chris, December, 1974.

20
Interview with Richard, former member of New York Newsreel, Los Angeles, April, 1974.

21
Interview with Chris, December, 1974.

22
Interview with Allan, Third World Newsreel, New York, July, 1974.

23
Interview with Chris, December, 1974.

24
Sherry Lyons, "Third World Newsreel," The Paper (student newspaper for the City College of New York), December 12, 1974, p. 12.

25 Interview with Ernie, December, 1974.

26 Ibid.

27 Interview with Robert, July, 1974.

28 Interview with Allan, Third World Newsreel, New York, December, 1974.

29 Nichols, *Newsreel*, pp. 58-59.

30 Interview with Chris, December, 1974.

31 Among these groups are the Revolutionary Union, The October League, The New American Movement, The *Guardian* newspaper, and The Black Workers Congress. By the end of 1975 the Revolutionary Union (RU) had become the Revolutionary Communist Party, the Black Workers Congress, the Revolutionary Workers Congress, and additional groups like the August 29th Movement had also arisen.

32 Interview with Chris, December, 1974.

33 Interview with Robert, July 1974.

34 Lyons, "Third World Newsreel," p. 12.

35 Interview with Chris, December, 1974.

36 Interview with Ernie, December, 1974.

37 Interview with Chris, December, 1974.

38 Interview with Ernie, December, 1974.

39 Amiri Baraka, "Sectarianism, Undermining, Secret Agents and Struggle," *Unity and Struggle* (Newark, New Jersey), December, 1974, p. 16.

Chapter Three

THIRD WORLD NEWSREEL'S FILMS

In fact, we even had a term called "A Newsreel Film" for those independent productions that people brought in consisting of a righteous, heavy political rap illustrated with a few pictures.

Tom Brom, worker for
American Documentary Films (defunct)

I've noticed that a lot of people are put off by our teaching because we know the answer to everything. Couldn't we, in the interests of propaganda, draw up a list of questions which appear to us quite unresolved?

Bertold Brecht, Anecdotes of
Herr Keuner

Third World Newsreel has faced a difficult task in overcoming the stigma it acquired during the period from 1968-1970, before most of the present members were actively involved. To what degree they have been successful in this regard will be one of the considerations put before this examination of the films Newsreel currently distributes. Since these films are selected by Newsreel and by their renters in terms of subject-matter, it will be useful to arrange them in a summary fashion indicating general theme, whether they were made by Newsreel or only distributed by them, the year of production, and their source or film-maker if not made by Newsreel. It will also be useful to arrange them in such a way as to separate the bulk of the films discussed in this study from those not included. Excluded films will include those well-known films for which Newsreel is a secondary distributor unless they are of particular relevance, early films (before 1971) discussed in Newsreel: Film and Revolution unless they have been given special emphasis more recently, and films announced for distribution but not yet available or without English sub-titles:

Films Distributed by Third World Newsreel Arranged by Theme

I. Institutional Oppression

        #
(1971 to present)   (up until 1971)

    A. Prisons

        *We Demand Freedom (73, 55 min.)
        *Teach Our Children (72, 35 min.)
        *In The Event Anyone Disappears
          (73, 50 min.)
        *Attica (Cinda Firestone,
          73, 80 min.)

    B. The Military

        *Only the Beginning (71, 20 min.)   Army (69, 25 min.)
        *Winter Soldier (71, 20 min.)   ROTC (69, 20 min.)
        *G.I. Jose (Realidades, WNET-TV,
          74, 20 min.)
        *U.S. Techniques and Genocide in
          Vietnam (Vietnam People's
          Army Films, n.d., 35 min.)
        *Selling of the Pentagon (CBS
          News, 71, 54 min.)

    C. Community Services--Housing, Schools, etc.

        *Rompiendo Puertas (Break and   High School Rising
          Enter) (71, 42 min.)   (69, 15 min.)
        *Homefront (Jenny Goldberg,   Lincoln Center
          74, 25 min.)   (68, 12 min.)
        *Los Gamines (Gustavo Ignacio   Lincoln Hospital
          Ayala, Columbia, 74,   (70, 15 min.)
          10 min.) NA#   (People's Park)
                                                (69, 25 min.)[+]

I. Institutional Oppression (cont'd.)
   (1971 to present)# (up until 1971)

   D. Due Process--Laws, Civil Rights, Trials, Police

   *So the People Should Know
   (Pentagon Papers Project,
   72, 30 min.)
   The Murder of Fred Hampton
   (Mike Gray Associates,
   71, 90 min.)
   Mangrove Nine (Franco Rosso,
   70, 40 min.) NA

   Los Siete de la Raza
   (S.F. Newsreel,
   69, 30 min.)

II. Women's Liberation

   *Childcare (70, 20 min.)
   *A Space To Be Me (Maureen
   Sherlock and David Weinkauf,
   74, 20 min.)
   Growing Up Female (Julia
   Reichart and James Klein,
   70, 60 min.)
   Red Detachment of Women
   (People's Republic of
   China, 71, 105 min.)

   The Woman's Film (S.F.
   Newsreel, 71, 40 min.)
   Make-Out (70, 5 min.)
   Salt of the Earth
   (H. Biberman, dir.,
   54, 90 min.)
   Women of Telecommunica-
   tions Station #6
   (North Vietnam,
   n.d., 20 min.)
   My Country Occupied
   (71, 30 min.)

III. Ecology

   *Earth Belongs to the People
   (Boston Newsreel, 71, 17 min.)

IV. The New Left Movement

   *America (70, 45 min.)

   Columbia Revolt
   (69, 50 min.)
   (People's Park) (S.F.
   Newsreel, 69, 25 min.)
   San Francisco State:
   On Strike (S.F. News-
   reel, 69, 25 min.)

(1971 to present)#   (up until 1971)

V.   Working Class Struggle

    *Felix (69-70, 8 min.)   Finally Got the News
                                            (Black Star Produc-
                                            tions, 70, 55 min.)
                                    Richmond Oil Strike
                                            (S.F. Newsreel, 69,
                                            15 min.)
                                    Lincoln Hospital
                                            (70, 15 min.)
                                    Wilmington (68, 15 min.)
                                    Salt of the Earth
                                            (H. Biberman, 1954)

VI.   National Liberation Struggles**

    *Black Power (L. Henny,   Interview with Bobby Seale
      69, 15 min.)   (S.F. Newsreel, 69,
    *El Pueblo Se Levante (The   15 min.)
      People Are Rising) (71, 40 min.)   People's War (69, 40 min.)
    *FALN (Dawn Films, 65, 30 min.)   Struggle For Life (NLF,
    *Nossa Terra (uncredited,   South Vietnam, n.d.,
      73, 40 min.)   20 min.)
    *A Luta Continua (Robert Van   79 Springs of Ho Chi Minh
      Lierop and Robert Fletcher,   (S. Alvarez, Cuba,
      71, 32 min.)   71, 25 min.)
    *Revolution in Dhofar (Jimmy   Hanoi, Tuesday the 13th
      Vaughn, prod., 73, 55 min.)   (S. Alvarez, 69,
    *Nigeria: Nigeria One (Facts   42 min.)
      Africa, re-edited by Newsreel,   Laos: the Forgotten War
      73, 45 min.)   (Cuba, n.d., 20 min.)
    *We The Palestinian People   Bay of Pigs (Cuba, 61,
      (a.k.a. Revolution Until   20 min.)
      Victory) (S.F. Newsreel,   Golpeando En La Selva
      73, 45 min.)   (Cuba, 67, 15 min.)
    Proclamation of the Nation of   Now (S. Alvarex, 68,
      Guinea-Bissau (uncredited,   5 min.)
      73, 40 min.) NA   Black Panther (S.F. News-
    Borroka: The Struggle (Ken   reel, 68, 20 min.)
      Kirby, 74, 55 min.) NA   Madina Boe (Cuba, 67,
    The Guns Should Be United   40 min.)
      (by the Democratic Popular   Fuerra Yanqui (n.d.,
      Front for the Liberation of   15 min.)
      Palestine, 73, 20 min.) NA   Vietnam, Land of Fire
    Don Pedro: La Vida de un   (French, 66, 15 min.)
      Pueblo (Norberto Lopez,   Cancer of Betrayal (Facts
                                            Africa, 72, 15 min.)
                                            NA

VI. National Liberation Struggles (cont'd.)

(1971 to present)　　　　　　　(up until 1971)

　　　　　　　　　　　　　　　Viva Frelimo (edited by
　　　　　　　　　　　　　　　　Newsreel from Dutch
　　　　　　　　　　　　　　　　television, n.d.,
　　　　　　　　　　　　　　　　30 min.)
　　　　　　　　　　　　　　　My Country Occupied
　　　　　　　　　　　　　　　　(70, 30 min.)

VII. Views of Socialist Societies

　　A. Cuba

　　　　　　　　　　　　　　　Cyclone (S. Alvarex,
　　　　　　　　　　　　　　　　n.d., 20 min.)
　　　　　　　　　　　　　　　Por Primera Vez (Cuba,
　　　　　　　　　　　　　　　　n.d., 10 min.)
　　　　　　　　　　　　　　　Historia de una Battalla
　　　　　　　　　　　　　　　　(Cuba, n.d., 40 min.)
　　　　　　　　　　　　　　　Hasta La Victoria Siempre
　　　　　　　　　　　　　　　　(Cuba, n.d., 20 min.)
　　　　　　　　　　　　　　　Isle of Youth (Cuba, 69,
　　　　　　　　　　　　　　　　15 min.)
　　　　　　　　　　　　　　　Cuban Teachers (Cuba,
　　　　　　　　　　　　　　　　n.d., 22 min.)
　　　　　　　　　　　　　　　Children of the Revolu-
　　　　　　　　　　　　　　　　tion (Jane Sellers,
　　　　　　　　　　　　　　　　65, 30 min.)
　　　　　　　　　　　　　　　Cerro Pelado (S. Alvarez,
　　　　　　　　　　　　　　　　67, 60 min.)
　　　　　　　　　　　　　　　Bay of Pigs (Cuba, 61,
　　　　　　　　　　　　　　　　20 min.)

　　B. North Vietnam and Liberated Sectors of South Vietnam

　　　　　　　　　　　　　　　Struggle for Life (NLF,
　　　　　　　　　　　　　　　　South Vietnam, n.d.,
　　　　　　　　　　　　　　　　20 min.)
　　　　　　　　　　　　　　　Women of Telecommunica-
　　　　　　　　　　　　　　　　tions #6 (North Viet-
　　　　　　　　　　　　　　　　nam, n.d., 20 min.)
　　　　　　　　　　　　　　　Day of Plane Hunting
　　　　　　　　　　　　　　　　(North Vietnam, n.d.,
　　　　　　　　　　　　　　　　20 min.)
　　　　　　　　　　　　　　　Young Puppeteers of South
　　　　　　　　　　　　　　　　Vietnam (NLF, S. Viet-
　　　　　　　　　　　　　　　　nam, n.d., 25 min.)

VII. Views of Socialist Societies (cont'd)

   C. People's Republic of China

      (Red Detachment of Women)
      (71, 105 min.)

Brief Synopsis of Films Listed as NA:

  Proclamation of the Nation of Guinea-Bissau--a record of the
    official proclamation by the leaders of the armed liberation
    movement in the bush of Guinea-Bissau.
  Don Pedro: La Vida de un Pueblo--Grandfather Pedro explains the
    heart and soul of his nation, Puerto Rico, to his nine year
    old grandson. Scheduled for broadcast on WABC it was withheld
    pending changes in the English voice-over. Newsreel's version
    uses the original Spanish soundtrack.
  Los Gamines--focusing on one child the film shows the daily ordeal
    of the urban orphans of Colombia and by implication, other
    Latin American countries.
  Borroka: The Struggle--a description of the work and principles
    of the E.T.A., an underground organization in the Basque
    country between Spain and France. Made clendestinely with
    the aid of the E.T.A.
  Mangrove Nine--develops the background and judicial struggles of
    9 Blacks in London arrested during demonstrations protesting
    the harassment of Blacks at a community restaurant, the
    Mangrove.

KEY:

   #
     Includes older films that have been strongly re-emphasized.

   *To be discussed in this study. Uncredited films were made by
   New York or Third World Newsreel. The only recent San Francisco
   Newsreel film distributed by Third World Newsreel, We The Palestinian People, is discussed in Chapter Five.

   **Included here are films dealing with the struggles of minority
   groups in the U.S. for self-determination.

   +
     Films in brackets are listed under more than one category.

   NA
     Films marked NA were not available for viewing as of December,
     1974, the time of my last screening visit to Third World Newsreel. They are described in a new catalogue, printed in Fall,
     1974, but some of the films are not assigned credits. Brief
     descriptions of these films follows the main outline.

The remainder of this chapter will be sub-divided into studies of these different categories of films, but before doing so, there are a number of points that should be made in relation to this table. Newsreel's latest catalogue does not arrange films by subject-matter for the most part, the first page listing films from five different categories in the table. Their most recent catalogue from Fall, 1974, announcing their recent acquisitions (many of which are listed as Not Available in the table), does include a selection of film programs by subject: "Pan African Struggle," "Third World Women," "The United States Military," "Black History," etc. Nine of the fifteen programs focus on Third World subjects. Perhaps this clarity of what to emphasize has helped move Newsreel toward a more systematized method of listing their films.

Newsreel's catalogue is overwhelmingly concentrated in two categories: Institutional Oppression (22 films, 15 of them new--since 1971 or older but re-emphasized) and National Liberation Struggles (28 films, 13 new). Of the latter, the great majority deal with Third World countries. Although the struggles for self-determination by minority groups in the United States are included here, only 5 of the 28 films treat this subject. The principle of self-determination can be felt, however, in many of the other films dealing most directly with other topics: all three of Newsreel's own prison films make some effort to link up the prison system and the general situation of Third World people in the United States. Some of this stress, though, is clearly due to the central importance of the Vietnam War since Newsreel's inception and Newsreel's active role in introducing many Cuban films into America in the late sixties. In fact, a Newsreel catalogue in 1969 listed over a dozen Cuban films; many of them are still distributed while the acquisition of newer ones has tapered off. There is also more competition now from groups like Tri-Continental, Impact Films, and, for a time, American Documentary Films whereas in the late sixties Newsreel was virtually the only source of Cuban and other Third World films. Barnouw, in Documentary, underscores the importance of a film like People's War (1969) at a time when the news media were presenting only the government's version of the war.[1] Unfortunately, then as now, the exposure of manipulation and distortion in the government's use of the media has not provoked a stampede in the direction of Newsreel.

Institutional Oppression is a category that has fewer roots in the early days of Newsreel. That in itself is interesting since one line of thought in the New Left was that the New Working Class would shape up around revolutionary battle lines drawn across the institutions in which this class of white-collar, middle-rung bureaucrats labored. The battle lines have been drawn but not as the New Left imagined. The lines are between the institutions and those they ostensibly serve, largely urban, Third World peoples. The new working class seems to have become the old petty-bourgeoisie--stuck in the middle its members vascillate and wind up in one camp or the other. Hence the perspective in these films is from the outside, a view of how institutions fail to serve the needs of people and of how people struggle to make their voices heard and their needs met. Newsreel's most recent acquisitions, the films marked NA, all fit in these two categories as well.

The fate of older Newsreel films is also quite interesting. The paucity of films under the category The New Left Movement is indicative. Most of the films to which Brom and Biskind were alluding in their epitaphs have disappeared. Those that remain are of two types: those of noteworthy quality as films that still speak to important issues or record historic events such as Army, Make-Out, Richmond Oil Strike, Black Panther, etc. and those of marginal quality (technically and/or aesthetically) but concerned with subjects of primary importance to Newsreel today such as Wilmington, Lincoln Center, Los Siete de la Raza and ROTC.[2] Newsreel has gone a long way toward extirpating the stigma that had become attached to their name.

Two fairly weak categories, Working Class Struggle and Ecology, are probably weak for very different reasons. Chris' comment, "If you want to speak to workers in New York City, you can't talk about point of production," (page 18, Chapter 2) is perhaps an indication of the primary reason for the weakness of the first category. New York (and San Francisco to an increasing degree as "urban renewal" takes its toll) is simply not a center in which the working class plays a very large role. New York is a center of finance capital with most of its lower class concentrated in service industries where the most immediate focus may be institutional oppression rather than the point of production. This is certainly the assumption lying behind many of the films in the category of Institutional Oppression and also applies to two of the four recent films under Women's Liberation (Childcare and A Space To Be Me), films dealing with the need for day care centers from the perspective of working class mothers.

The presence of only one film in the Ecology category is symptomatic of the neglect of this issue by the Left as a whole. To a much greater degree than women's liberation, ecology remains a subject of concern to middle-class liberals whose articulation of the problem does little to mobilize working class and/or Third World support. The roots of the ecological crisis in the capitalist mode of production--a system based on the destruction of its environment must eventually destroy itself--have not been exposed in such a way as to link them up with the other forms of revolutionary struggle. Earth Belongs to the People is an honest but limited effort in this direction and Third World Newsreel's production in progress, Gallons Per Minute, on the "energy crisis," is nothing if not timely.

It is also worth noting that relatively few of the recent films have been made by Third World Newsreel and those that are Newsreel-made were mostly done in 1971 during the period of transition from New York Newsreel to Third World Newsreel. Production was suspended for almost two years as the group rebuilt and this has meant that for the time-being their identity is largely a function of the films they distribute rather than the films they make.

When Newsreel first was formed its place on the Left and within independent filmmaking was very clearly defined, largely because there were no competitors. The American underground filmmakers, experimental filmmakers, or the New American Cinema--all names for the independent filmmaking tradition chronicled by P. Admas Sitney in Visionary Film (New York: Oxford University Press, 1974)--was pointed in a very different direction from the strident, battlefield militancy of the early Newsreel. Its concerns were primarily aesthetic, formal, and personal.

Although the work of some of its members (Sharits, Landow, Conner, Brakhage) may raise important theoretical questions of how film communcates, there is little sense of a political consciousness, almost none of a Marxist analysis and a general aversion to Newsreel's initial forte: agit-prop. Nonetheless, some of the momentum of this tradition helped launch Newsreel and was internalized as an ongoing tension by the inclusion of several members who has previously identified primarily with experimental filmmaking. This is a tension that has been previously overlooked, adding a more friable quality to the relations between the founding members whom I previously characterized as the "nucleus": "Having been part of the founding group, let me say emphatically that we were not friends, and that there was considerable repressed mistrust among this early group precisely because people did not know each other, and because many of the people who played an early role in Newsreel came from very different backgrounds OR were involved in very different life-styles ...."[3]

Despite this tension, though, Newsreel stepped into a virtual vacuum as a filmmaking collective distributing its own films (and providing first-time access to films from Cuba and North Vietnam) as organizing tools for the New Left movement. As this movement has dissipated so has Newsreel's original distinctiveness. Since 1968 several other filmmaking and/or distributing groups have been formed, some of them functioning on a collective basis with a Marxist orientation fairly similar to Newsreel's. There is at least one important difference, however, that is clearly a function of Newsreel's internal development over a period of several years: all of the other groups that have come into existence are predominantly white. As such they sometimes face the same problem Newsreel faced early in its development: to what degree can white filmmakers document a struggle whose most intense contradictions take place among Third World people? Answers to that question vary among the groups and also from the kinds of answer given by Newsreel previously, but in so far as Newsreel is now primarily a Third World radical collective combining filmmaking and distribution in the service of a revolutionary struggle, it retains a distinct position in relation to other groups and seems to continue to play a barometric role in relation to the development of a radical left movement in America.[4] From the staunchly Marxist-Leninist radicalism of Single Spark Films to the generally middle-class feminism of New Day Films, the range of political points of view among primarily white, independent filmmaking groups is indicative of the broad and perhaps diffuse leftist front in America. Newsreel fits within this diffuse pattern but by acting as the only Third World collective making and distributing films by and for Third World people, Newsreel continues to indicate where the movement is honing its sharpest edges.

* * *

Third World Newsreel's Prison Films

We haven't benefitted from America's democracy. We've only suffered from America's hypocrisy. If you're black you were born in jail.

Malcolm X, in <u>We Demand Freedom</u>

Third World Newsreel's emphasis is perhaps partly an indication of their continuing support for lumpen-proletarian ideologies.[5] The Black Panthers, leading exponents of a lumpen analysis, were also very quick to introduce the prison issue into the center of the political arena. And as Malcolm X indicates, jail stands as a synonomous term for the conditions in which racial minorities live. The degree to which members of a prison population will form the vanguard of a revolutionary struggle remains open to question. The degree to which prison represents a vivid and often all-too-real symbol of Third World oppression by a capitalist system is beyond doubt. It is the vividness of prison's symbolic significance that perhaps accounts for some of the romanticizing of prisoners and their situation along with the more general tendency of white radicals to romanticize all aspects of Third World struggle.

As a group whose political importance was largely ignored during the sixties, prisoners can still benefit from liberal concern of a civil rights kind; as a group which has come to see itself in political terms, prisoners can be articulate spokesmen and women on racism, the need for self-determination among Third World groups and armed struggle It is this latter prospect that can provoke a liberal and even left-wing backlash that Newsreel may need to face more squarely in future prison films.

Gary Wills, who often excels at the liberal game of chastizing other liberals, summarizes the functions of prison into three categories: 1) revenge: the payment of penalties to the social order. This function controls the behavior of guards, "It would be logical suicide for a guard whose job is to inflict pain if he had to prevent it as well."[6] 2) deterrence: again pointing to the paradoxical nature of prison Wills comments, "The deterable are mainly deterred by other things short of prison and the imprisonable are by and large undeterrable."[7] (He neglects to mention that his distinction is fundamentally a class distinction, not one of human nature.) 3) rehabilitation: and yet, "Solitude, deprivation, the breaking up of families, the loss of meaningful work, the denial of heterosexual congress--all the staples of our prison system--do not 'reform' human beings but destroy them. We no longer have any excuse for not knowing that."[8]

Since prisons perform these three functions in a contradictory way, it makes sense to see if there is some more coherent perspective on their social role. But Wills can go no further and a left-wing commentator, Dan Georgakas, writing in a radical film magazine, Cineaste, will not even admit of the sympathetic perplexity that dominates Wills' analysis: "Violent crime in the streets is not simply a right-wing slogan but a fact of everyday urban living." "... it is unrealistic to expect a sympathetic response when inmates complain about the quality of food or medical treatment or even when they speak of being beaten up by guards."[9]

Georgakas is political enough not to want to wind up simply endorsing moral sympathy, but not political enough to present a case for how and why prisons actually do function in our society. It leads him to a more outright form of revulsion for prisoners and the prison issue but one which is not different in kind from that which emerges when Wills offers up his own solution to the prison mess in a letter to one of his critics: he proceeds by arguing that what society needs is a system of <u>effective</u> deterrence and to this end puts forth a policy of repression by force, "Deterrence would take the form of more cops on the street to guard against muggers, better patrolling of homes and shops against theft, more police cars to deter murderous driving-- activities of established deterrent effect. Money and manpower would not be wasted on prisons which demonstrably do <u>not</u> deter."[10] In either case the solution to the prison question seems to be to keep Them away from Us, precisely what the prisons already do so efficiently.

Prisons are a particularly brutal manifestation of the brutality rooted in our social system. They are a graphic illustration of how boundaries are established and maintained by moving across them: a system defines itself in relation to its environment by exchange with that environment. What is not Us is Them or It. Prisons represent an exclusionary principle, a source of identification, a fortification on a line of defense against everything alien, everything not yet molded to the patterns of a system. Prisons are a point where definition by elimination, identity by opposition, is upheld most obviously by a forceful imposition of a boundary. Michel Foucault speculates on the interest in prison by asking,

> Isn't it because the penal system is generally where authority, as authority, shows itself most clearly? Imprison someone, keep him there, deprive him of food and heat, prevent him from leaving, from making love, etc., this would definitely be the most delirious manifestation of authority imaginable.[11]

But the identity society, or the dominant ideology as embodied in law, gains through the prison-as-boundary, is a general or systemic effect which also operates at a specific and immediate level in terms of the prisoners themselves. Insofar as prisoners are allowed to recross the boundary, it is with the proviso that they accept the locus of the Other as the source of their identity. This is measured primarily by the internalization of guilt. The prisoners demonstrated their personhood (identity) by accepting responsibility and punishment for a crime wholly their own. All contributing factors of a structural or systemic nature are disavowed. To not see a system is not to threaten it. Upon this condition a prisoner can be deemed rehabilitated, a process brilliantly demonstrated in the Chilean film El Chacal de Nahueltoro where an illiterate peasant is first taught to accept his guilt before he is executed. To refuse to accept this proviso and its consequences is to become a revolutionary. It is this fact that partially explains the violent overreaction of the prison "authorities" in the suppression of the Attica rebellion.

We Demand Freedom was made by Allan Siegel during 1972 when he was not a member of Newsreel. Siegel had been one of the original members of Newsreel and when he rejoined the group late in 1972, Third World Newsreel undertook to distribute his film.[12] It is the most sprawling, the most all-encompassing of Newsreel's prison films, but also one of the most dizzying. The single strongest impression upon walking away from it is of confusion, and yet within a structure that rambles and formally undercuts itself, We Demand Freedom offers a series of invaluable mini-lessons on the nature of the American prison system.

The film itself does not seem to have clear divisions, formal guidance to its internal or logical arrangement of sections. For the purposes of discussion, however, the film can be divided into five sections that span most of the key issues regarding prisons. The opening section makes clear the broad concerns of the film. It is designed as a series of metaphorical impressions indicating the way all our lives are confined, isolated, controlled. A female narrator announces that the film is about "prisons and all other institutions like prisons." She asserts, "We create our own ecological, spiritual, political, economic boundaries." It is time to be free of these boundaries, especially those involving prison. But to speak of boundaries at this general a level with no allusion to the dynamic of how they are maintained or by whom (in whose interests) is to make of freedom a rather amorphous alternative.

Travelling shots of prison cells shift to a montage of images that accompany Bob Dylan's "Desolation Row." Linked to the same music the montage seems to suggest an equation: it exemplifies how we are imprisoned outside prisons, in our everyday lives. The camera roves through a record store, a MacDonald's drive-in, a bank, then cuts to a notorious clip of Vietnamese war footage--an American soldier slams his rifle butt into the collar bone of a Vietnamese prisoner sitting on the ground, his hands tied; the man falls forward; the American kicks him in the groin repeatedly. The camera returns to America and tracks down a storefronted street in what appears to be an urban ghetto.

This sequence in the first section illustrates several of the problems that plague the remainder of the film. The general point is important and clearly worth arguing: prisons are a logical extension

of normal relations, not an unfortunate anomaly struggling to cope with
abnormal (criminal) relations. But the entire sequence is controlled
by the music. It begins and ends with Dylan's song and the length and
rhythm of the visuals seem to have been conceived to fill the time necessary to play the entire song on the sound track. As the dominant code,
though, the music is essentially ambiguous. It makes no clear point,
but evokes a general impression. As the dominant it reduces the ambiguity of the images and tends to foreground their similarity in terms of
isolation and oppression, but it does so without the capacity to discriminate between levels or types of oppression or to associate these
examples with the larger argument about prisons. The song's own original ambiguity prevents it from being the ready-made provider of specific
knowledge about a specific issue. Hence the sequence is a combination
of two ambiguous motifs--that of the song and that of the images--and
although the song functions as the dominant code, it does so without
distinction.

A further source of confusion in this sequence is the total lack
of synchronous sound. None of the images are accompanied by any sound
other than that of the song. Sync sound can be an important means of
pouring specificity into an image, of compelling the viewer to work
through the precise actions and sounds of a given moment. To deny synchronicity is often to deny an image specificity, especially if it is
replaced by a homogeneous sound band that extends over a series of
images. This homogeneous sound then tends to guide the viewer in his
selection of significant detail, and to suggest a more generalized
reading of the images as typical or symbolic. If the overall argument
is of a general nature as it is here, then this combination may simply

repeat the general assertion (that everyday life is a form of imprisonment) without providing examples of a more concrete, specific nature. The argument becomes closed at an abstract level. Although stated somewhat dogmatically, Tretyakov's comment on this point in 1927 remains relevant:

> The documentary needs clear indication that the image on the screen represents a particular man at a particular moment in a particular place doing something specific. The loss of this "specificity" of the image generalizes the object and the viewer observes it as a depersonalized and "type" representation.[13]

The choice of Dylan's music itself is, ironically, confining. Dylan's following is primarily white, middle-class, college-educated--where the roots of the New Left first (and finally) sank. His music is used frequently during the course of the film, often is large chunks that include whole or nearly whole songs. Although it is mixed with Latin music, jazz, electronic, soul, and Peruvian flute music, this very mixture becomes another source of confusion since among this array of musical styles no one style clearly dominates. In attempting to be all things to all people there is a very strong risk of becoming the opposite.

The first section elaborates upon the general impression of confinement with statistics that emphasize the immense number of people incarcerated within the United States, more than in the rest of the world combined. Interestingly, the numerical information does not include class or racial breakdowns (although the fourth section makes clear these aspects) nor does it indicate the particular familiarity of prison for the lumpen-proletariat. This latter omission is characteristic of the film as a whole and is somewhat puzzling given the emphasis placed upon this class by the Black Panthers and other groups. Although this emphasis appears to be part of the impetus behind the film's creation, it does not figure into the actual political analysis of the film which tends to straddle the working class/lumpen debate (about which group would constitute a revolutionary vanguard) in favor of a more general emphasis upon the oppression of all Third World peoples by the prison (capitalist) system.

The second section develops some of the reasons for prison beginning with footage of a black chain gang that suggests both the extraction of large amounts of surplus-value and the tyranny of authority. The former point receives additional emphasis through a montage of work situations involving unskilled or manual labor couples to a song whose refrain is,

>   Work all day
>   Don't get paid.
>   Money, money, money.
>   Give me my money.

The same problems of ambiguity apply to this sequence as applied to the Dylan sequence. It is preceded by a title that reads, "Crime is inevitable where wealth is unevenly distributed," but one thing an ambiguous series of sounds and images cannot show is inevitability. That workers are the principle resevoir of criminals is the unstated assumption but the legality of "free labor" is one of the foundation stones of capitalism and the relationship between it and crime could use further clarification, especially in terms of how crime is defined, what kind of crimes are most frequently committed and against whom.

Another level of the question of legal justice and whose interests it serves is introduced by a montage using stills of lynchings and hangings, primarily of blacks. Again the specific nature of vigilante justice, or racial violence, is glossed over and this montage is coupled to another Dylan song. The section concludes with an image of Nixon and the rhetorical question, "Who are the real criminals?" The reasons for answering the question with a class analysis are well evoked yet so central to the entire argument of the film that it is unfortunate they are not developed with even greater clarity.

Although there is frequent voice-over narration--by different voices of both sexes--the narration is seldom used to provide logical bridges from one section to the next or even from one idea to the next. More often it is used to indicate a topic or to provide certain forms of substantiation (e.g., statistics). This localizes the voice-over narration, which formally could operate at a higher level, as an aspect of a particular sequence. While not opting for a cinema-verite format where voice-over narration is generally abandoned for other forms of logical and narrative development, We Demand Freedom does not employ voice-over in its classic role of organizing or welding together the larger units of the film--in this case the sections and the sequences which compose them.

For example, the next section of the film simply flows out of the tail of the previous one with no bridging device to suggest that once we have seen how crime is class-defined and works against the poor that we should then look at exactly what a prison does to the poor people locked inside it. This doesn't destroy the power of the arguments or the impact of the sounds and images within a section, but it does contribute to the overall fuzzy impression that the film leaves.

The third section examines the institutional oppression of prisons as it is experienced and articulated by prisoners themselves. The section is devoid of voice-over narration entirely. Although the voices of the prisoners are heard voice-over they are at the level of characters, not narrators, and do not pretend to any kind of overview. What they emphasize is day-to-day oppression: the endless waiting, the loss of individuality, the internalization of guilt through everyday contacts. As one prisoner comments, "They train people not to realize what the real problem is." The prospect of finding employment after prison is about as low as the prisoner's self esteem, "Everything is programmed; after a while you just wait to be told."

For Third World people there is an additional layer of oppression --the perpetuation of racial conflict within the prison system and by the prison system. A male prisoner describes how whites are given more and better paying jobs (although average wages in prison fall far below the Federal minimums), "It's not so much that the whites are pressing for these jobs, it's that the guards and prison administrators give whites more jobs than they should be holding so that they are pitted against the blacks. Administrators try to keep this animosity going."

As elsewhere in the film this statement is not "balanced" by the administration's point of view; the views of the prisoners speak alone and for themselves. The visuals show prisoners working but do not clench the case either. Although statistical information may be available, We Demand Freedom, to some degree, assumes the viewer will accept such statements on the basis of her personal experience of American life. To make such an assumption regarding Third World audiences, as Malcolm X's epigraph suggests, is more than reasonable. For such an audience it would be a non-racist situation that would require documentation. Hence the manner in which racism in prison is treated is less an example of facile propagandizing than of directing the film toward a particular audience.

The fourth section is an extremely valuable survey of the history of the prison institution and its uses. It is a history told primarily in terms of the treatment of racial minorities and workers in the United States beginning with the Native American. A number of quotes are used from Native American chiefs and leaders beginning in the last century to suggest that the treatment of the Indian has been equivalent to that of the prisoner. Black Elk, Sioux chief, stated, "We are Prisoners of War," and the images of Indian conquest and consignment to reservations (primarily through the use of stills) illustrates this point of view. The Native American has indeed played a major role in the definition of America by exclusion, by the creation of a boundary between civilization and savagery across which only bullets pass. This point is not extended further but instead serves as a backdrop for a summary of the use of the legal system in the battle between capital and labor. The use of the conspiracy laws of 1806 and the criminal syndicalism laws of the 1920's to thwart worker militancy are described voice-over. The description is accompanied by historical footage of bloody confrontations between striking workers and police or privately recruited goons. The music, though, is strangely lively as if awakened by the sound of fighting in the streets and suggests the New Left's infatuation with violence more than the consequences of these particular acts of violence. The music, in fact, is very similar to the score from Shaft and its bold, defiant beat is at variance with the historical effect of this repressive use of the legal system. This section concludes on the same broad note on which it began, alluding to the Afro-American's experience of the legal system instead of the Indian's however. The shift between the structural function of law as buttress for an economic system and the experience of law as racial oppression is not made explicitly. The voice-over commentary does not address the relationship between these two perspectives, only their internal qualities. Unless the relationship is itself made the subject of discussion, it will be understood on the basis of assumptions brought to the film rather than arguments advanced by the film. Relationships which spring logically from a Marxist analysis of deep structure would seem to be shifts in particular need of the kind of direct attention which voice-over narration can provide.

The section ends with a voice-over commentary by George Jackson describing his family background and how he came into contact with the law and prison system. The sequence makes an effective transition from a more abstract level of consideration back to the personal. George Jackson is an eloquent insightful speaker and his description of the gradually deepening spiral of legal entanglements that wrapped around him culminates in his account of how he plea bargained a charge of robbery: in exchange for admitting guilt he would get a light sentence. The sentence was one to life.

With that the commentary, the sequence and the section end. The camera tracks along a dirty grey road toward the Federal maximum security prison at Rahwey, New Jersey. Electronic music accompanies a montage that shoots off into a lyrical equation of the most disparate images: astronauts entering a rocket, Vietnamese women firing antiaircraft guns, a MacDonald's hamburger store, college protest rallies including one with Mario Savio from 1965, the 1968 Chicago Democratic convention's street violence. These images and more fly past while the dazzled spectator wonders what happened to George Jackson. How does all this add up? The film provides no explicit answer and of all the sectional transitions this is the most bewildering--going from a tight, chronological autobiography to the broadest possible association of major historical events. It is not until the film has advanced some distance into the final section that it becomes possible to recognize that this section deals with the state of the prison struggle today in both literal and metaphorical terms.

There is one level on which the abrupt transition makes sense. After Jackson announces the result of his plea bargaining and the scene shifts to the tracking shot of the prison at Rahwey, prison remains the controlling focus of the spectator's attention even though the personal account of George Jackson disappears. And Jackson disappears at the point when he accepts the locus of the Other, the authority of the prison system, by entering into a bargain with them that only they have the power to alter. Once Jackson forfeits his right to question his guilt, once he accepts his guilt and uses that as a basis for bargaining, then George Jackson as an individual disappears and we are only left with the prison system that has vanquished him. This would certainly be an appropriate analysis of Jackson's fate at this point in his life, but it is a form of analysis that is difficult to recover from the welter of sounds and images that launch the final section at this point.

The fifth section is divided loosely into two parts. The first part is primarily metaphorical and deals with liberation struggles that are similar to the struggles of prisoners. This section centers upon the Vietnamese war of national liberation and features a lengthy quote from the Declaration of Independence of the Democratic Republic of Vietnam (1945). The visual montage of various forms of protest, struggle and war are accompanied by a montage of musical selections that run from jazz to Latin drum music to semi-Asian melodies. This part of the section is more or less concluded by another lengthy quote, from George Jackson, who describes freedom in terms of basic human needs and ends with the ironic assertion, "We will have this freedom even if it costs a total war."

A transitional phase again invokes a point of view similar to Malcolm X's; using an extract from a speech by H. Rap Brown, it underscores the victimization and oppression of Black people as a race. This serves as a prelude to the concluding part which is a capsule summary of the events at Attica, September, 1971.

L.D. Barkeley, one of the spokesmen for the prisoners, describes what led up to the Attica rebellion by describing the working conditions under which prisoners earned 25¢ or 50¢ per day. When five prisoners filed a legal petition they were locked up in solitary and beaten by prison guards. Barkeley's conclusion: "There's no such thing as peaceful change." Some additional visuals sketch out the Attica battlefield but there is no further analysis or description and the film concludes on a freeze frame of prisoners in the Attica yard, waiting, waiting for time to kill them.

* * *

The first sentence of Georgakas' critique of We Demand Freedom reads, "(the film) is an unfortunate example of how not to make a radical film."[14] Its metaphors are "incoherent and boring."[15] "Almost every segment is much too long."[16] But Georgakas' complaints can only pose as an alternative some vague notion of artistry: "(We Demand Freedom and Teach Our Children) have striking visual moments and moving personal testimony but neither of the films stands up as an artistic whole."[17] Without a theory of documentary film, Georgakas falls back upon bourgeois standards of taste: why can't the film be as artful as the films we are taught to accept as artful? It may be symptomatic of the state of leftist film criticism that his reviews are printed in a radical film magazine, Cineaste.

There are clearly problems with the film but it should also be clear that We Demand Freedom succeeds in reaching an audience of primarily Third World people and in explaining an oppressive institution's functioning in terms of the experience of individuals held within its grasp. It succeeds in signalling the movement from surface to deep structure, to a conceptual model that situates prisons within the social system inaugurating and perpetuating them. These points should be clearly stated for it is only within the context of that success that questions arise about the relative effectiveness of certain strategies.

At a formal level these are to a large degree the result of the initial decision to make the film as a compilation film using clips from a variety of previously shots films coupled with voice-over commentary and narration and a wide variety of musical selections. This choice, perhaps dictated by economics, has eliminated the possibility of sync sound cinema-verite type material, of sync sound interviews, and of music designed specifically for the film. This makes the principle means of communicating information the juxtaposition of sequences and sections and the music recruited to the film. The music, though, not only carries meanings that accrue to it through its general circulation and that may conflict with the meaning intended by the film, it is also primarily a source of mood or tone rather than logical or theoretical analysis. It falls into the general pattern described by Klughez, "The movement (in film) is from image to image, from sound to sound--a series of psychological rather than logical connections."[18] Further, the arrangement of sequences and sections lacks a clear-cut, logical progression, and the voice-over commentary, which could fulfill such a function, is confined to the internal explication of sequences and sometimes sections. Although the film seeks to make conceptual analogies and offer a Marxist analysis of how and why prisons function, its formal tools are actually a form of handicap.

* * *

> Five or ten inmates ran into this tunnel we had dug.
> The pigs proceeded to shoot inside. They shot so many
> volleys in there no inmate could have survived. Blood was
> running off so deep it was this high. Blood was so deep
> the pigs had to wade their way in there in order to find
> out how many people were dead.
>
> They are violent when their interests are at stake.
> When you or I want a little bit of freedom, we're supposed
> to be non-violent.
>
> Attica inmates,
Teach Our Children

We Demand Freedom was the work of a seasoned radical filmmaker. Teach Our Children, on the other hand, was the first effort of two Third World women in Newsreel during a period of intense turmoil for the group as a whole, as we noted in Chapter Two. Nonetheless it is a particularly compelling film which makes many of the same points as We Demand Freedom in half the running time.

Teach Our Children divides roughly into three sections which go together to develop the view of prison as a microcosm for the general oppression of Third World peoples under capitalism. The initial sequence begins where We Demand Freedom ends, with the demands of the Attica inmates during the rebellion of September, 1971. These are spelled out and include such things as legal representation at parole board hearings, an end to the segregation of prisoners on the basis of their politics, support for the families of prisoners, and an end to the quota system of paroles for black and brown prisoners.

The demands are reminiscent of the Black Panthers 10 Point Program which was also quite modest in its focus upon the need for immediate reform in the everyday living conditions of Afro-Americans. There was no reference to revolution, socialism, or the use of violence in the program itself. Request such changes peacefully, however, and nothing happens. Demand these changes forcefully, and the response is directed at the forceful display and not the demands themselves. Either way, the petitioner loses, underscoring all the more clearly the oppressed condition of those who seek change.

This introductory section is quite brief and leads to an account of the conditions leading up to the Attica rebellion itself. These are described essentially as they were in We Demand Freedom and conclude with a statement by a prisoner, "We call upon all conscientious citizens of America to help put an end to this situation that threatens you as well as us." Upon this call the film shifts to the second section.

Newsreel footage of the riots in Newark, New Jersey in 1967 are introduced with special attention to the deluge of wounded persons at the emergency room of a Newark hospital. Although the point is not made explicitly, the footage makes an effective transition based on the idea of demonstrating just how much of a threat the situation actually is to Americans who are not behind bars. Justice is no more guaranteed in the community than it is in jail. People are vulnerable to violent attack in either place. Protest is met with silence; outrage with tear gas and night sticks. By equating the situation in and outside the prison in terms of the use of violence to contain and suppress dissent, however, the transition overlooks the distinctive function of the prison as a formal means of exclusion, a clear-cut means of forcibly isolating a given population from the larger society for the protection of part of the society. The prison system operates at a plane comparable to that of the university prior to World War II: it is outside of any direct relationship to the forces of production. This is not true of the urban, Third World ghetto many of whose inhabitants holds vital positions within heavy industry and services industries. It is more true if we concentrate primarily upon the urban lumpen-proletariat in the ghetto and Newsreel's equation of the prison and the ghetto is perhaps another indication of their indebtedness to the lumpen ideologies of the late sixties.

Teach Our Children devotes most of this longer second section to elaborating upon the prison metaphor and the injustice of the judicial system. Like We Demand Freedom it draws upon images from a large variety of sources and also mixes together an assortment of different film styles from sync interviews to animation. One particularly effective sequence involves an ironic commentary on equal justice under the law by means of animation: cut-outs from newspapers and magazines are placed upon a pair of scales. The scale tips. In each case it is the image representative of the oppressed that rises up, lifted by the heavier image of the oppressor: a white boyscout outweighs a Third World boy; Nixon outweighs a Native American; a businessman outweighs a woman worker. It is an ingenious visual argument despite at least one critic's irritation: "You can't drop Jules Feiffer into the middle of a Humphrey Bogart film and expect it to be effective."[19]

The sequence indicates in visual terms the overdetermined nature of the image; it brackets or communicates about one image by means of another image, through time. By showing us one image rise and another fall on the scales of justice, the film demonstrates how context controls meaning, how one image, or one person, is not equal to any other. The film succeeds in some small measure in doing what Godard poses as a theoretical problem in Winds from the East: how to negate or bracket an image by means of another image.* Godard attempts an answer by drawing an X through a picture of Stalin to "negate" Stalinism, to demote his icon to a lower level than that of the surrounding images (e.g., Mao), but Godard still relies upon a conventionalized symbol, an arbitrary sign (the "X") rather than another image. Although Newsreel does not seek to express the difficult concept of negation here, they do succeed in utilizing images alone to establish logical boundaries, levels of control within the visual pattern.

This middle section ends with a funeral parade for an unidentified individual where most of the mourners are Third World people and express militancy with clenched fist salutes. From this death the film returns to Attica to specify what kind of threat prison and the assumptions rooted in the prison system hold for Third World people. The third section examines what happened at Attica, particularly the storming of the prison, the actions of those who attacked the prisoners (a

---

*The image track as a motivated sign system lacks the precision of an arbitrary sign system. Principally, it lacks a means of negation other than by conventionalized signs such as an "X". Images bear an analogous relationship to their referent unlike most words and are hence founded on presences, on the materiality of the referent, and require the supplemental work of a language system to express negation. What Susan Sontag says of photography applies in most cases to the moving image track as well: "All possibility of understanding is rooted in the ability to say no. Strictly speaking, it is doubtful that a photograph can help us understand anything." Susan Sontag, "Photography," The New York Review of Books, Vol. 20, no. 16 (October 18, 1973), p. 63.

sampling of which is provided by the first epigraph) and the contrast between how these events are described by the prisoners themselves and how they are described by the prison authorities.

The section and the film conclude on a note of surging determination despite the bloody toll exacted against these particular prisoners. Even the recountings of the massacre carry at an inflectional and rhythmical level a poetic, transcendent quality that is partly a direct consequence of having Third World prisoners speak for themselves since the quality is a part of the natural speech patterns and is missing or largely effaced in Anglo-Saxon speech. (Something of this quality is suggested even by the transcribed words of the epigraphs.) The final images once again reinforce the metaphorical pattern: a prisoner exercising with weights in a prison yard, Third World guerrillas in action, ghetto children playing in an abandoned lot. Fittingly, the film does not include Newsreel's traditional logo (machine gun sound with a flickering image of a machine gun on which "Newsreel" has been printed); instead, the film is quietly dedicated, "For all our brothers and sisters."

Georgakas aptly evaluates the film: "(it is) more ambitious than Firestone's Attica and does a better job of showing how the institution of prison relates to the entire capitalist structure of power."[20] Teach Our Children may have been a learning experience for the two women who made it, but they learned quickly and efficiently and have shaped a densely packed, explosive challenge to more compartmentalized concepts of prison and the reformist palliatives that accompany them. The film lashes out at all the forms of oppression that affect Third

World people and movingly presents the case for collective, organized defense, defense which will be most effective when it becomes an offense.

One of the film's greatest problems, however, is also related to one of its strengths. One strong strand throughout the film is the material relating to Attica, much of it conveyed through sync interviews with participants. The implications of this event are then broadened not through its own reverberations or those which a formal organization of material restricted to Attica might be able to evoke, but through the various forms of metaphorical statement that link other material to Attica and prisons in general. The scales of justice animation sequence has already been discussed as a particularly effective and provocative metaphor. Others are more problematic and serve to raise questions about the implications of the use of metaphors.

An example occurs in the second section of the film where the visual montage associates images of slaves, workers and prisoners. To erase the distinction between slave and worker is to forget what may have been capitalism's most progressive aspect: the founding of an individual freedom (immediately recuperated by exploitation). To erase the distinction between worker and prisoner is to obliterate the line that defines those within and those beyond the capitalist system. Workers are integral to the forces of production; prisoners are not (even though prisoners have their labor super-exploited, it is part of an industry marginal to the overall economic system). A worker's oppression is a function of his exploitation--his status as worker; a prisoner's exploitation is a function of his oppression--his status as prisoner.

A similar problem crops up in the third section when the film associates images of garment district workers in New York City pushing racks of clothing through the streets with images of slaves and other workers. There is first of all the problem suggested above, but there is also the problem of an iconography of labor: What is the meaning of an image showing manual labor? What should it be? These questions must be answered historically. To the Russian filmmakers of the twenties and early thirties manual labor was cause for celebration and work, machinery and sweat are celebrated in films like The General Line (Eisentein, 1929) or Road to Life (Ekk, 1931). Here work is presented as oppressive by likening it to slavery. The context controls our response and foregrounds negative connotations. But why is manual labor chosen and why is oppression emphasized over exploitation? Perhaps because the oppressiveness of manual labor under capitalism is easier to show than the exploitation of any labor, but easiness does not seem adequate justification. First the metaphor relies on the assumption that the viewer will regard capitalism as oppressive (in conjunction with the formal context: the conflicting messages that a viewer would receive who subscribes to the work ethic are not fully controlled). Second, it emphasizes a subjective and emotional factor--oppression--over the factor that makes labor under capitalism distinctive: exploitation. By not showing the relationship between the worker and surplus-value the film leaves no opening to explain the economic determination of the prison system as protection against those who threaten the systematic production of surplus-value by elimination from not only the forces of production but from the society (as defined by the dominant ideology).

The metaphors therefore create confusion, they fail to operate with sufficient precision to situate the prison system within the larger social system. Instead, the prison system becomes a kind of free-floating metaphor whose own location remains indeterminate. Likewise the metaphors usually operate at the level of emotional or psychological similarity: the similarity of violent response to anti-war rallies, ghetto riots, and Third World guerrillas is meant to solidify these images into one amalgam. This is achieved, however, at the expense of logical differentiation. Although the response is similar, these events are prompted by different aims, principles, and tactics. The effect is to generalize the experience of oppression and to define revolution as that which promotes a violent response. Metaphors can be made and made well but it may be more important to make them at the level of deep structure than of experiential affect. For instance, prison's function as a means of imposing the locus of the Other upon those who are readmitted to society could be compared to the function of the patriarchal family; its exclusionary principle could be compared to the role of imperialistic wars. These kinds of metaphors would require a more conceptual treatment of montage and perhaps more careful attention to the relationship between sound and image. They would clearly require an incorporation of the filmmaker's understanding of deep structure, or of dialectical materialism in a more classical terminology, into the formal structure of the film itself. Without such considerations the attempt to move from surface phenomenon to deep structure within the course of the film generates a sense of bewilderment comparable to that generated by everyday encounter with the phenomena of a capitalist social system.

* * *

In The Event Anyone Disappears was recut from 50 to 25 minutes when it became apparent that people had difficulty sitting through the longer version. It is available on videotape and is distributed on tape as much as it is on film.[21] Of Newsreel's three prison films, In the Event is the most controlled in terms of subject matter. It makes few of the metaphorical allusions to society-as-prison which abound in the other two films. It concentrates its attention upon the experience of being in prison but in such a way as to liken this experience, implicitly, to that of the Third World person struggling to survive in the outside world.

In describing the film, Chris stated, "Mainly, what we tried to show was the exploitation of the work force inside the prison."[22] That may be too strict an interpretation of the film's emphasis, however. Like the other Newsreel prison films, In the Event seeks to discuss a great many subjects. Of these the exploitation of the work force is one. Others include the oppression of prison labor as it is personally experienced, the oppressive conditions under which prisoners live whether working or simply surviving, and the nature of the prisoner/prison interface as represented by guards, rehabilitation programs and medical services. The overall effect is on the one hand to absorb the discussion of exploitation into the general and subjective experience of oppression rather than ground the latter in the consequences of the former and on the other to homogenize the experience of Third World people whether in prison or outside in terms of oppressive realities one of which is economic exploitation. To do so is to neglect the distinctive functioning of prison which has been discussed previously and to make of it only a more intense, more blatant form of the same experiences found outside the prison walls. Even when Newsreel's film dwells exclusively upon what happens inside those walls, the notion of the prison as metaphor seems to remain controlling.

The film is organized around interviews, most of which are in this case sync interviews although there are frequent cut-aways to images of the prison system at large. Sound plays an important role in the overall development of the film; the added specificity and credibility gained through sync interviews is one important aspect of it. Additionally, music is again relied upon heavily for tonal effect but it does not shoulder as great a burden here as in We Demand Freedom since the interview material provides a skeletal organization around which it can build. Locations sounds, or noise, also play a major part in the creation of mood, especially the sounds of the prison work shops and small factories. The noise is incessant and deafening. Although there is sometimes voice-over commentary it is frequently engulfed by the ambient noise. The overall effect is make the voices of the prisoners appear to bob up during the sync interviews from beneath a sea of drowning sounds. It makes an effective device for communicating the alienation of labor and the isolation of the prisoner within his environment.

One somewhat problematic use of music involves the selection of material to accompany images of prisoners at work. The mood of the music is often upbeat and imparts a more positive aura to the labor than Newsreel may have desired. Had the music been part of the location sound--music provided by the prison officials or by a prisoner's radio--its affirmative quality would have been understandable. But as a textual code provided by Newsreel it seems oddly optimistic without in itself providing grounds for such optimism. Music may be a very crucial means of escape or self-defense for an oppressed worker, but as a textual code its primary effect is to ameliorate the oppressiveness of the image of labor for the viewer rather than to demonstrate how the worker himself copes with an oppressive situation.

Discussion of the exploitative nature of prison work is carried out by interview. A black prisoner states, in tight close-up to the camera, "I make 85¢ a day." The wage scale at his prison runs from $1.00 to 60¢ per day which he explains pits the prisoners against one another. A little later in the film a prisoner speaks about prison work shops as "big business." These comments are tucked into the middle of the film and do not occupy a structural position within the film that could allow them to be controlling. They are well-made points, tied to convincing shots of the prison work shops that evoke the iconography of eighteenth century sweat shops, with sound added, but they clearly make economic exploitation an epiphenomenon not in relation to the distinctive functions of prison but in terms of the common experience of oppression among Third World people wherever they might be.

Other prisoner interviews relate additional tales of oppression. These include a description of prisoners left to die when medical aides refused to administer treatment outside normal clinic hours; of overcrowding in prison cells; of an education program taught in English to a prison population made up largely of Puerto Rican men who only spoke Spanish; and of guard brutality. The last topic is developed in some detail through a series of sequences that bring together several points of view. The sequence begins with a black security officer in an office with rows of books behind him. He discusses how little he knew of the psychological and sociological factors affecting people before he took up prison work. A slow wipe erases half of his image and replaces it with a shot of a guard touring a cellblock. The officer goes on to add that a guard should serve a four year apprenticeship in order to understand fully the needs and problems of prisoners.

The wipe is completed and the images of the guards are replaced by a black prisoner who describes how the guards can and do use anything they want against the prisoners. He gives an example of a guard who called a prisoner out of his cell to take a phone call then beat him up. Toward the end of the film, this theme is taken up again by a prisoner who warns us, "In the event any of us disappear, just remember that we all got good hearts."

The overall sequence creates an effective transition from the liberal facade erected around security work to the raw reality experienced or feared by the prisoner himself. The wipe becomes a useful device to suggest peeling away, unmasking. The black officer, educated and concerned, appears more and more naive as the sequence develops and his naivite takes on more and more the function of disguise, hiding from himself and the usual forms of prison system rationalization the events that he can only understand as aberrations but which to the prisoners constitute the most basic, everyday reality. Through its sustained development and the retroactive effect this had upon earlier statements and points of view, this sequence is one of the most cinematically powerful in the entire film. It nails down by manipulation of the textual codes Foucault's description of how prison authorities must think,

> You have handed over to us robbers and murderers because you thought of them as wild beasts; you asked us to make domesticated sheep of them on the other side of the bars which protect you; but there is no reason why we the guards, the representatives of "law and order," we the instruments of your morality and your prejudices, would not think of them as wild animals, just the same as you.23

* * *

In general, Newsreel's prison films make the group one of the most important single sources of film material on this subject. These three films represent the bulk of Third World Newsreel's filmmaking work since the transitional period when the group's name and identity changed. The films are invaluable organizing tools and have met with considerable success in the hands of community and political groups.24 Although the exact nature of their political thrust can be debated, as I have done here, they are all pitched at a level to which most people can relate. The choice of emphasis upon oppression and upon the commonality of Third World people's experience with capitalist institutions may be a debatable choice but it allows for debate to take place among precisely those people Newsreel wants to reach rather than isolating it within more marginal groups (such as film critics or cadre-type political organizations).

At a more formal level, looking at the three films together helps pinpoint a series of problems relating to the use of sound in documentary, particularly the use of speech. There are two basic modes into which the use of speech falls: direct and indirect address. Direct address involves an acknowledgment of the presence of the camera (and hence the viewer); it is the narrational* mode most familiar in the form of the first person omniscient narrator--the Voice of God, as it is often called. The possible forms of this mode are the voice-over narrator (voice of God), the direct sound or sync narrator (the voice of authority), voice-over character (the voice of witness, with images of illustration) and sync character (the interview).

Modes of Address in Documentary Film

Direct Address:

	synchronous sound	non-synchronous sound
narrators	Voice of Authority	Voice of God
characters	Interview	Voice of Witness / Images of Illustration

---

*In this study the words "narrator," "narration," and "narrational" are all used to refer to spoken commentary. They are distinguished from "narrative" which is reserved for the principles and procedures of story-telling.

Indirect Address:

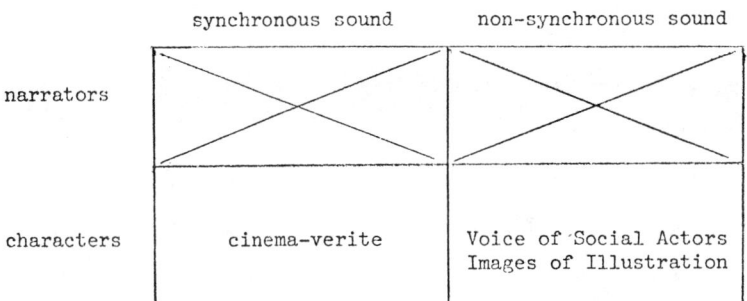

Indirect address disavows or ignores the presence of the camera (and hence the viewer); it is the narrative mode (as we normally think of it in terms of fiction where characters play out their roles of oblivious of our presence) or the non-narrational mode. Using terms of Louis Marcorelles, if direct address is the lived word, then indirect address is the living word.[25] Indirect address precludes the voice-over narrator, a form distinct to direct address. The sync narrator is only possible when the narrator speaks as a character--when a television commentator makes a blooper, for example, and suddenly becomes an apologetic person speaking his own words. The most representative form, though, is the sync character--the classic form of cinema-verite where characters, or idnividuals carry out their lives as though the camera were not recording them. Whatever effect the presence of the camera has is deflected into alterations in everyday behaviour patterns instead of in how the camera is addressed. Also common is the voice-over character where images of illustration are coupled to the character engaged in his more or less normal patterns of social interaction (the character as social actor).

Newsreel's prison films do not involve appreciable use of any of the forms of indirect address. In this regard they belong to the more established historical traditions in documentary filmmaking where the film by addressing itself directly to the viewer declares itself apart from the conventions of the fictional film and normally assumes the status of a truth. (This distinction between fiction and documentary is purely a matter of convention, however; both modes of speech can be employed by either form.) To address the viewer is to acknowledge more than his or her sheer presence, though. It is also to acknowledge the viewer as actor, as one who comes to the filmic event with human intentionality, human desires. Foremost among those needs customary acknowledged is the desire to know. Direct address is therefore a mode generally directed toward problems of exposition.

Exposition functions on two levels in the textual system--within the textual codes and within the extra-textual codes. At the level where the extra-textual codes are dominant exposition is primarily about the immediate referent of the speech of the narrator or character --what it is like to work in the prison work shop, how much a person is paid, what happened during the Attica rebellion, etc. The film image is conventionally spoken of as a window onto this world outside itself; its own function as signifying practice is obscured. Relatively autonomous sequences of interviews or narration localized to references about a specific topic are typical means of bringing this form of explication into the foreground. It should be apparent that this is the level at which the Newsreel's films seek to fulfill the need to know most of the time.

Exposition at the level where the textual codes are dominant is primarily about the relationship between individual sequences or sections and the film as a whole. It is the level of formal relationships within the film, the level of part-whole relationships, and is a function of the filmmaker's manipulation of the textual codes. It is the level at which she/he reveals his/her epistemology. (These two levels also operate within the mode of indirect address but since Newsreel seldom uses this mode, their consideration wull be deferred.) It should also be apparent that this is a level at which the Newsreel films are relatively weak.

Newsreel relies primarily on the more local effect of interview situations or voice-over commentary by characters or narrators where the extra-textual codes retain dominance. Newsreel seeks to link their film to the real world and real conditions but by doing so too hastily, at the local level of the sequence, they leave the relationship between the film as a formal whole and the film as a series of part-part, part-whole relationships undetermined or indeterminate. Since it is the formal whole that exists at a conceptual level, the effect is to reduce the firmness of Newsreel's grasp upon the conceptual level at which both the film and the real world operate, the level of deep structure. Newsreel's choice of the mode of direct address seems to indicate their awareness of the importance of the need to know and their own desire to fulfill that need. Indirect address generally lacks any form of explicitly stated overview at the level of the extra-textual codes (it simply follows characters who live through their immediate present); and at the level of the textual codes it can fall prone to a return to fictional formats--the similarity of the crisis structure in Drew Associate films (Leacock-Pennebaker) to the classic dramatic curve and to the films of Howard Hawks in particular has been well demonstrated by Stephen Mamber.[26] Newsreel seeks something more, but by failing to devote themselves to the problems of the textual codes, the need for a formal whole compatible with their conceptual model of the functioning of society (dialectical materialism), Newsreel undercuts the overall effectiveness of the films, returning at the formal level to the more or less conservative patterns of omniscient narration and personal testimony.

These patterns seem more akin to the assumptions of a logical positivism than dialectical materialism. They assume the underlying validity of rational explanation; they assert the dominance of the digital over the analog in a non-dialectical, static manner.* They reduce the overdetermined status of the visual image and human interaction to a logical determination. They subordinate the formal patterns of the film as a whole to the film-reality relationship of the individual sequence. In doing so they couple the twin dangers of empiricism and dogmatism into a single package, even though the particular forms News-

---

*Analog and digital communication constitute the two basic forms of all communication. Analog communication involves continuous quantities with no significant gaps. There is no "not" nor any question of "either/or": everything is "more or less" (e.g., images, gestures, inflections, rhythms, and the context of communication itself). Digital communication involves discrete elements and gaps, and forms the matrix for all denotative, linguistic communication.

reel chooses (the voices of non-leaders among both characters and narrators, the emphasis upon the spoken word rather than the written one) are a markedly important shift from the far more dogmatic format of Voice of God narration and stilted interviews.

An attempt to escape some of the implications of these choices, particularly the choice to emphasize the local level at which extra-textual codes may be dominant, may be seen in Newsreel's extensive use of music as a dominant especially in We Demand Freedom. Although this does help break with the empirical notions of rationality that in political terms generate the paradox, "The working class is capable of reason. If reasoned analysis leads to the conclusion for the necessity of revolutionary struggle, then why doesn't the working class revolt," music is not capable of functioning at the level of exposition as a dominant code. Its dominance is indicative of an abandonment of explication in favor of evocation which evades the problems of formulating a Marxist theory of social relationships at the formal level of the textual codes in film.

There is an interesting attempt at a solution to this problem of the organization of the textual codes to create a formal whole that responds to the need to know generated by the mode of direct address in the films of Emile de Antonio.* There is also a very provocative attempt at a quite different solution in the mode of indirect address in

---

*De Antionio's films are the most rigorous attempt to structure a pre-established line of reasoning in direct address but without narration that I know of. His films include: Point of Order (1963), Rush to Judgment (1967), In the Year of the Pig (1969), Millhouse: A White Comedy (1971), Painters Painting (1973), The Weather Underground (1975).

the films of Fred Wiseman. And Although Wiseman's work is remote from the immediate issues here (being in a different mode altogether) and de Antionio's only marginally related, there is a prison film distributed by Newsreel themselves that can serve as a useful point of departure for comparing Newsreel's own method with that initially proposed by de Antonio. It is a film by a former editor on de Antioni's films, Cinda Firestone; the film is <u>Attica</u>.

<u>Attica</u> is distributed primarily through Tri-Continental Films. Newsreel is only a secondary distributor and had no direct involvement in the making of the film. Hence there is little reason to discuss it exhaustively although it is useful to point out some of its political differences from Newsreel's own prison films and to take up the problem of formal organization in some detail. "The film had its beginnings as a pamphlet Cinda Firestone and Jessica Segal were writing for the Liberation News Service. Firestone then decided to make a 5 minute film; and as more information and footage was made available and fed into it, <u>Attica</u> grew to a feature length documentary." 27 The film consists of footage shot by state troopers during their assault, footage shot by Firestone at Attica subsequently, footage of the McKay commission hearings, and interviews with prison officials and prison inmates.

The political thrust of the film is considerably more diffuse than Newsreel's films. Argument by analogy is not employed and none of the interviewees make a reasoned case for the distinctive function of the prison system. As a Newsreel member commented,

> In a capitalist society, there have to be prisons. Otherwise the system cannot function, and that was not pointed out. There have to be prisons, there have to

be military forces, and with prisons and those military forces, they have to confine people. They have to control. Otherwise there will be a threat to civil society. If you're no good you go to jail. And that's the basic point that wasn't clear in Attica.[28]

This is a shortcoming which Georgakas also perceives, "There is only the dimmest perception of a system working according to its own logic, a system which needs prisons like Attica."[29]

Newsreel, though, does distribute the film, a choice dictated by the major importance of Attica in dramatizing the conditions of the prison system (almost literally insofar as the rebellion made a conscious attempt to speak through the media--an attempt that backfired when the media took at face value the reports of prison authorities regarding what happened when the prison was stormed). And, although the film does not present an analysis, it does, like the Newsreel films, let prisoners speak for themselves, a wide-range of prisoners who by speaking in their own words capture a specificity that is usually lost when leaders speak for causes.

Although Attica is inferior in its political analysis, as a film (as a formally organized whole) it is superior. (A good example of this inferiority is when the McKay Commission asks an official, "Could your plan have saved the lives of the hostages if the inmates were determined to cut their throats?" After an evasion fails, the official responds, "I doubt it." The film then moves on, failing to draw any conclusion about the motivations for an attack that was willing to sacrifice the lives of hostages.) This superiority resides in how the mode of direct address is organized into a formal whole, a narration made up of tiny fragments of speech from a vast array of sources that in its totality tells the story of what happened at Attica in September, 1971. In looking at this organizing of material, stress will first be placed upon the techniques employed to indicate the possibility of achieving a totalization that has so far eluded Newsreel. The implications of this particular technique, however, seem primarily negative and call less for imitation than reflection upon alternative tactics.

By breaking up the narration and assigning it to characters rather than narrators, Firestone runs the risk of generating great confusion. This is overcome by the rigor with which individual facets of the narration are coupled so that cuts between shots or sequences developing a point are linked logically to one another. Normally they relate in terms of (1) amplification—a series of inmate interviews describing oppressive living conditions; (2) chronology—different individuals telling what happened next; (3) motivation—characters explaining conditions catalyzing the rebellion, other characters describing the response to the rebellion, others describing the aftereffect of the response, etc.; and (4) contrast—one explanation for a given decision or event juxtaposed with a radically different explanation. This latter form of cutting normally operates between testimony at the McKay Commission by prison authorities and the testimony of prisoners for the film itself. Editing is therefore controlled by the demands of exposition and sacrifices other possibilities like emotional affect. Firestone's method, and by extension de Antonio's, thereby shapes "raw material," the individual facets of the narration, into a finished product, the overall film as narration. There is none of the sense of confusion at the end of Attica that there is at the end of We Demand Freedom. All of the parts are carefully orchestrated into a formal whole.

Several problems arise. The individual facets suffer a double loss of credibility: first, from the consequences of the mode of direct address (discussed below) and second, from their particular kind of subordination to a formal whole. The kind of transparency, of immediate, local dominance of extra-textual codes found in the Newsreel films is lost in favor of a less immediate dominance by the whole. This is not entirely regrettable insofar as the local dominance of the referent--that to which the film refers in the real world--tends to mask the film as signifying practice and pretends it is a neutral, "truthful" presentation of how things really are. The problem cannot be resolved by arguing in favor of local dominance over subordination to a dominant whole as Tetyakov did in asserting, "When a fact becomes a brick in a construction of a different kind--the pure documentary concept disappears; everything depends upon montage."[30] (That is simply to subscribe to the ideology coded into assumptions of film as a neutral recording medium.) The problem can only be resolved by examining precisely what kind of whole the parts are subordinated to and what the epistemological assumptions of that whole are. The question becomes to what degree the formal whole of the film allows access to the deep structure of phenomena in the real world, of historical processes or events. To what degree does Firestone's conceptual model correspond to a materialist model of social action? To what degree to other models?

Much of the problem revolves around the exclusive use of direct address. This mode ruptures the pattern of relationships between everyday events and individuals in favor of a relationship directed toward the camera but without taking account of the camera itself. In other words the subject of direct address is not the relationship of the character to the camera, but his relationship to the real world. We are thereby provided with information that is from the start second hand. We garner empirical data that is in fact already interpreted twice over: by the character who relates it and by the filmmaker who selects who to relate it and how. In a sense it repeats the problems identified with the voice-over narrator in direct address but through the form of character testimony. Problems touched on here are echoed in discussion of <u>We the Palestinian People</u>, <u>38 Families</u>, and <u>Redevelopment</u> in Chapter Five where direct address proposes a logical analysis of a process but fails to develop a formal model adequate to the task. Leacock explained the problem of direct address this way, "When you interview someone they always tell you what they want you to know about them .... What I want to see is what happens when they are not doing this."[31] Indirect address at least removes half the problem: characters do not tell us what they did, they show us what they are doing.

De Antonio's and Firestone's method of organization recruits the smallest fragments--shots and sequences--directly into the largest constellation--the film as a whole. The film is a narration; each fragment's position is determined by its logical, narrational linkage to what precedes and follows it. This places the greatest emphasis upon the editing and upon the relational importance of each fragment. The narration becomes the dominant principle and reduces each fragment to a part of itself. The multiplicity of meanings inherent in the motivated aspects of the shot (visual information, non-syntactic verbal information, music, sounds) are subordinated to a strictly digital linearity. They are not recaptured at a higher level for the narration itself is one-dimensional, flat. It is consistently dominant and whatever ambiguities or conflicts exist within it are not pitted against one another; other possible dominants do not challenge its status. Ambiguity is simply absorbed into narration that does not interact with any other textual code on an equal basis. (Epistemologically, it becomes a kind of essentialism that reads into events a narrational pattern discovered by the filmmaker. The actual forms of relationship between phenomena are not seen as over-determined, nor does this kind of conceptual model allow for overdetermination. There is an essence, a truth, to which the filmmaker is privy and which he repeats for us by a reduction of the pro-filmic event to the dictates of a single textual code.)

<u>Attica</u> ends up with an uncomfortable aura of ambiguity about it. A viewer might well suspect that she/he could combine facets of sync interviews into a very different pattern, telling a very different story. The film's narration becomes similar to courtroom testimony where one story becomes interchangeable with another, only the viewer lacks the lawyer's invaluable right to cross-examine. In seeking to escape the dogmatism of the omniscient narrator, Firestone lapses into the relativism of conflicting witnesses.

* * *

Perhaps Marcorelles is right when he suggests that neither direct nor indirect address alone is sufficient:

> An ideal mixture of Leacock's method, which is purely
> cinematic, and Perrault's, which is more poetic and more
> literary, involving the "living"--which is more or less
> spontaneous and more or less organized--and the "lived"--
> with its historical structure, its sense of becoming--will
> one day produce an autonomous cinema that has finally broken
> completely with established methods of expression, but this
> still is a dream.[32]

Firestone's film demonstrates the great need to think very carefully about formal patterns of organization to the overall film while not providing a very satisfactory solution. How to combine the "living" and the "lived" word to achieve a conceptual model that would be commensurate with Newsreel's goals remains in question. (The possible solution offered by Wiseman is perhaps both more sophisticated and acceptable than de Antonio's but it is also incomplete.) The form of the film seems to require a self-reflexive mode that can both present or show what people actually do and also organize or intervene upon that presentation to indicate the controlling patterns of a deep structure. Firestone shifts from an empiricism which records events in the real world to an empiricism which records testimony about those events, a solution that finally collapses back into the problem since it neither interrogates the codes of neutrality in the cinema that allow it to appear to leave what it records unaltered (film as signifying practice) nor yields a formal deep structure that breaks with the ambiguity inherent in an empirical point of view. As an explanatory model it is no more adequate than the solutions proposed by Newsreel's own prison films. The twin perils of empiricism and dogma remain very much with us.

* * *

Newsreel's Military Films

It's not our war. It's the rich people's war, the people whose sons don't have to go.

They kept using words like Cong, slopehead, slant eyes, and I said, "Hey! These are the same kind of words they use in the States against me, against all Third World people!

We don't want to fight anymore, but if we have to fight again, it will be take these steps!

Anti-War G.I. Veterans,
Washington, D.C. Rally, 1971
from Only the Beginning

Consideration of the other films distributed by Newsreel will be somewhat briefer. The prison films suggest many of the political directions and most of the formal problems that characterize Newsreel's work. Neither the prison films nor the other types of film provide clear-cut, definitive answers to these problems. They do offer amplification of tendencies in political direction and elaboration of formal challenges. The remainder of Third World Newsreel's films will be looked at from these twin points of view.

Only the Beginning and Winter Soldier were both made by Newsreel in 1971 before the composition and orientation of the group shifted completely to its present Third World emphasis. As such their structure and lines of emphasis make an interesting comparison with G.I. Jose, a film acquired in 1974 although not made by Newsreel themselves.

Both films are records of public events designed to be communicated by the media. In this regard they resemble the records of the events at Attica, although these events do not contain the life-and-death risks that haunted Attica. In Only the Beginning the event is an anti-war rally in Washington where former G.I.s filed across a speaker's platform on the Capitol steps to throw away their military decorations and denounce the war. In <u>Winter Soldier</u> the event is publically staged testimony of 300 G.I. Vietnam veterans regarding war crimes under international law which they personally witnessed in Vietnam. In both cases Newsreel seeks to make the broadest possible associations, especially in <u>Only the Beginning</u>, and runs into some of the same kinds of problems that beset the prison films.

<u>Only the Beginning</u> operates in terms of two more or less parallel bands of sound-image track. The first involves the event itself and the sync sound words of the G.I. veterans either at the time of the event or in interviews for the film around the same time. The second involves footage from Vietnam and is used to illustrate or amplify upon what the veterans say. The second band of material is accompanied by voice-over commentary from the interviews or occassionally by narration, but does not have synchronous sound of its own.

The footage from Vietnam was not shot for this film but edited into it from other sources.[33] The absence of sync sound here immediately establishes a hierarchical ordering in which it operates on a subordinate level to the first band of testimony presented in synchronous or voice-over direct address. There is a somewhat disturbing implication behind what was probably an economic necessity: that the Third World struggles exist to be interpreted from the point of view of the other, in this case an other who has changed sides but who nonetheless remains apart in essential ways from his Vietnamese brothers and sisters. The ordering may also appear to "make sense" in terms of reaching an American audience, but on second thought, it should be apparent that concerned Americans should have no trouble in understanding the point of view of the Vietnamese themselves. Behind what seems to be a pragmatic and sensible facade, this choice of formal organization masks a ethnocentrism that is characteristic more of the earlier New York Newsreel than Third World Newsreel. The effort is made to identify with the Vietnamese and their struggle for liberation but it is carried out, at a formal level of organization within the textual codes, in an ethnocentric manner. The tone of moral outrage characteristic of the New Left is thus not a surprisingly dominant note, in sharp contrast to the calm, objective, patient tone in U.S. Techniques and Genocide in Vietnam, a film made by the Vietnamese themselves.

The band of non-sync material from Vietnam is used to illustrate the daily lives of the Vietnamese liberation forces, their tactics and morale. Parts of it are used to document U.S. aggression and brutality --burning villages, torturing prisoners. One major portion of it is used to draw a parallel between the treatment of the American veteran and his South Vietnamese counterpart. A narrator tells us that disabled Vietnamese veterans petitioned for supplemental benefits and were denied. They planned a demonstration in Saigon and were told it was forbidding. They carried it out anyway, since "they didn't believe that the government would use force against veterans disabled in the service of their own country." The footage documents the result when these crippled, prosthetic-limbed veterans are clubbed and tear gassed by Saigon police and army units. The footage makes a convincing attack upon U.S. and South Vietnamese policies, priorities and actions.

Most of the sync interview material shot in the time immediately surrounding the public rally details examples of racist and genocidal Army policy as witnessed by the veterans. It also becomes a revealing record of how the veterans viewed their own situation that stands in marked contrast to the official depiction of the American G.I. Subversion in both passive and active forms was common. Patrols would be faked, the soldiers hiding just beyond the perimeter of their own camp. Officers would be fragged (killed) mysteriously by soldiers who had their fill of patriotism.

Oddly, though, this line of development, exploring the attitudes of G.I.s at the time when they are objectively functioning as instruments of U.S. aggression, is not pursued very far. The reports addressed to the camera of internal subversion of Army morale and discipline are left to tell the whole story. For the anti-war movement it is an encouraging story, but for young men who lived that contradiction of supporting a war effort (however subversively) and also detesting it, the exact manner in which the contradiction tore at their emotions, the intense struggle they must have gone through to understand their role instead of rationalizing it must have cut far deeper than these almost bravado tales of resistance would suggest. And for a movement looking for avenues toward radicalization beyond the walls of the campus, this process could have served as one important model had it been explored in detail.

At least two factors may have stood in the way of this line of pursuit. The first is the tendency to generalize toward abstract commonality, in this case between U.S. veterans and South Vietnamese veterans, between anti-war veterans and anti-war civilians, between personal testimony of atrocities and generalized symbols of such acts. It is a tendency also marked in We Demand Freedom and perhaps is indicative of the New Left's effort to identify with revolutionary movements through vicarious emotional empathy rather than theoretical or analytical argument. This tendency is one large reason why Only the Beginning amounts to a series of indictments of the war more than a structured analysis of the war and its larger implications and motivations. The moral outrage expressed by the veterans is doubled by that expressed through the footage from Vietnam added by Newsreel. It becomes less a call to understand the war in terms of the capitalist system that spawned it or in terms of the personal experiences of those who fought it than an invocation to denounce it for its offensiveness. It is this kind of choice that has made common the complaint that early Newsreels speak only to the already convinced.

The second impediment is the difficulty that the New Left had in dealing with the personal element throughout its history. The women's movement may have been a singularly important contribution from the New Left but it was also a major factor in razing it. As the movement sought identification with a revolutionary movement taking place somewhere else, it denied its most immediate reality, except insofar as this reality provided metaphorical evidence of similar forms of oppression (and sometimes exploitation) as those motivating genuine revolutionary struggle. This was a major point of departure and one with sizeable consequences for the New Left's ability to take its own experience seriously in any form other than metaphorical. Hence in numerous

Newsreel films there is an almost measurable urge to move beyond the immediate into the metaphorical, to tie things up with vague and amorphous allusions that are not rooted in close analysis either of the structural similarities between phenomena nor in the controlling dimensions of personal experience--the general or the specific modalities of a deep structure. The imaginary (ideological) identity by opposition between Them and Us which these soldiers have struggled to break through and transcend by meta-communicating about it (even if we only see this in the secondary form of direct address to us rather than in practice), is not integrated into the film. Instead, this ideological opposition is repeated at another level: the battle between Them (the imperialists, the U.S. government) and Us (Third World people and those who identify with their plight). The oppressiveness of such an opposition for the G.I. is not directly analyzed or discussed, and so the film runs the risk of reinstituting this oppression as part of the dominant value structure of an oppositional movement.

Moving beyond this form of bind without rationalizing the subtle forms of control They can exert over Us is exceedingly difficult and it is partly the New Left's impatience to get on with it, with the revolutionary moment, that impedes its confrontation with this difficult problem. In the final analysis, however, it is a crucial problem, well summarized by Anthony Wilden:

> If dissent is to escape its own self-alienation, if it is to escape the automatic response of liberalism that all new ideas are equal or that a new theory is simply "an interesting point of view," then dissent must transcend the status of negative identity. In a word, <u>all dissent must be of a higher logical type than that to which it is opposed</u>.[34]

The failure to achieve this form of dissent is one of the shortcomings of the New Left as a whole, perhaps inevitably if personal experience can only be admitted at a metaphorical level.

> The general attitude of the officers--I was a Lieutenant at the time--was there's someone senior to me and if this wasn't standard operating procedure, he'd be doing something to stop it. Since nobody senior ever did anything to stop it, everyone assumed that this was what was right.
>
> G.I. veteran,
in Winter Soldier

Winter Soldier is a more tightly controlled film than Only the Beginning and restricts itself to one spatial and temporal continuum: the testimony of veterans regarding war crimes in Vietnam. The mode is always direct address, either in front of the cameras and microphones of all the press attending the event or for the Newsreel film crew specifically. There is no narrational structure and no attempt to insert metaphorical commentary. The testimony speaks for itself as a devastating indictment of U.S. policies and their implications; the repetition of similar stories from numerous veterans only serves to heighten the credibility of each story. The film mounts these eye-witness accounts into a powerful emotional condemnation of a war fought by G.I.s who have come to realize it was totally outside their own interests to do so.

The veterans introduce themselves and summarize their testimony in terms of precise war crime violations in the first part of the film. Crimes that are mentioned repeatedly include slaughter of civilians, torture of prisoners, destruction of the property and possessions of civilians, rape, use of forbidden chemicals against people and crops, mutilation of bodies, and the falsification of information. Virtually all of these crimes indicate the degree to which Army training--normal, systematic training, not some aberration of it--prepares soldiers to see the enemy as an entire race that is sub-human and fit for the most bestial of punishments. One soldier tells of a training officer who took a rabbit, killed and disembowled it in front of his men saying that it might look innocent and trusting but that only by this way could it be trusted. It was the last lesson he had before leaving for Vietnam.

Another veteran tells of an ambush that resulted in the deaths of 25 civilians. The commanding officer then put out an order for all enemy weapons being held by his men to be turned in. These weapons were then placed with the bodies and the dead civilians were counted as Viet Cong. Others testify that a V.C. was commonly identified as any Vietnamese with a weapon or any Vietnamese who was dead.

The film is a powerful document in its collage of voices bearing witness to atrocity. The formal organization is weak, consisting of little more than introducing the veterans and their charges and then following up a number of them in more detail. The local effect of individual sequences dominates over the formal effect of the film as a whole. The whole becomes an accumulation of these effects and does not shift to a pattern of formal control through the textual codes. The extra-textual codes remain dominant and yet carry such weight and impact that there is little immediate sense of incompleteness. On the contrary. There is a sense of surfeit, of having learned too much, having heard too much about harsh realities that our dominant ideology teaches us are best left ignored or relegated to unfortunate anomalies.

In retrospect the lack of formal organization to the film somewhat undercuts this point since the systematic nature of these war crimes is clearly indicated and yet not tied into an understanding of how the functioning of imperialist policies is inextricably related to such a systematic demotion of the other, the one outside the norms of the dominant ideology, the one who is identified with the environment which the system is pre-ordained to conquer (exploit). Such a unifying statement would require a meta-communicative form of discourse from the veterans themselves or a manipulation of the textual codes to arrange their testimony into such a pattern. The veterans have discovered the horror within the truth of what they have been trained to do, but neither their voices nor those of the film fully explain why these horrors must be taught, why their experiences are not aberrations, and why such wars can only be perpetrated on the assumption that they are. At the pragamatic level of providing a valuable organizing tool, especially in relation to an anti-war G.I. movement, Newsreel has again succeeded admirably. At a broader level of providing insight into the functioning of the system that selects and promotes certain kinds of war over others, Newsreel has again postponed the more analytical task in favor of the immediate response.

> The military cuts a line between you and your family. It's a terrible thing. I got two purple hearts, for getting my ass blown away. This is what I get for fighting a bull-shit war. I was 190 pounds when I went in, and 110 pounds when I came out. My family doesn't even know me anymore; it's nothin' like those World War II movies ever

were.

> Puerto Rican G.I. veteran
> in <u>G.I. Jose</u>

<u>G.I. Jose</u> was acquired for distribution by Third World Newsreel in 1974. It was originally made by Norberto Lopez for "Realidades," a Spanish-speaking program on WNET-TV in New York. Although it makes many of the same points as the two films made directly by Newsreel, it also approaches its subject from a noticeably different direction which seems indicative of the shift in emphasis between New York Newsreel and Third World Newsreel as well as of differences between Newsreel and a major television station's programming interests.

<u>G.I. Jose</u> is not built around an event, symbolic events being a form of political action particularly well identified with the New Left. It does involve the personal testimony of a number of Puerto Rican young men about their experience of the U.S. Army, but restricts itself to their testimony without adding any metaphorical cut-aways. The focus is exclusively upon Third World men, Puerto Ricans to be precise, and the personal element which so often initiates leftist concern only to be displaced to a metaphorical level is here treated with persistence and insight.

The first section of the film is a virtual textbook of false consciousness as several young Puerto Rican men describe "in their own words," why they are volunteering to join the Army. The words are only partially their own, most notably when they cite the absence of any viable alternatives within their immediate environment, less so when they invoke the myths of patriotic duty, excitement, adventure and

travel they have been taught to associate with military service. The
section ends with an effective cinema-verite sequence recording the
swearing-in of a dozen or so volunteers. Much of the time the camera
remains behind the back of the swearing-in officer (who is white); his
upheld hand dominates the foreground while behind it the earnest volunteers "repeat after me." It is an effective use of textual codes
(of composition in this case) to communicate a critical attitude toward
the pivotal event--the induction of Third World volunteers into the
United States Army.

The second section of the film begins when we see another individual, still dressed in civilian clothing as were the would-be volunteers,
say, "The uniform don't mean nothing. It's all shit." Retrospectively,
we learn that the speaker is a veteran and this section details the impressions of the veteran to the experience that could only be imagined
in the first section. The juxtaposition of the two sections is also
an effective means of creating a formal whole out of a before and after
comparison. The experience of the war becomes an absence, a gap in the
film, rather than a metaphorical insert. What we discover is the trace
of that experience in the radically altered attitudes of the Puerto
Rican veterans.

The intensely personal level at which the lessons of military
service are learned is well indicated by the epigraph. The impulse to
make reference to the functioning of a system is even more remote here
than in the Newsreel films, and yet the intensity with which the veterans discuss their personal experience and its effect upon their lives
and relationships goes some distance toward suggesting that a powerful

force is at work shaping the lives of men, that it could scarcely be coincidental. By plunging further into the personal the film ironically penetrates further into the socio-political than those Newsreel films that try to straddle both camps.

The veterans demolish the false consciousness of the first section. The macho pride that is casually assumed in the first section becomes the source of tragic waste in the second: a veteran tells of a brother who is wounded by shrapnel and yet insists on going back out on patrol. He has too much pride to remain in a "safe area." His first time out after returning he is blown to bits by a land mine. The veteran tells the story rapidly, poetically, with a barely suppressed fury that cannot be ignored. Glory through conquest is rapidly demoted into the folly of macho pride.

G.I. Jose is also a film that utilizes the direct address format of the interview to good advantage. It avoids the omniscient tone of the narrator in favor of the everyday voices of people speaking from intense personal experience. It captures through the juxtaposition of interviews from two different points in time, the shifts in articulated values that are a product of the passing of that time. By concentrating on articulated values it stresses what interviews can do best--reflect what a person can articulate when asked to directly address an observer rather than evoke participation in the events that realized those values. G.I. Jose thereby communicates many of the same ideas about the effect of the war as does Hearts and Minds when it follows different veterans who typify pro- and anti-war sentiments but in a tighter, more succinct pattern. It sacrifices a certain amount of resonance, of complexity, in doing so, but it is a modest price for a short, 20 minute film to pay when it is able to retain as much impact and possibility for provoking discussion among a well-defined audience and a more general one as well. By dwelling so forcefully upon the personal effect of Army service, G.I. Jose goes a long way toward suggesting the systematic and ideological assertion of power that enables an institution like the Army to have such a devastating effect on individual lives.

U.S. Techniques and Genocide in Vietnam and The Selling of The Pentagon form an interesting contrast to the first three films. Both utilize variations of sound/image relationships that are revealing not only of the aims and tactics of the U.S. military but also of the filmmakers themselves. Both offer a broadened scope in their examination of large issues involving the U.S. military--the false front created by Pentagon propaganda in the one case and the naked reality of armed warfare in Vietnam in the other.

U.S. Techniques was made in North Vietnam and is representative of the Third World films which Newsreel introduced into the United States in the late sixties when there were few, if any, alternative sources. Even today when groups like New Yorker Films and Tri-Continental offer numerous Third World films, Newsreel remains an important source of non-theatrical, hard-hitting documentaries like U.S. Techniques.

The film is simply organized. A Vietnamese narrator describes the American government's policy in Vietnam as genocidal. Accompanying footage depicts a bombing run on a village and the ruinous aftermath. The remainder of the film is a blow-by-blow description of the weapons utilized by American forces to carry out this policy, weapons that often contravene international war conventions and invariably have little value except as indiscriminate anti-personnel devices.

A combination of Newsreel footage showing the actual use of various weapons, animated material detailing their technical features, and medical documentation recording their effect upon human beings is used to examine the deployment of steel fragment bombs, dum-dum bullets, spider mines, flechettes, anti-personnel mines and napalm. The visual material is shockingly graphic, detailed, painfully blunt. The narration is cool, scientific, detached. It is reminiscent of the narration to Land Without Bread insofar as the disparity between its detachment and the horror of what is shown works to subvert our faith in the spoken word. There is a realm of experience that cannot be captured in the digital net of words, and that experience looms awesomely over the film.

And yet by not directly insisting upon the atrocious policies that promote such tactics, by not denouncing the military tactics frequently and righteously the narration escapes the temptation to which so many Newsreel films succumb: the attempt to indeed present in words the sense of moral outrage that such tactics and weaponry can evoke. The narration could almost be that of the technologists who developed these weapons except that instead of a modest sense of pride there is only a blankness, a numb sense of loss. In this regard the narration approximates that of Night and Fog.

The narration of U.S. Techniques thus becomes a guide through an experience that is on the brink of the nightmarish even with this calm, detached point of entry. It leaves space for the viewer to ponder and react rather than insisting upon a reaction at the cadence of the narrator. It leaves space for a kind of internal subversion where the image tracks ultimately dominates and betrays the tone of lucid objectivity which the narrator dons. Such a stance is only a pose, a pose with important tactical functions in the film, but one which must be finally unmasked. This the images do, peeling away the veils of distance, the rationalizations of efficiency and moral neutrality. Through this form of internal subversion the film penetrates even deeper in our consciences than a more straightforward attack on U.S. policies could hope to do. U.S. Techniques exemplifies the manipulation of textual codes--the relationship between sound and image--to achieve an effect far more powerful than that available when such formal considerations are demoted in importance.

The Selling of the Pentagon also makes use of sophisticated sound/image relationships but to distinctly different ends. The film is a classic example of the voice of God tradition in which images and additional sounds are mustered in support of a narration that remains dominant throughout the film. There are no opportunities for subversion, for interplay between different dominants. Everything has been carefully orchestrated to at all times give credence and substance to the narration. The final words of the film's narrator, "This is Roger Mudd," are intended to impart a human, fallible quality which the remainder require us to take on faith.

There is an ironic illustration of the voice of God concept that is in itself also one of the most damning examples of Pentagon propagandizing in the film. Roger Mudd interviews a former Pentagon press officer who describes how press conferences were set up in Vietnam to conform to a "one-voice concept." Prior to the actual press conference on bombing runs in the North this individual would select the most handsome, most articulate pilots he could and then brief them on the "one-voice concept," rehearsing their stories so that there would not be "any divergent views." The result: "Great; the pilots represented the way we conceived the air war was being fought." (The interview with this press officer is also a good example, like the interviews in G.I. Jose, of effective use of this format: he describes how something was done, the conscious motivation behind it, rather than report at second-hand what happened factually.) Not only does this tactic parallel the design of the film itself, the news crew who "bought" this one-voice concept was from CBS (Mudd's own network).

The function of this kind of narration is well summarized by David Denby: "The narrator's function in those films (standard network documentaries) is often as much psychological as it is informational; his presence implies a balanced, judicious authority which the viewer can trust, relieving him at the same time of forming his own relationship to the material (if all the difficulties haven't already been edited out."[35] It is a point not lost on the Pentagon itself: many of their own cold war films utilize narrations by Walter Cronkite, Chet Huntley and other newscasters in the voice of God tradition.

The digital component of the verbal message retains tight control throughout the film; a story is told to which we passively assent. There is even less participation than in the narrational technique of the de Antonio and Firestone films (and Davis' Hearts and Minds which also follows de Antioni's strategy). In those films the viewer is left to construct the narrational connections between fragments not originally shot to fit into such a pattern. In this film, everything has been pre-arranged to fulfill a narrational pattern that can be followed with minimal effort. There is a flattening out of the over-determinations, the multiple meanings residing in the images and the sound/image relationships into a single meaning of reinforcement for a logo-centric and subject-centered narration.

Formally, The Selling of the Pentagon thus conforms to a conservative tradition in documentary and its overall thrust politically is decidely less radical than the Newsreel's films. It is well capsulized by Mudd's pronouncement that, "This propaganda barrage (from the Pentagon) is the creation of a run-away bureaucracy that frustrates attempts to control it." There is a hint here that reform will not be easy, that it may even be impossible, but it is the only alternative allowed to be posed. The more radical critique of the devastation by the military of personal lives or entire races for imperialistic purposes is never broached.

Despite this reformist orientation, similar in kind to that of Attica, the film is of definite usefulness to Newsreel. It effects an exposure of the propaganda machinery of the Pentagon that is beyond the resources of Newsreel (even though CBS used only publically available material, that material is more available to some "publics" than to others), and thereby throws into well-documented question the kinds of arguments which Newsreel's own films seek to refute. The film's examination of the Pentagon as a mass medium of its own (reaching an estimated 50,000,000 Americans during the sixties) and its manipulative relationship to the other mass media goes a long way toward unmasking the forms of distortion that hide behind the name of news. Together with U.S. Techniques and the two earlier Newsreel military films, Army and ROTC, The Selling of the Pentagon describes the large-scale effect of the military machine upon the everyday lives of individuals as well as the sophisticated tactics that go into the make-up of so powerful an institution.[36]

* * *

Newsreel's Community Service Films

> The new films are moving away from the two things which created (Newsreel's) stereotype: reporting "significant events" (riots) and explaining their significance. Today's demand is for information about ourselves and our relation to the Amerikan machine and for a new solidarity against it, for us. Newsreel serves these needs as it unites the filmmaker and the subject, and as it makes new films about people's lives rather than events.
>
> Rebecca Pulliam, "Newsreel," The Velvet Light Trap, no. 4 (Spring, 1972), p. 8.

Since working-class people are often unable to buy essential services on a free market, these services are provided at reduced cost by governmental, tax-supported means. These include medical services, schooling, housing, and direct aid (welfare). In many urban areas, though, as the tax-base of middle-income individuals diffuses into surrounding suburban areas, these services which even in the best of times place self-perpetuation and stop-gap measures above genuine service, begin to break-down. Older Newsreels like Lincoln Hospital and High

School Rising demonstrate the effect of this on medical and educational services. Two more recent Newsreels, Rompiendo Puertas (Break and Enter) and Homefront, demonstrate how the basic need for shelter falls prey to the same economic determinations that play havoc with these other vital elements of a true community.

The tendency in Third World Newsreel to make films "about people's lives," as Pulliam describes it, is pronounced throughout their repetoire of films dealing with institutional oppression as that very category might suggest. This is further conditioned by the difficulty discussed in Chapter Two of organizing in New York City around the point of production.[37] And the shift to a local and personal level of emphasis is one which has characterized much of the work on the left since the demise of the New Left.[38] This is not surprising when much of this surviving left is based upon Third World leadership for whom oppression does not need to be evoked by a montage of national liberation struggles in the far corners of the globe. It is as close as the broken bottles in the street and the cockroaches in the kitchen. Like the trade-union at the point of production, community organizing becomes an immediate, personal, first-line of defense in the struggle for survival and self-determination.

These Newsreel films are similar in tone and purpose to some of those made by the Film and Photo League during the 1930s. The depiction of the Anacostia Flats in Washington, D.C. in Bonus March, 1932 and of hunger marches in Strike Against Starvation were also intended to muster community solidarity and illustrate the deprivation inflicted by an economic system seemingly incapable of correcting its own cyclic declines. With the addition of sound they gain the very valuable tool of being able to allow working people to speak for themselves, to more telling effect than any narration could devise: "What the intellectuals have recently discovered, however, is that the masses don't need them in order to know. They know perfectly well, and much better than the intellectuals--and they say it very well. But there is a system of power which checks, forbids and invalidates this discourse and knowledge."[39] By bringing the extra-textual codes through which working-class, Third World people communicate in everyday life into the textual system of the film, Newsreel not only draws attention to the problems endemic to the community but also to the very means of articulating these problems and the strategies of attack upon them that are adopted by the community members themselves. The mute images of workers could seem dangerously revolutionary to the sponsors of the British documentaries in the thirties, but images alone cannot explain or analyze with the power and immediacy of the image plus the spoken word.

The stress upon the personal, articulated by community members more than spokesmen, is not without its dangers. There are two that are appropriate to this discussion, one involving the textual codes and the other the political implications of this choice of emphasis. The former involves the limitations of direct address that have been referred to previously. The voices of the masses are validated but at one remove from their actual participation in everyday life. There remains a compelling urge to label problems and spell out solutions that requires the mode of direct address and runs the risk of the kind of reductionism that leads to dogma. The utilization of many voices rather than that of one narrator, the choice of characters who speak in direct address but do not themselves assume the role of narrator (retaining an extra-textual identity in favor of a textual one), and the strong role that music plays in many of these Newsreel films all work to deflect the risk away from the end point of dogma but nonetheless tend to reduce the multiplicity of determinations and meanings that make up everyday life into those that can be articulated in direct address. It is a short cut to deep structure that also makes of it a more threadbare thing than a structure that can more fully account for the overdetermination of everyday life, of phenomena as they are experienced.

A related problem is the extent to which this focus further promotes the tendency in Newsreel from its inception away from the theoretical or analytical in terms of the formal organization of their films or of broader political questions than those of the most immediate, action-oriented nature (the general neglect of false consciousness, ideology, and deep structure as areas of prominent concern, for example). This may be due to a general current of anti-intellectualism in American life, but part of it is certainly due to the way in which the personal was treated by the New Left, an approach well criticized by Russell Jacoby:

> Only human subjectivity--the personal--seems real and potent; the personal, it is said, is political, the political, personal. The identity of the two eliminates the need to pursue either separately. Theory and objective thought make way for human relations, feelings, intuitions. The immediacy of these kills to the quick the core of theory and thought: mediacy.[40]

This kind of relationship to the personal does not seem to pertain as strongly to Third World peoples and the absence of a theoretical dimension from the speech of characters in Newsreel's community service films may be more an indication of the beginning stages of revolutionary consciousness still prevalent than of a confused identification of the personal and the political. The confusion, though, does seem to still figure into Newsreel's own impulse to witness and celebrate important political events or situations without an equivalent commitment to organizing this material into more theoretically sound textual systems through the manipulation of the textual codes. The solution clearly does not lie in the denial of the personal (or the theoretical) but in their fusion in a rigorous manner, a goal even further from realization in San Francisco Newsreel than New York.

> When you're tired, you have to stand up, even in your last years of life. They only want your money. If you want something to eat, you have to pay tax. If you want to go to the bathroom, you have to pay tax. Where do the taxes go? To Vietnam and the moon. They should take the money and put it into housing for us, the poor people. What are they doing in Vietnam? They didn't lose anything there.
>
> Elderly Spannish-speaking woman in Rompiendo Puertas

Rompiendo Puertas (Break and Enter) was one of four films made by New York Newsreel during the period of transition to Third World Newsreel in 1971.[41] Along with El Pueblo Se Levante (The People Are Rising) it gives a strong indication of Newsreel's commitment to Third World people's struggles while its actual structure reflects a deepening immersion in the immediate context for struggles that had in the past been all too readily abstracted into more diffuse, metaphorical significance. As Ruth McCormick notes, "The crew who worked on this film lived side by side with the squatters, got to know their struggle from the inside, and consulted them constantly about what they felt the film should say. The result is both real and informative."[42]

Break and Enter deals with the occupation of condemned buildings by black and Latin people, mostly Puerto Rican. The city of New York condemned the buildings in order to make-way for high-rise, middle-income housing, evicting scores of families in the process and then allowing the buildings to lie fallow for years while funds were acquired for the next stage of the project. The story of the gradual rise of community ire over this project is told by interviews with the participants, a limited amount of voice-over narration (stressing vital facts as in We Demand Freedom more than serving a bridging function) and the visuals themselves which show the community discussions, the actual occupation, the hammering away of sheet metal closing off the windows, the police attacks to re-evict the squatting families, and the continued solidarity of the people despite harassment.

Except for isolated montage sequences evoking the flavor of New York from a working-class perspective, the film owes little or nothing to the city symphony tradition. Its concerns are too immediate, its politics too specific for the formal reflectiveness of that approach. The film does incorporate, however, sequences that are one of the rare examples of Newsreel's subscription to the newer technique of cinema-verite. These sequences do not play a dominant role within the overall film, however. Nor do they move into the kind of detailed examination of everyday life which is possible. For the most part, the cinema-verite sequences are reserved for planned demonstrations or actions, such as the inauguration of "Operation Move-In" with the occupation of a condemned building. Cinema-verite's acceptability seems to be reserved for those situations in which Newsreel knows what is going to happen, where that element of fore-knowledge allows them to incorporate verite footage into a format that is pre-conceived in terms of political direction. It almost becomes an inscription of cinema-verite technique into the mode of direct discourse, rather than an endorsement of a technique that moves away from the reductionist dangers of direct address (but toward those of an indeterminate empiricism).

Another technique that figures into this film and into several others (We Demand Freedom, Teach Our Children, Black Panther, High School Rising, Richmond Oil Strike, and America) is the lateral tracking shot. It is as though Newsreel discovered the significance of this shot independent of Godard and used it over and over to present a parallel view of surface phenomena whose determinations they sought to alter.[43] The shot suggests analogies to a movement paralleling the dominant social structure, attempting to overcome it, and not yet being able to turn onto a collision course from which it can emerge victorious. This sense of being held at bay, of seeing (and implicitly knowing) what constitutes the other world, what makes it work and should be changed, of fixing on it as a locus of one's desire (for change, for identity) yet not being able to transcend it emerges repeatedly, whenever the shot is used. It does not hold as strongly critical a set of connotations as it does in Godard's films, perhaps because it is rooted in sound/image relationships far less rigorously than Godard's theoretical mind and fictional format allows. The tracking shot here (of high-rise buildings, of condemned buildings and razed city blocks) and elsewhere in Newsreel calls forth a more ambivalent response as though Newsreel were involved in a tug-of-war (with their aesthetic, with a political system) that neither side was winning, yet.

The diversity of the individuals who speak to the camera in Break and Enter is one of the film's strongest points. The woman whose words are featured in the epigraph spoke in Spanish, but with a clear understanding of how much opportunity America offered her and the people around her. Most of the speakers are women, many of them are middle-aged or elderly; many do not appear glamorous by media standards. As in The Woman's Film this serves as another form of validation in which people can see themselves filling the role in textual codes normally reserved for the star, the hero/heroine of classic Anglo-Saxon beauty. A particularly effective sequence demonstrating this commitment to the members of the community and women first involves a woman who describes problems of childcare in her apartment while in the far background of the shot a man sits caring for a young child. The negative space usually reserved for the "little woman" is here cleverly subjected to a role reversal.

This sequence and others is also of interest in that it does take place inside the home, off the street where Newsreel's predilection for "street action" often prompted it to dwell. Although the format is not cinema-verite, the movement into the home signals the settling in process that McCormick refers to. The setting of discussions about the oppressive living conditions inside the very apartments that embody this oppression makes a far more compelling background than a speaker's platform and also help lend a more mellow, less didactic tone to the words we hear.

Although the Young Lords Party (a Puerto Rican revolutionary group in New York) contributed to the organizing of the community, they are not featured as the vanguard of the people. We do not even see any indication of their presence until 15 or 20 minutes into the film. There is no clearly defined vanguard proposed by the film, but if any group comes close to assuming that role it would have to be the women of the community. Newsreel's own description of the film indicates that 80 percent of the squatters were women with large families.[44] The women not only provide the impetus for the occupation and the bulk of the interview material, they also provide the allusions to a broader perspective of a Marxist analysis with which to locate this particular struggle. It is a working mother who introduces the connection between oppression and exploitation when she discusses her work in a button factory and makes the comment, "In order to bring $40 to my house, I have to bring in $400 in profits for them." It is another woman who concludes the film by arguing that to break and enter is not a crime; it's the only way to get anything done and that next on the agenda will be occupying some of the luxury apartments in the city.

Although exploitation is again presented as an off-shoot of a more pervasive oppression (accurate experientially, but somewhat askew theoretically), the women who make these observations have a very firm grasp on the realities of their own situation and know how to communicate that reality and how to change it with bold clarity. Like <u>The Woman's Film</u>, much of the power of <u>Break and Enter</u> comes from the plain, non-rhetorical speech of the people who live the contradictions of capitalism every day of their life. When working people decide to take possession of the points of production or reproduction (the factory or the living unit) rather than simply withhold their labor or their rent until modest reforms are agreed to, then the stage is set for an escalation or polarization in the conflict between proletariart and bourgeoisie. The ominous concluding warning that the luxury high-rise buildings are next is precisely to the point. It is little wonder that Newsreel continues to encourage distribution of this film when many other early Newsreels have fallen by the wayside.

> I believe that people should have enough self-respect to fight for their own decency. They give the landlord power by being afraid of her. They make her the tyrant she is. They permit her to rule their lives and to determine the quality of their lives and yet they will complain among themselves, but not have the self-esteem to follow it up with something that's a true hardship for the landlord like depriving her of the rent ....
>
> A Tenant in *Homefront*
>
> After three years on strike most of the violations have been repaired. No one has been evicted.
>
> Printed title in *Homefront*

Homefront is Newsreel's other recent film about community housing and organizing. It was shot in 1972 and 1973 by Jenny Goldberg who originally made it as a project at New York University; after seeing the film Third World Newsreel decided to distribute it.[45]

The film operates on a smaller scale than *Break and Enter* where Operation Move-In involved taking over 38 buildings. *Homefront* depicts the struggle of ten tenants who are without the benefit of a mass community organizing effort to confront their landlord and win minimal improvements in the quality of their apartments. The introductory section graphically documents the unsafe, deteriorated condition of the building by following occupants through their apartments as they point out gaping holes in the plaster walls and ceilings, refrigerators that do not work, dangerously run-down stairwells and hallways where their children often play. The middle section details the struggles of the tenants to confront the landlord and focuses upon the efforts of Lisa, the most militant tenant, to encourage the others to stand with her in a rent strike.

The final section broadens the perspective first by indicating that this kind of isolated incident is related to larger community problems. The camera tracks down an entire city block on which only a few individuals are seen: it has been condemned to make way for urban renewal. An interview with an architect provides an explanatory level to this visual record: landlords do not care about maintaining small apartment units for reasonable rents when they can make greater profits from other projects: as a speaker at a community rally concluding the film says, "Why do you think money isn't being spent on something as basic as housing? Because investors can make more profit by lending their money in other areas like industrial plants, high-rise office buildings, luxury apartments. If they can't get their profit from housing, they don't go into it." The broadened perspective offered by this concluding section is, in fact, the most direct link between this film and Newsreel's own work and probably explains their willingness to distribute it.

The development of the second section is perhaps the most interesting aspect of the film, however, insofar as it confronts that initial stage of political consciousness where reluctance, fear, and rationalization play major roles as impediments. Most often Newsreel films present individuals who feel very clear about their priorities and the kinds of action that political change require even if these individuals are presented as typical or average rather than as leaders or organizers themselves. The tenants shown in this film are not at the point where they feel clear and unequivocable about their committment to political issues or even to a direct confrontation with their landlord. The arguments raised by Lida and by the more hesitant tenants thus provide an extremely valuable tool for inaugurating similar types of discussion among people just on the threshold of a political awareness of their situation. Fear of being harassed and intimidated, fear of losing time on the job (and perhaps the job as a result), fear of losing money in organizing expenses, fear others will back out and further expose those who participate--these are real fears that need to be considered and confronted when dealing with community organizing rather than glossed over with the certitudes of those who have moved beyond them. Break and Enter attempts to deal with these kinds of problems indirectly, providing examples of people who have overcome them; Homefront tackles them directly, making it and The Women's Film the two Newsreel films that broach the difficult subject of false consciousness to any appreciable extent.

In this regard the film resembles some of the efforts of the Challenge for Change program in Canada although it did not include the kind of community feedback into the making of the film that characterizes these efforts and many other Newsreels as well. It does, though, present the level of consciousness that exists when problems are first perceived, when solutions and tactics are debated and people seek to raise their consciousness to a higher level, a task which the film itself can contribute to quite positively. Unlike the Challenge for Change films, though, Homefront does not remain at the level of mirroring existing levels of consciousness but instead, in its concluding section, points to a more theoretical overview that can further direct consciousness-raising in a Marxist direction.

The main problem raised by the middle section is that the consciousness of Lisa, the militant tenant, is also relatively low in that she does not make the kinds of associations offered in the final section while she puts the question of the rent strike into the form of a ego-challenge, a matter of pride more than politics. (The comment in the first epigraph is representative of this tendency.) This problem does not perturb Newsreel which sees the discussion process that takes place around their films as an opportunity to put this in perspective:

> The film shows the contradictions that exist among the people. They can see their own contradictions when they see the film. Now when (Lisa) is talking unsisterly, this is really obvious to someone else when they see the film. Someone from her peer group will also see this. Hopefully that will serve to help them raise their consciousness a bit higher and alert people who are not political.46

This point seems particularly apt for a film that is directly concerned with levels of consciousness so that discussion would naturally move in that direction as well. For other films that operate on a more theoretical level and attempt to present some kind of analysis of what forms of understanding and action are most appropriate, this sort of open-ended approach could place too high a burden upon the spectator who may feel confusion between elements that are presented in order to be criticized and elements presented in order to serve as models. Newsreel's willingness to be open to viewer criticism as a vital process of extracting meaning from the films rather than as a device for repeating a catechism prescribed by the film (as was too often the case in earlier Newsreels) signals a significant breach with the more dogmatic, "correct line" attitudes of New York Newsreel in its early stages. The willingness to show false consciousness at all rather than efface it with revolutionary rhetoric also seems to indicate another level on which the increased degree of commitment to the personal involves a very hard-nosed look at what people are actually thinking and how they relate that to any program for social change.

Neither of these films presents great strength in its formal organization; the most impressive facet of each is the depiction of personal struggles to stand up with determination against oppressive living conditions. This is primarily a function of the extra-textual codes incorporated into the textual system—the voices, inflections, gestures, expressions, the codes of decor and furnishing, especially as they are communicated by the women whom both these films feature. This is again indicative of Newsreel's priority to make progaganda of immediate use rather than tackle long term issues; it is symptomatic of the New Left's anti-intellectual, anti-theoretical bias even though its more bristling edges have been considerably softened.

An observation about the emergence of a political, underground film distribution system in England in the late sixties gives a good glimpse into how widespread these priorities of immediacy and spontaneity were on the left at that time:

> (The third circuit of political distribution) was essentially pragmatic. There was relatively little interest in the theoretical aspect of alternative cinema: the need to re-examine the nature of film, to re-appropriate the cultural and political function of film, to politicise film aesthetics, were hardly considered. The politics of the third circuit was based on a sort of organization reformism, one that was lacking in a solid, ideological perspective.[47]

Unlike the third circuit, Newsreel never confined itself to reformism but it did share the anti-theoretical bias. Newsreel saw film as a direct and leading force in the class struggle, referring to film in terms of "can openers" and "hand grenades."[48] The approach of many political filmmakers in France after May-June, 1968 did not gain acceptance with Newsreel until the early seventies and even then with less theoretical bite: "The cinema is not outside the class struggle, but it does not participate in it directly, in that it is not a specific means of political practice."[49]

But the groundwork for this approach was flimsy. The largest tradition of socially conscious filmmaking, the British documentary under John Grierson, had eschewed aesthetics for relevance. As Grierson himself confessed, "It (documentary film) ceased exploring into the poetic use of the documentary approach with us in the '30s."[50] This is an attitude that continues to plague efforts to set documentary film on as firm a theoretical footing as fictional film or its own divorced helpmate, experimental film (in the hands of filmmakers like Godard, Snow, Gehr, Sharits, or Resnais). It is rooted as deep as habit and continues to pop up in serious discussion of documentary: Henri Breitrose asserts in reviewing Barnouw's history of documentary, "It is an aesthetic of content that drives the documentarian, and the rule that for the audience a documentary is as good as its content is interesting is difficult to falsify."[51]

The problem is that without at least intuitive creative instincts of how to shape a whole from parts, the documentary film collapses into being only as interesting as its content. It becomes nothing more than a duplication of extra-textual codes that are not even recognized as codes that are subject to manipulation: the filmmakers thinks he has caught reality. It is at this point that some of the rudimentary concepts of a semiology make their entry: "The concept of a reality mirrored in some kind of independent natural state has already been demolished. <u>Symbol systems in themselves are the original forms into which the world as we know it is organized. The object in front of which the painter sits down to paint is already a 'way of taking the world'</u>."[52] Ignoring this insight usually means that local dominants in a film are not organized into an overall pattern by means of the textual codes. The total becomes a sum of the parts. The parts are seen as mirrors of an external, natural world. They are not seen as signs in a signifying system—film communication.

The challenge is twofold. First to recognize that the "natural" world is made-up of signifying systems dialectically related to our own intentionality and governed by a deep structure resulting from that intentionality. Second to recognize the importance of the filmmaker's manipulation of the textual codes in order to shape the kind of textual system best equipped to indicate this set of relationships. It seems to me that only through coming to grips with the second point will it be possible to explore fully the implications of the first, to escape the twin horns of empiricism and dogmatism and shape a dialectical film form commensurate with a Marxist analysis of real conditions of existence. These conclusions must remain speculative, at least in terms of Newsreel, however, since they are prompted by absences, by what is not addressed by films like <u>Homefront</u> and <u>Break and Enter</u>. To what degree it will be Newsreel and to what degree other filmmaking groups that solidify possible approaches to these theoretical problems remains to be seen.

* * *

Newsreel's Due Process Films

Due process has not been an area of major activity on the part of Newsreel recently, partly because its value becomes limited to the symbolic (a value of greater importance to the New Left) once the possibilities for significant social change by legal means are challenged and discarded. Hence the kinds of emphasis placed upon due process by the Civil Rights movement have shifted to a concern with the impact of a legal system upon the Third World community, especially its oppressive and repressive aspects (brought out particularly well in <u>Los Siete de la Raza</u>).[53] This shift is also a product of the emphasis given to the legal system by the Black Panthers and other lumpen-proletarian groups as a repressive system to be fought against at a day-to-day level rather than as a potential source of significant change. <u>The Murder of</u>

Fred Hampton, in fact, operates as a kind of legal brief detailing the complicity of the police and District Attorney's office in Chicago in the murder of a leading Black Panther. It presents the legal system as entangled by a web of systematic falsification and repression. It offers little if any hope for reform.

So the People Should Know was a film quickly made at the time of the Daniel Ellsberg-Michael Russo trial involving the disclosure of the Pentagon Papers. It was made originally for American Documentary Films but was recut, hastily, after ADF went bankrupt. The resulting film is distributed by Newsreel. The filmmakers now call themselves Resolution Films and are associated with San Francisco Newsreel where they made Redevelopment.[54]

The film's lasting value (beyond publicizing the issues in the trial itself) lies in its stress on the revelatory impact of the Pentagon Papers as a document of the level of American commitment to South Vietnam together with clear foreknowledge of its incapacity to stand alone during a period when these facts were being publically suppressed or denied. These points are spelled out through interviews with Ellsberg, Russo and their lawyers where they discuss the importance of the Pentagon Papers. They are also brought home on a more immediate level by Ellsberg's personal recollection of his experience with the war and what he learned from it.

In the late sixties, Ellsberg was commissioned by the Rand Corporation to do a study on "Viet Cong Motivation and Morale." His travels in Vietnam convinced him of the exceptional morale of the Viet Cong, their wide base of popular support and the futility of attempting to defeat them without destroying the nation and/or its inhabitants. He also saw at first hand the degree to which it was a class war more than an ideological war of free world vs. slave world; the highest income areas in South Vietnam were also those areas most loyal to the Saigon regime. (His impressions of the Viet Cong's determination seem to be accurately portrayed by a parallel experience in Godfather II, when Michael witnesses the courage of the Cuban revolutionaries. It is an interesting example of fiction borrowing from fact.)

The facts brought out by the film also serve an important retrospective function in vindicating much of what was argued by the left regarding the war when the mass media were still repeating governmental press releases is not brought out by the film explicitly but could be readily supported by a matching up of leftist commentary with material found in the Pentagon Papers.

A final but more problematic value of the film is in the series of street interviews that are intercut with the interviews of the defendants. These are conducted by Ellsberg and Russo and attempt to take the pulse of what the "man on the street" thinks about the war in general. One woman respondent is particularly impressive in the incisive political edge to her replies stating, for example, that the war was obviously an "imperialist war." The difficulty is the lingering doubt on two levels: whether the interviews have been in any way pre-arranged and to what degree what is said matches up with what the individuals do in any case.

To accept articulations of belief for behavior in practice is a danger that most social scientists know all too well and spend considerable time attempting to circumvent by ingenious forms of scientific control built into interviews and questionnaires. There are no such controls here. The goal here is akin to that expressed by Leacock but without Leacock's distinction between levels at which values can be discovered, "To me, it's (the use of cinema-verite) to find out some important aspect of our society by watching how things really happen as opposed to the social image that people hold about the way things are supposed to happen. And by seeing discrepancies, by revealing the things that are different from what is expected, I think people can find out something very important about themselves."[55]

This use of the interview form of direct address does not seem highly rewarding. It is further weakened by the hit-or-miss, take-it-on-the-fly nature of street interviewing. If ideology operates most fundamentally at an unconscious level--in terms of habits and modes of perception--then expressions of belief cannot reach it. We are presented with rhetoric, opinions rather than lived values---the very form of presentation that becomes so much a part of the politician that instinctive distrust is not without reason. The importance of recognizing this distinction is further obliterated by the treatment of the textual codes, by demotion of the signifying aspects of the pro-filmic event in favor of the impression of "capturing" reality by means of these candid interviews. At a formal level this compounds the problem. As Fargier argues, "The first thing people do is deny the existence of the screen: it opens like a window; it is transparent. This illusion is the very substance of the specific ideology secreted by the cinema."[56] We are not encouraged to recognize the presence of ideology within the textual system, either at the level of the speech itself or at the level of the textual codes.

By relying solely upon the methods of the voice of authority and the interview in the mode of direct address, the film is dominated entirely by the verbal, digital code. Visuals substantiate or interpret, but are not strongly enough organized to achieve dominance of their own. Ellsberg becomes a self-referential authority, challenged, subverted, or dominated in no way. It is ironically fitting that when one interviewee finishes speaking she asks Ellsberg his view. He then answers his own question, guaranteeing himself the last word in a literal as well as a metaphorical sense. The film's limits are thus Ellsberg's limits, stranding it on a level of consciousness that remains below the more radical critique of capitalism as a pervasive, non-reformable system (reform, especially a populist version where "the people" regain a say in their existing form of government lies implicit behind much of what Ellsberg says.) This may be an example of Newsreel's more openended approach to audience response as an act of serious political interrogation. It is clearly an example of filmmaking tied to the beliefs of those it chooses as subjects through a relatively minimal exploitation of the textual codes.

* * *

Newsreel's Women's Liberation Films

Women's liberation poses problems for a Marxist film group. Much of the energy within the women's movement has been directed toward reform and equal rights, especially among white, middle-class women.

Women's liberation at the other extreme in the form of radical lesbianism disavows working relationships with men. Neither of these approaches has very great appeal among Third World working-class women. Reform and equal rights seem like remote goals given the immediate problems and like impossible goals given the history of Third World oppression. Radical lesbianism seems a ludicrous alternative when much of working-class survival still depends upon the nuclear family and when male-female relationships are an important form of mutual aid.

As a result it is not surprising that a great many Newsreel films give considerable attention to the role of women in working-class struggle at a variety of levels of which women's liberation per se is but one. Films like Teach Our Children, Homefront, El Pueblo Se Levante (The People Are Rising), Break and Enter, My Country Occupied and several other films on national liberation struggles all pay serious attention to the voices and actions of women as they participate in a common struggle. And even of all the films listed under Women's Liberation only Growing Up Female is exclusively about women's consciousness raising and even in this case considerable attention is paid to socio-economic factors and their effect upon the women's perception of what liberation means.

Other films in this category place considerable emphasis upon corollary issues: Childcare and A Space To Be Me—day care centers in relation to the working mother; Growing Up Female—career expectations in relation to socio-economic background and societal conditioning; Red Detachment of Women—a filmed ballet from China on collective solidarity in the face of feudal oppression; The Woman's Film—feminism in relation to a revolutionary working-class movement; <u>Salt of the Earth</u>--women's vital contribution to working-class trade union struggle; <u>Women of Telecommunications Station #6</u>--women's contribution to the struggle for national liberation in Vietnam; <u>My Country Occupied</u>--imperialism as witnessed by a Guatamalan woman.

Of the new films in this list, <u>Red Detachment of Women</u>, like <u>Growing Up Female</u>, is only secondarily distributed by Newsreel; its emphasis upon peasant women and their struggles, and perhaps especially its portrayal of Third World women, makes it a logical candidate for Newsreel distribution. Similarly the two films for which Newsreel is the primary distributor, <u>Childcare</u> and <u>A Space To Be Me</u>, place appreciable stress upon the problems of the working-class Third World woman. Both deal with the question of day care. The former was made by New York Newsreel in 1970, and the differences in emphasis between the two are quite revealing.

<u>Childcare</u> is now distributed with reservations. The film itself simply recounts the problems faced by working women in New York City who finally band together and open a day care center. The women speak highly of this collective solution and are optimistic of applying it in other areas such as a food co-operative. Newsreel's most recent catalogue warns,

> This film is a beginning point for discussing community child care .... It presents the special problems of working mothers and the pitfalls of corporate child care, but it doesn't go into the government's expanding involvement in day care and what that's all about. It doesn't portray the righteous struggles for community control for several of the day care centers receiving government funding in N.Y.C.[57]

Newsreel's concern revolves around the degree to which day care has become a potential tool of governmental efforts to force welfare mothers to accept day care over which they have no direct control, and to compel unemployed women to work at such centers for minimal compensation.[58] The surfacing of this concern on the part of Newsreel is a good example of how their films, being tied to immediate issues and events, can also gain or lose in political importance as these issues and events continue to develop.

Childcare follows a fairly straightforward and simple format in making its case, utilizing the mode of direct address most often with voice-over speech by characters (primarily the women involved) and images of interpretation (showing oppressive mother-child relationships and more joyous ones before and after the creation of the child care center, respectively). Shots of a working mother attempting to shop with her children in tow is a particularly effective example of how the lack of child care affects both mother and child. The transition to the solution is also well handled as the viewer first hears the women discussing, in voice-over interview, the possibility of setting up a center, the difficulties, and then the resolve to simply do it. Once this resolution has been articulated and the women launch a campaign to draw wider support from the community by leafletting and speaking on the streetcorners the film then cuts to the first affirmative image showing the women at work on the streets. By delaying the images of affirmation until after the resolve to do something has been articulated, the film conveys the important point that things do not simply happen but are a result of very concrete human intervention. It is a happy combination of political message with formal arrangement.

A Space To Be Me is about the same topic, day care centers, but approaches it from a very different perspective as a result of an array of different choices at the level of the textual codes. Originally made by a couple independently and then acquired for distribution by Newsreel, the film is similar to Growing Up Female in developing a series of case histories of women's lives. In this case it is a series of five working mothers who are shown and in each case the stress is upon the degree to which total responsibility for child care handicaps the women from pursuing other roles than those of mother and housewife such as earning enough money to make ends meet. The women are both black and white and all from what appear middle class backgrounds. They live in a suburban area and their homes are decorated with some of the tasteful consideration that becomes possible once sheer survival is no longer at issue.

Again we learn about the women in the mode of direct address, frequently during this first section of the film from sync interviews as they explain their problems of caring for their children by themselves. These extra-textual codes like decor and dress become our only cues to the social milieu in which they live since. As in the experiments of Kuleshov, the women are isolated from social interaction and instead stitched together to form a new formal pattern peculiar to the film, one that concentrates upon their relationships with their children. We see and hear no one but these five women and their children, and only occassionally see them outside their homes. Even then it is in situations of minimal social contact such as driving a car.

This deflection away from the window-onto-the-world dominance of extra-textual codes at the local level toward a more formal pattern, as in the case of Attica, is not in itself a negative achievement. But as in Attica the kind of formal pattern constituted leaves very serious questions in the viewer's mind.

These questions may be fairly inchoate during the first section of the film. The separation of the women from each other and from their own environments is quite noticeable but the stress upon their family relationships (none have husbands with them) effectively suppresses prolonged concern. It is the transition to the second, concluding section that precipitates graver doubts.

An abrupt cut places the viewer in medium long shot in front of a bright new day care center. A voice-over narrator describes the center. We later learn the narrator is actually a character, the center's director whom we also hear in sync interviews. But the suddenness of this transition is only compounded by the voice-over commentary by the five women who all deliver glowing testimonials to the value of the day care center. There is no indication of problems, no suggestion of difficulties. If there is a strong enough need for such centers then they will magically appear in an ideal form satisfactory to everyone.

The formal structuring thus moves into a clearly idealist direction. The day center appears deus ex machina in sharp contrast to the method of introduction found in Childcare. There is no indication that the women featured in the film had any involvement in its creation whatsoever nor any awareness of the importance of a resolve to work collectively to create and control such a center. In fact, the day care director specifically indicates that the center draws upon federal funding for day care centers and from the Project Headstart program. As in the John Ford classic, The Grapes of Wrath, a benevolent government steps in to ameliorate the hardships of the people whenever their personal suffering becomes too intense. And this magical benevolence from above is all the more effectively protrayed for its being structured into the manipulation of the textual codes. By being a better film formally than some of the other Newsreels, A Space To Be Me becomes a more dangerous film politically, an unfortunate but inescapable lesson in this particular case.

In discussing The Woman's Film, Rebecca Pulliam comments, "The key to the film is synchronous sound; the women can thereby talk for themselves and they do so powerfully."[59] Although this is definitely true of The Woman's Film, analysis of these other two films suggests that sync sound in itself is not quite the monolithic force Pulliam claims. The relationship between the speech of characters and the images--whether sync images or images of interpretation---is also important as is the nature of the formal structure shaped from individual shots. The operation of the textual codes at the time of the pro-filmic event is likewise crucial since the exclusion of social interaction in A Space To Be Me becomes a major problem by the time the day care center is simply dropped into these women's lives in the film but when we are given no cues via composition or editing as to the actual relationship of this center to the women outside the film. (There is not even an establishing shot of the center that fixes it in the same community, a community never specifically identified in the film.)

The insistence upon using the voices of the characters in the documentary rather than that of a narrator, particularly the single, omniscient narrator is a very important advance and a major asset in numerous Newsreel films. Its ultimate importance, however, cannot be ascertained in isolation but only in terms of its contribution to an overall formal pattern, the textual system, as well as its local interplay with other relationships between textual and extra-textual codes. Childcare and A Space To Be Me address a very important problem for the working mother. They make a valuable addition to Newsreel's repetoire of films concerning women's liberation. And the specific utilization of formal elements in each provides further insight into the crucial importance of a documentary film theory as well as practice.

* * *

Newsreel Films on Ecology, the New Left Movement,
and Working-Class Struggle

These three categories are grouped together since there are only three new films to be discussed among them. Some of the reasons for the relative weakness of these categories were suggested in the thematic discussion of films distributed by Newsreel (Chapter 3, pp. 8-9). Of the films not discussed here, Finally Got the News is almost certainly the most important. It marked an important shift in Newsreel's emphasis in that it dealt with exploitation among black auto workers in the Detroit area from a very explicitly Marxist-Leninist point of view. There was little trace of the New Left in it, but there was considerably more Marx than in Third World Newsreel's own films. Dan Georgakas, in his review of the film, notes that the person most responsible for the film's structure, John Watson (an auto worker and organizer, not a member of the filmmaking team that originally came to do the film from New York), "insisted that the film be created within a teaching rather than a reporting framework and that its explicit Marxist message be directed toward an audience of black workers."[60]

This insistence unfortunately makes the film another example of narrator didacticism and dogma discussed amply in reference to other films although the rigor of the Marxist analysis and the insistence upon exploitation as the root of experiential oppression give the film a lasting value far greater than many of those films more specifically rooted in a particular event to which some Marxist analysis is grafted

The three films representing these three categories do not introduce new considerations into the discussion so much as amplify upon problems previously raised. Hence it will be sufficient to give some indication of their political perspective and the formal problems that they highlight.

Felix the Cat was made by New York Newsreel and is simply conceived by replacing the original soundtrack to a Felix cartoon with one of Newsreel's creation. The result is to transform the serial plights of undauntable Felix into an allegory of class conflict in which Felix is threatened with extermination by City Hall politicians but wins the day through a cat and mice alliance that brings the masses onto their side. It is not a perfect allegory by any means (the people, for example, side with Felix so that the cats will once again control a rampaging mouse population), but the strength of the verbal transformations are sufficient to make it both an enjoyable and serviceable work.

The shift in meaning through a change in sounds with no corresponding change in the images or their arrangement once again illustrates the over-determination of the image-track and the capacity of the soundtrack, especially words, to foreground one possible set of meanings over others. This shift also indicates the latent presence of a conflictual relationship between classes (though perhaps somewhat different types of classes than those of a Marxist analysis) in the original cartoon. This could hardly be argued to function as a "structuring absence" in the way politics is in Young Mr. Lincoln in Cahier du Cinema's reading of that film,[61] but does suggest that a process of suppressing the political dimnesions of art may operate in a more pervasive, and rudimentary, manner than their very singular study of one film implies.

America is also an older Newsreel but one which has received recent emphasis as an "historical document" pointing out the interrelationships between a series of events occurring in 1969.[62] (The film is discussed in Newsreel: Film and Revolution as well (pp. 88-89); at that time it was called Amerika. The change in spelling is a small clue to the drift away from a confrontational, polarizing stance that was more typical of the left in the late sixties.) Unfortunately, America is a substitute for a retrospective analysis of the New Left or the broader pattern of events during the late sixties; Newsreel, like most other movement groups, still tends to plunge into the most immediate, most pressing problems with only a brief glance back over their shoulders at what has gone before. This is one major difference between Newsreel and more formally pre-occupied filmgroups like the Dziga-Vertov group (Jean-Luc Godard and Jean-Pierre Gorin): "... unlike other militant film groups such as Newsreel or Chris Marker's SLON or the French CGT labor union film group of Paul Sebar, the Dziga Vertov group rejects the "reflection of reality" notion of the cinema and therefore refuses the 'go out and get footage' approach ... at the expense of a thorough analysis of the causes, effects, relations and contradictions of events."[63] *America* itself is not primarily analytical and for that reason (discussed further below) cannot serve as an adequate tool for an analysis of the events of the late sixties.

The greatest strength of *America* lies in the voices of revolution that it records (via sync interviews). These range from relatively immature harbingers (the voices of relatively "apolitical" youth on the streets of New York who nonetheless see the political implications of drugs and other changing cultural values) to established political leaders (the voice of Eldridge Cleaver, for example). It is Cleaver who provides a useful analysis of the level of political consciousness among many potentially revolutionary people and what connections remain to be made:

> People say, "All those riots are causing my life to be miserable in all areas," you know? They don't focus in on the fact that it's the pigs and their mentors, the people who control them, the power structure, bald-headed businessmen and the Chamber of Commerce. See. They're not turned onto that power structure. They just know that life is becoming increasingly miserable for everybody.

Another very important voice heard on several occasions through the film is that of the G.I. Several G.I.s who also appear in Army, sit in a G.I. coffee-house near Fort Dix, New Jersey and rap about the effect of their tour of duty in Vietnam:

> When you go over there you find nobody has any respect for the Vietnamese people because the Army has prostituted their whole life style and doesn't even think of them as human beings. Because the Army makes you not think of them as human beings, when you get a chance to open up on a village--the Cong fire a few rounds at you and the villagers shelter them--so after a while you get pissed off at these people in the village. They're supposed to want you there to protect their freedom and they're helping get you dead. So, you look for an excuse. So at night, during the free fire zones, you call up and say, "There's troop movement out there."

These moments give the film considerable power at a local level, at the level of individual sequences, where interviews are used to good advantage to explain attitudes and share reflections rather than capture beliefs as though they were true or summarize what actually happened or was done. They give America considerable value and make it an early indication of the kind of extended attention given to the voice of the G.I. and veteran in Only the Beginning and Winter Soldier.

America exhibits a musical variety as great as that of We Demand Freedom ranging through Dylan and soul music to heavy rock and roll and inidgenous Third World music. This is not surprising inasmuch as the same individual had primary responsibility for both films, Allan Siegel. They generate a similar type of confusion in this case as well and fail to provide the kind of overall dominant that the film needs.

Another recurring problem is the use of visual montage coupled to musical selections to suggest commonality between a vastly disparate

64

series of protests, demonstrations, guerrilla battles and repressive retaliation. This results in a loss of specificity similar to that noted in We Demand Freedom and a collapsing of aims, tactics and goals into the same amalgam. This is a strategy often employed by Cold War propagandists who seek to make all protest appear to be Communist motivated. It is also a strategy that can lead to the gradual diffusion of the specific meaning of an act or symbol into a non-threatening vaguery. The working of such dilution through time by a bourgeois ideology is well indicated by Leo Hurwitz during an interview:

> Q. Often in the 1930s the socialist perspective of works of art arose out of the interconnection of the work with the context of social struggle within which the work was presented .... This can be overlooked today.
>
> A. It was understood then. For example, in Woody Guthrie's song, This Land is Your Land, the line, "This land is meant for you and me," meant socialism, not litter-free national parks.[65]

America's montage sequences of revolution effect a similar destruction of specificity from within. By mounting together a series of images with associations leading to different phenomena and different modalities of deep structure and failing to provide a precise enough rationale for their combination, this form of montage pushes the film back toward the analytical muteness of the photograph: "photography ... is able to relate a tin of canned food to the universe, yet cannot grasp a single one of the human connections in which that tin exists."[66] This is not true of film which has many more textual codes at its disposal, but to attempt to make such connections in sequences as weakly controlled formally and poorly organized conceptually as Newsreel's "revolutionary montage" sequences is to make the attempt with both hands tied behind your back.

Earth Belongs to the People was made by Boston Newsreel in 1971. Boston was one of the numerous satellite Newsreel offices throughout the United States involved exclusively in distribution. This film on the nature of the ecology crisis was their single filmmaking contribution.[67] In contrast to several of the other categories where Newsreel has chosen to distribute certain films and not others, their choice to distribute this film is not necessarily revealing of their political orientation toward ecology: Earth Belongs to the People is the only Newsreel film on this subject and one of the very few films from any source to treat ecology in Marxist terms.

The strength of the film lies in its concrete political challenge to more liberal assumptions about ecology. The film utilizes an on-camera narrator to argue its points and he begins by asserting that overpopulation is a myth. There are not too many people in countries where population density is far below that of the United States (Third World countries); there is not enough food to feed them because of the inequities of wealth between countries. The narrator mounts a scathing criticism of agri-business, arguing that like any other industry its motivation is profit. People's basic need for food must conform to that priority.

Other points made by the film are that three-fourths of the pollution is caused by industrial sources, and that technical innovations are, like food, packaged to maximize profit, not to sustain any form of ecological balance. The growth of the automotive industry and the demise of the urban public transit systems is cited as an example, one graphically illustrated by the loss of a vast electric streetcar system in Los Angeles once General Motors (sole maker of public transit buses in the U.S.) acquired major interests in the system's stock.

These are very important issues, deflecting the problem of ecological responsibility away from volunteer and small-scale remedial actions toward the very heart of the capitalist system--industrial production and production for profit. As such the film is capable of providing a valuable springboard for lively discussion and allows Newsreel to reach into audience markets, as it were, for which some of their other films would be less suitable. The only drawback is the film's own deficiencies.

These are two. The first is a simple problem of technical weakness. The sound is often garbled or has not been related as tightly as possible to the image track which is itself a fairly random collection of images of pollution, the Vietnam war (inevitably) and crude animation illustrating different aspects of problem. This may be attributed to the status of the film as a first effort, but there is nothing so offputting to the average viewer as technical deficiency.

The second problem involves the formal organization of the film around the omniscient narrator. Such a style carries with it a clear advantage: "The two major styles of cinema--fictional narrative as most predominantly shaped and expressed by Hollywood, and documentary--depend on narration, and almost always a third-person narration which transforms what is seen on the screen into otherness, into objectivity, and which creates a kind of instant credibility."[68] Narration is the dominant since it is of a higher logical type, controlling that which it explicates, shaping the level of the diegesis to the pattern of its internal logic.[69] But this is to raise the problems of logo-centric and subject-centered discourse which have been previously discussed. The narrator tells all and thereby dulls the viewer's sense of active participation in fulfilling his need to know. It is a device assuming the infallability of He Who Knows (the narrator) and is in some ways a logical extension of the ideological assertions that the free and equal individuals of a capitalist (democratic) society are also the end points at which knowledge collects in a pure form. The reliance upon the narrator, however effective it is in communicating information, fails to challenge the concept of the individual as a function of the society constituting that concept: "The individual as an autonomous being was ideology even as bourgeois society announced it."[70] This failure then locks the film into a mode of explication which is non-ecological, in which the eco-system, the relations between a system and its environment, becomes segmented into the relation between He Who Knows and the Problem.

This is to place a false bracket around the problem, assuming that the individual remains outside it, autonomous, rather than being inextricably rooted in a network of ecological relationships, communication systems like economic exchange and language. At a formal level the film recapitulates the false distinction between Them and Us (capitalist pollution and the people) that underlies capitalism itself. This is a recurrent problem with Newsreel's films (and one common to most other documentaries that share a leftist perspective but have not applied it to the manipulation of the codes of the textual system themselves) that takes on additional irony when the problem addressed is ecology. Earth Belongs to the People, at a formal level, then provides strong evidence for the argument that, "A 'break-out' from the form and content of bourgeois thought and its expression in the arts or in a discourse cannot occur in and of itself: such a breakthrough in presentation is dependent on an equivalent breakthrough in the modes of perception and attitude of the receiver."[71] Formal questions cannot be neglected, but neither they can be resolved solely at a formal level. The eco-system must be seen as a whole and the place of the filmic event as an opportunity to reshape perception and attitudes given its rightful importance through a consideration of the formal structuring most capable of achieving a rupture with bourgeois ideology.

* * *

Newsreel's Films of National Liberation Struggles

The stress in this category upon liberation struggles in Third World countries is partly a function of seeing these struggles as one of the two major contradictions in capitalism today: the determination of Third World people to be liberated vs. the need of an imperialistic capitalism for colonies.[72] (The other being the contradiction between workers and owners in the developed countries.) The stress on Third World countries rather than America may also be a function of Newsreel's relative inactivity in terms of filmmaking since several of the films that have been made recently carry overtones that align them with this stress (e.g., the emphasis in the prison films upon Third World peoples and their pervasively oppressed condition under a capitalist system).

Third World Newsreel's specific concern with the problems of Third World people, including their interest in both expressing political solidarity with these struggles and in reaffirming the cultural and historical links between Third World people in the United States and the Third World, makes this stress quite logical. The concern with a racial and national identity distinct from that of white America gives added appeal to films that may include but are not limited to class struggle within developing countries (in contrast to the more strictly working-class analysis of Finally Got the News). The differences between a working-class analysis and one revolving around national and racial identity are not necessarily contradictory, especially when the differences between developing Third World countries and developed western nations are considered. When these two approaches vie for dominance in reference to a revolutionary movement within the United States or any other developed country, debate often intensifies. Newsreel's own openness and non-sectarian approach to this potential conflict is well-indicated by the differences between Black Power and Finally Got the News.

Newsreel's own attitudes toward the distribution of Black Power have been indicated (Chapter Two, pp. 18-19). The importance of what Stokely Carmichael has to say about black oppression in the United States and the history of that oppression outweigh the extreme emphasis upon race that dominates his speech. Newsreel's willingness to promote the film despite its departures from Marxist-Leninist orthodoxy reflect an open-endedness similar to that of the filmmaker's who described the function of revolutionary films in terms of an educational dialogue: "The films provide a 'lighthouse' function: people can assess their own position vis a vis a certain problem and can learn to assess the position of other people."[73]

Black Power was originally made for American Documentary Film by Leonard Henny, who was teaching at Washington University in St. Louis in 1969 when the film was made.[74] It consists of two intercut sections, one devoted to a sync recording of a speech by Stokely Carmichael in the Oakland Auditorium on Huey Newton's birthday, the other a recording of the Uzozi Aro'ho Dancers performing a variety of African dances. It is never clear whether these events occurred at the same time and place, but since the dancing footage has no speech track of its own (only the music to which they dance) it is dominated by the speech track of Carmichael's address and serves primarily as a set of images of interpretation, underscoring the cultural heritage of the Afro-American to which Carmichael refers.

Carmichael's speech is powerfully insistent and seeks to drive home oen basic point: "We are talking about how our people can survive America, about the survival of a race, nothing else." From this point of view, Carmichael summarizes the history of the Afro-American in America as the history of a race's genocide: "If you do not think he's capable of wiping us out, check out the white race. Where ever they have gone they have ruled, conquered, murdered and raped whether they are the minority or the majority." "The major enemy is the honky and his institutions." This last statement is a telling phrase for in it pride of place goes to the racial question, the honky, and only secondarily is the capitalist system invoked and then vaguely as, "his institutions."

This insistence upon the racial question produces a virtual reverse racism. Carmichael is insistent that all blacks unite to face the white man, that no divisions, no class lines be allowed to keep blacks apart from one another. Blacks must be patient with their less conscious brothers, the Uncle Toms in their midst, and not turn to white allies in preference to winning the support of their blood brothers: "Every Negro is a potential black man (sic)." (Feminism plays little role in Carmichael's address and the subordinate position of the dancers, who are female, in the textual codes seems to correlate well with the role of the female in cultural nationalist strategies such as Carmichael's or the Black Panther's during this period.)

The consequences for a working-class united front and an orthodox Marxism are spelled out clearly by Carmichael:

> The ideologies of Communism and Socialism speak to class structure. They speak to oppressed people from the top down to the bottom. We are not just facing exploitation; we are facing something much more important. We are facing the fact that we are victims of racialism. Communism and Socialism do not speak to the problem of racism. And racism, for black people in this country, is far more important than exploitation, because no matter how much money you make in the black community, when you go into the white world, you are still a Nigger.

The answer Communism does offer to the racial question—that it is a tactic used to divide workers among themselves and a source of super-profits—is rejected without even being considered. Carmichael makes the distinction between oppression (racism) and exploitation, between national liberation (survival of blacks in America) and working-class revolution into a contradiction and opts for one side only: "If we got a gun in our hand, it's either Them or Us. We have to begin to organize our people. Nothing else."

The film itself is thus one of the least open-ended films in Newsreel's catalogue and while Newsreel does not openly criticize Carmichael's line, they do emphasize the historical importance of the film as an important step toward awakening a sense of positive black identity and breaking out of the identity by opposition in which blacks are defined by their relationships to whites. Unfortunately, Carmichael himself does not break far enough away from it, simply moving to the other side of the same Them/Us opposition. Through his speech, however, the seeds of a black consciousness can be planted, and through discussion around the film, viewers can decide, as Chris described it, "what is correct and what incorrect." Newsreel's renewed emphasis of a film that was not highly promoted when first made (not surprising given Newsreel's mainly white, college-based constituency at the time), does give some idea of how strongly indebted the group remains to lumpen-proletarian arguments and the high priority placed upon racism with its attendent emphasis upon national liberation.[75]

El Pueblo Se Levante (The People Are Rising) initially arose out a particular incident: the death of Young Lords member Julio Riordan.[76] Involvement in this event led Newsreel to a fuller awareness of the Young Lords' struggle to establish a breakfast program for the Puerto Rican children in their East Harlem community. This in turn led them to realize the still broader questions of self-determination and community control at the root of the Young Lords efforts.[77] This prolonged involvement with specific issues until a larger pattern emerged establishes a sharp difference between El Pueblo Se Levante and many earlier Newsreels. The beginnings of a movement toward a staunchly Third World orientation in 1971 were fundamental to Newsreel's continued development and are clearly indicated in this film, Break and Enter, Childcare, Only the Beginning and Winter Soldier. As McCormick notes there is an appreciable difference in the qualities of the Young Lords members and "the type of white radical generally given the most publicity in the media--the long-haired, hung-loose, dope-smoking, endlessly talking anarcho-liberals of the leftish Youth Movement who have been the subject of many earlier Newsreel films."[78]

El Pueblo Se Levante actually seems to benefit from its divided origins, gaining a sense of immediacy and crisis through its focus on specific events and a sense of historical development through its broadened perspective. It was as though Newsreel had independently learned the lesson Lewis Jacobs applied to several meandering cinema-verite films: "But overall what ultimately emerged--despite the disclosures of some fundamental truths about the human condition--was the realization that it was not enough for films to be committed to so inflexible and ingenuous a belief in the significance of surface detail and to trust so implicitly in chance to gain an imaginative coherence."[79] Reflecting the tendency found in The Woman's Film to portray the lives of ordinary working people rather than their most articulate spokesmen, the film nevertheless links up the massive discontent and active protest among masses of people with a vanguard group struggling to heighten the levels of consciousness even further.

The tactics of occupation and appropriation for human needs that were depicted in Break and Enter recur here and their partial origin in the Young Lords' own tactics is indirectly suggested by the continuity between the films. The squatter movement itself is referred to as one of the ongoing struggles of the moment, and detailed attention is also given to the occupation of Lincoln Hospital primarily by Puerto Rican people after a woman, Carmen Rodriquez, was killed by the hospital staff. (This is the charge; she had a heart condition and yet was given medicine for arthritis that sped up her heart and killed her. The hospital version was that she "failed to respond to treatment.") The hospital staff, mostly Third World nurses and orderlies, attempted to keep the hospital functioning and with the support of some of the physicians were successful in winning a number of important concessions. The Young Lords assisted in the take over, but here as elsewhere in the film, we see the hospital employees directing the occupation and giving their description of the events rather than focusing upon the involvement of the Young Lords. As one orderly remarks, "Now we can see what socialism is all about," and like the comments by the white workers in Richmond Oil Strike [80] it is an observation worth a thousand well-prepared speeches.

A major portion of the film centers around the conflict between the Young Lords and a Puerto Rican church in the community. Newsreel's first involvement stemmed from a confrontation in which the church leaders called in the police to drive the Young Lords out.[81] The film actually opens with a speech by a Young Lord from the pulpit of the church that occurred at a later time, chronologically, but which effectively sets the mood in its poetic homage to the memory of Julio Riordan

and other Puerto Ricans who had died under suspicious circumstances
(such as suicide in the Tombs--New York City's infamous detention center):

> They work seven days a week.
> They work. They work. They work and they die.
> They die broke. They die old.
> They die never knowing what the front end of the
> First National City Bank looks like.
> Pablo, Miguel, Iago, Olga, Manuel
> All die yesterday and today and will die again
> Tomorrow.
> All die waiting for the Garden of Eden to open up again
> Under a new management.
> All die dreaming about America waking them up in
> The middle of the night screaming ....
> Always broke, always owing, never knowing
> That they are beautiful people.

The eulogy resembles the visceral, dramatic poetry of The Last Poets. The cadence, the rhythms, the symbolism are vividly Third World. The power of the digital message--the literal meaning of the words--is multiplied many times over by the density of the analog messages amplifying it. The sequence is pointed proof of the power of cinema-verite techniques (even in the direct address mode here where the distance between the film audience and the church audience is minimal) to display a pro-filmic event with a compelling facticity beyond the means of re-creation or voice-over commentary. The sequence is also a vivid demonstration of the cinema's ability to record and situate distinctive, ethnic forms of speech within the context where they arise. What Guiseppe Ferrara said about Visconti's La Terra Trema seems to apply just as well to El Pueblo Se Levante:

> Visconti's determination to keep pure the mother-tongue of
> the inhabitants of Aci-Trezza goes much further than any
> literary enthusiasm. It is first of all a kind of revenge
> against the reactionary purism that hates a cinema filled
> with dialect expressions, and it is therefore a victory for
> the language of humble people, of those who are never

listened to, and in the end will express themselves without censorship and without false translations.[82]

After the film establishes the difficulties the Young Lords had in launching a Breakfast Program and then shows them carrying it out in the "liberated" church kitchen, the immediate problems of this particular political group fade into the background. The struggles of the working people, the everyday problems confronting them become the central focus of the film as it highlights four major areas of concern--education, health, food, and housing.

The film is careful not to isolate the situation in New York City from the more general pattern of exploitation confronting the Puerto Rican people. When a woman narrator (women are featured very prominently in this Newsreel) begins to discuss the racial oppression found in the neighborhood schools, she doesn't stop at the borders of the community. Instead she links this oppression to the situation in Puerto Rico itself where school children learn that culture means American culture, that there is no native culture, where massive poverty co-exists with luxury hotels for foreign visitors. The woman, speaking voice-over and in a sync interview, reminds us of the Puerto Rican women's contribution in maintaining a sense of history and dignity, and the immense hardship they face. We see stills of the Puerto Rican grandmothers who fired several pistol shots from the Congressional gallery back in 1950 and the more disciplined parading of male and female Young Lord cadre through a New York street. Some of the images of interpretation also show the women at work organizing the squatter movement. The question of education is also conceived in the broadest terms and calls into question the most basic assumptions about cultural heritage, sexual roles and racial identity transmitted in the school system: "By contrasting the people in New York and the people back home on the island, the film demonstrates that Puerto Rican identity and dignity can only be restored by national liberation and self-determination in the United States."[83]

The subjects of health and food are largely dealt with by the descriptions of the hospital occupation and the Young Lords' breakfast program. In the treatment of the last major topic, housing, the film again stresses the connection between the sub-standard condition of housing in New York and in Puerto Rico. A Puerto Rican woman, interviewed in front of an East Harlem tenement say, "It's not housing, it's a dump." She describes how she has to teach her children to take an umbrella with them when they go to the bathroom in order to protect themselves from falling chips of lead paint. These scenes are contrasted with shots taken in Puerto Rico in which squalid shanties droop themselves along the bank of a muddy canal while luxury hotels soar upward in the background. Another woman interviewee mentions that 35 percent of the Puerto Rican people subsist on charity, 40 percent of the housing is classified unsuitable for human occupation, 20 percent of the work force is unemployed, and that armed intervention is called upon when protests threaten to rock the government (as they did in 1965). Inadequate housing is not simply an isolated phenomena but integrally connect to the working conditions of the majority of the people and to the government's unwillingness (as an extension of American imperialism) to create a climate of change. The conditions that make for inadequate housing in Puerto Rico are not eradicated by the pilgrimage to New York;

in fact, they are made all the more intense by the more extreme climate and by the more extreme contrasts between wealth and poverty.

The film's conclusion circles back to its beginning after a young woman member of the Young Lords explains the circumstances of the death eulogized at the onset. Julio Riordan was arrested and then found hanged by his own belt (an item usually removed from prisoners). A massive funeral was planned and several hundred people joined a procession that led finally to the same church the Young Lords had occupied several months before only to be driven out by the police. The film concludes as a woman member of the Young Lords predicts that the struggles of the Puerto Rican people will soon link up with those of other oppressed people both inside the United States and abroad. As she speaks the image track cuts away to the funeral procession leaving the church and making its way to the nearby cemetery. The particular events surrounding the work of the Young Lords have now been drawn into a wider perspective and the withdrawal of the image track from its interior sync accompaniment to the larger context of the community and the funeral procession lends extra weight to this totalizing impetus.

El Pueblo Se Levante is distinguished by its almost exclusive use of women characters on the sound track, its combination of Latin music with visuals that systematically demonstrate the destruction of that culture from which the songs come, and the careful integration of the work of a vanguard, revolutionary organization with the less programmatic but equally compelling concerns of the community-at-large. A common culture binds together the one-third of the Puerto Rican people who live in mainland America with those still living on the island itself. This

Newsreel film, perhaps better than any other, is an eloquent testimony to common struggle against a mutual enemy that retains a sense of the diversity, complexity and determination of people who have been spared the lamentable fate of many documentary characters, being turned into fodder for political sloganeering. As in The Woman's Film, Break and Enter, Childcare, Homefront and portions of the prison films, it is the typical working person who shines through and becomes the expression of a necessary consciousness rather than the arbitrary accompaniment to an axiomatic dogma.

* * *

Newsreel's National Liberation Films

Newsreel's films of national liberation struggles in Third World countries (FALN, Nossa Terra, A Luta Continua, Revolution in Dhofar and Nigeria: Nigeria One) share a number of points in common and will be considered as a group. To one degree or another, all of them indicate that the government in power is reactionary, failing to fill the basic needs of the people, suppressing dissent and complying with the express interests of the imperialist countries who in turn provide economic, technical and military aid. Imperialist interests usually consist of the extraction of raw materials and the investment of capital to establish cheap production facilities (based on poorly paid, poorly organized labor). This pattern is basically the same whether the country has political independence as in the cases of Venezuala (FALN), Nigeria and the shortlived nation of Biafra (Nigeria: Nigeria One), and Dhofar (Revolution in Dhofar) or is a colony as in the case of Mozambique (A Luta

Continua) and Guinea Bissau (Nossa Terra).

Several of the films point out the failure of democratic procedure to redress wrongs. The vote's inadequacy as a tool for significant change is underscored in FALN when Romolo Betancourt was elected to replace the corrupt government of Perez Hermanez on the strength of reform promises that never materialized. A guerrilla leader sums up the lesson of that experience, "In this country nothing is solved by elections. Because an individual who is not a revolutionary and attains political power will not change the country's political, economic and social situation. This cannot be solved by individuals but by a change of systems and this cannot be brought about here except with weapons in our hands."

The inability of the system to fulfill the needs of the people and the failure of democratic processes to redress wrongs leads to the formation of guerrilla resistance units and the development of a revolutionary perspective in which redress can only flow from genuine national liberation, freedom from imperialist domination and, ultimately, freedom from internal domination by the indigenous ruling class. All of the films (except Nigeria: Nigeria One which is somewhat distinct in examining the origins of what it argues was a civil war rather than a national liberation struggle) trace the origins of armed liberation struggles to the repressive and oppressive policies of the existing governments. They are spawned in the social conditions of the countries where they emerge, not in the planning rooms of Moscow or Peking.

Considerable attention is then given in the films to the qualities of these guerrilla movements. There is little in the treatment in these films made in the countries where the struggles are taking place that matches the romanticization of armed struggle, the celebration of street violence and polarization to the point of violence that was found in the New Left's attitude toward the power structure in the United States. This attitude was often justified by reference to Third World liberation struggles and intense identification with such struggles frequently took place. Early Newsreels and the continuing tendency toward "revolutionary montage" sequences document this attitude vividly (see, e.g., San Francisco State Strike, Columbia Revolt, Summer '68, People's Park, Black Panther, etc.).

When we examine films designed to familiarize an American audience with the actual origins and nature of these struggles, armed struggle is firmly situated within a context in which the highest precedence goes to the quality of human life, even during the difficult period when a violent struggle is being carried out to overcome a reactionary government. These films indicate in no uncertain terms that guerrilla warfare is not the college radical's dream of macho adventurism but a grim, necessary component of a far more radical attempt to liberate human beings from exploitation and oppression. A Third World Newsreel member expressed this concern well when he said,

> There are so many levels of struggle. If you're a repressed individual fighting the revolution it's obvious that it'll be a type of revolution whose processes and goals will remain detrimental. The problem therefore has to be dealt with on all levels from the individual person, from day care centers up to the schools and community, to the cities, from the cities to the states, and then on up to monopoly capitalism. It has to be on all these levels. It's like Fanon talking about being colonized and being half a man. Well, what he's talking about is how to regain that other half, to become a complete human being.[84]

The qualities of the guerrilla movements that are stressed fall into categories similar to the four headings in El Pueblo Se Levante: health, food, education, and housing. In fact, all of these categories except housing receive considerable attention with additional stress placed upon the role of women within the liberation forces. The emphasis that dominates the voice-over explanations repeatedly is that the various liberation movements strive to serve the needs of the people and succeed far better than the regimes that hold official power.

This emphasis is largely a consequence of filming behind "enemy lines"--from the government's point of view. These films show us what it is like for people living in liberated, predominantly rural zones. As such they present a picture that no amount of speculation or conjecture could supplant. They provide a valuable counter-argument to the assertions of official spokesmen that the liberation movements indeed live up to the adventurist image of wild-eyed terrorists menacing a peace-loving populace. Although the counter-violence of armed insurrection clearly establishes requirements for military or para-military forms of organization, the predominant activity for these organizations is serving the people.

A Luta Continua, Revolution in Dhofar and Nossa Terra all underscore the changes in agricultural methods that take place in liberated areas. In A Luta Continua the point is made that the Portuguese imposed a system of cash crop production which neglected the more immediate needs of the Mozambiquan people for food. In liberated zones crops of coffee and cotton are plowed under to make way for corn. In Revolution in Dhofar a guerrilla unit works on the construction of a water reservoir for an entire village while in another area armed members of a small village watch over the country's only mechanically powered water pump. (For comparison, the film's narrator also indicates that the sultan's palace cost $5,000,000 to construct.) In *Nossa Terra* the narrator explains that cultivation has increased in liberated areas at the same time as the Portuguese have lost some of their economic incentive for retaining Guinea Bissau due to the loss of territory under their control. In each case the point is made that the production of raw materials (cash crops) had a higher priority for the colonialists than the nutritional needs of the people and that the struggles for national liberation have reversed this tendency.

Health is discussed in a similar way although here medical problems are divided into standard problems of community health and those special problems entailed by guerrilla warfare. Most of the care is provided by medical specialists among the people (as opposed to foreign aid) and occurs wherever and whenever the need arises. Thatched huts become surgical ampitheaters; the shelter of a tree a first aid station. Hygiene, diet and preventive medicine are taught on a regular basis among the liberated population. Treatment for wounds caused by bullets, shells, napalm, and booby traps is administered with whatever supplies are on hand, often relying upon captured Portuguese, or indirectly, American drugs and medical equipment for the more serious cases.

The catch-as-catch-can quality to something most westerners think of in terms of quite tightly stratified and esoteric institutions gradually develops a subversive quality through the course of these films. The simplicity of the institutional apparatus begins to pale in importance in contrast to the great importance given to individual care. Economic factors in relation to the patient's ability to pay never even enter the picture although the economic limitations of what can be done are clearly indicated. This directness and clarity about priorities poses a subtle challenge to those more sophisticated but perhaps no more beneficial forms of medical care that accompany advanced industrial society.

Concern for health is paralleled by a concern for education. In Dhofar, Guinea Bissau and Mozambique basic educational needs had been long neglected: 99 percent of the people of Guinea Bissau were illiterate prior to the advent of the liberation struggle. In each country a high priority is placed upon education with the institutional matrix again simplified to the point of providing a clear demonstration that much of what is often considered essential to a good education in more developed countries is more a function of ideological strategy than people's needs (the training of a well-educated, well-behaved work force, for example). Classes take place in jungle clearings; teachers and pupils work together to prepare meals and build temporary classrooms; pupils pass on their knowledge to newer (not necessarily younger) students. In Dhofar a large, mobile encampment of several hundred students constitute what is known as the Lenin School where they combine the learning of Hamitic, Arabic, and English with lessons in guerrilla tactics. There are no distinctions or privileges assigned to roles far more sharply differentiated in our own society. Young and old, educated and illiterate all struggle toward a common goal. As much as possible each individual is prepared to carry out that struggle on all possible fronts, from learning the alphabet to firing a captured M-16 rifle.

This de-differentiation of roles, which are often quite rigid in the tribal societies from which the guerrilla forces come as well, is nowhere more strongly emphasized than in the role of women. In each of these films, the narrator indicates that women are accorded equal rights from the formation of all-women military units to the distribution of previously strictly women's work (e.g., the pounding of grain and cooking of meals) between men and women equally. In Revolution in Dhofar a woman narrates some of these changes directly (in the other films they are mediated by the male narrators). Not surprisingly then it is in Dhofar that we hear a woman say, "Without the participation of women, no revolutionary change can be achieved."

To some degree Nossa Terra and A Luta Continua look upon this phenomenon with an eye for dramatic effect, sometimes at the expense of clear interpretation of the significance of the changes from the point of view of the women themselves. (The absence of women's voices is one indication of this.) Nossa Terra particularly has included a number of visual sequences that clearly play upon the assumptions of a western audience more than explicate how the women see the changes in their lives themselves. One extremely powerful sequence in the film involves a low-angle shot of bare-breasted women marching in and out of jungle shadows, gun belts over their shoulders and rifles in their hands. The rich, dark colors and striking iconography creates an overwhelming impression (conjuring up images of modern day Amazons) that is both inspiring and troubling. On one hand, the image speaks for itself, testimoney to the changing status of determined women. On the other hand, the image is absorbed into a (male) narration that makes of these women insubstantial symbols, abstractions illustrating a narration, a formal code, over which they have no control or even access. It is a more sophisticated example of the kind of attitude found in the much older FALN (made in 1965) where the narrator at one point speaks of a woman in her early twenties whom we see cleaning a sub-machine gun as "a girl" who used to be a student.

The emphasis given to the role of women in these films is certainly one of their most striking features and one of the most important indications that the liberation movements are overcoming not only colonial oppression but also some of the oppressive features of their own tribal systems. The degree to which this is presented from a male point of view (in contrast to the predominance of women commentators in El Pueblo Se Levante, for example), however, indicates that the consciousness of the filmmakers is not always as high as that of their subjects. The question of the degree to which these films present an outsider's point of view rather than a point of view for outsiders (an American audience, e.g.) encompasses more than the treatment of women, however, and will be taken up again when the films are discussed in terms of their formal structure below. (In passing, it is interesting to note that My Country Occupied, made in 1971, avoids many of these problems by describing the effects of colonialism or neo-colonialism in Guatamala from the point of view of a woman peasant. There is something about the tone of the male narrators in these other films that suggests such a point of view might be too "narrow" for the broad perspective that they seek.)

Each of the films further stresses that these activities are not variations of do-gooderism, but part of a clearly socialist perspective. A portion of the opening narration in FALN indicates the need to move beyond the conceptual horizon offered by compradors and colonialists:

> The wealthy float on the surface; living a certain way limits how you see and feel, limits the range of what you can understand. Do they know very much about what is below the surface? Hunger is in sight. Slums are in sight. One lives beside them. One stops seeing them .... Here, an imposed system keeps people from the power that allows people to begin to grow.

Through their recourse to the historical development of a national liberation struggle, the impossibility of less radical efforts to bring significant change to the lives of the majority of the people all of these films convey the sense that a socialist solution is the only practical solution even though its realization will be a long and painful process.

That the battle is being waged against an oppressive colonial and capitalist system which must be replaced is also underscored by direct statements that the enemy is not seen personally but as an impersonal, dehumanizing system: in Nossa Terra one of the guerrilla leaders says, "We are not making war against the Portuguese people. We are making war against the imperialist system." This is a point that becomes a principal focus in the San Francisco newsreel, We the Palestinian People.

One final thematic parallel between most of these films is the demonstration that retaliation by the government in each case follows a pattern much like that which unfolded in Vietnam. Villages are razed, people are relocated, napalm is deployed. The air belongs to the government's air force, imported from abroad. The land belongs to the liberation forces who have the support of the indigenous people. In

Revolution in Dhofar and in Nigeria: Nigeria One there are sync interviews with mercenaries hired by the government and the rebel Biafrans respectively who confirm the influence of foreign powers and the utilization of modern weapons like napalm. (Confirm in the context of the film; the actual state of affairs in relation to the film would require more exhaustive analysis than this study can support.)

National liberation struggles throughout the Third World develop similar forms of institutional life devoted to the preservation of human dignity, confront similar patterns of retaliation to those encountered by the Vietnamese, and seek to constitute a socialist form of society once the para-military organization required for liberation can be dispensed with. Although recent events, particularly in Portugal, have made dramatic changes in the current situation in many of these colonies and countries, the historical emphasis of the films themselves ensures them of continuing value as documents of a particular phase of a long-range struggle and of how that phase was understood and articulated, at least by visiting filmmakers.

The film which conforms least to these common thematic points is Nigeria: Nigeria One. In this case the struggle is not posed as a conflict between a repressive government and an oppressed majority. The national government of General Gowan is defended as being itself the product of a coup that overthrew a former, far less responsive government. The Biafran position as represented by General Ojuku is seen as using the fascade of self-determination for a national minority to serve the opportunistic interests of Ojuku's personal desire for power dovetails with the fears of foreign imperialists that General Gowan may nationalize the oil industry or otherwise impair their investments. Hence the Biafran cause wins support from Portugal, South Africa, Rhodesia and other nations more indirectly. This support allows Ojuku to wage a bloody war that only impedes the development of national unity and an anti-imperialistic foreign policy since Gowan too is compelled to seek outside help.

The film's overriding concern to explain the motivations behind the civil war leads to a more didactic point of view than that of the other films. There is less consideration of the quality of life realized by the government's efforts than there is of the liberation force's activities in the other films. Whereas the other films spend little time attempting to convince the viewer of which side is better serving the interests of the majority of the people, this becomes the central focus of <u>Nigeria: Nigeria One</u>. The overall history of the development of the Nigerian nation gets far less attention as a result than that of Guinea Bissau, Mozambique, Dhofar, or Venezuela although the actual circumstances surrounding this one event or period are examined more closely than any comparable period in the other countries.

In a complex situation where the filmmakers cannot assume their viewers understand the motivations or goals of the opposing sides and where a choice is made to report on the conflict itself rather than situate that within a larger perspective illustrating the priorities of the liberation forces, or in this case, the governmental forces, there may be a strong temptation to make points dramatically as much or more than factually. This is a temptation which Facts Africa, the producers of this film, have, unfortunately, not resisted as consistently as they might have.

At one point in the film the camera zooms in to a close up of a document which the narrator explains is a secret agreement between General Ojuku and a foreign government trading military assistance for mineral rights. The narrator argues that at this point General Ojuku was claiming freedom from foreign domination as one of his goals. At another point the film presents a sync interview with a white mercenary fighting for the Biafrans who had previously flown planes for Phoenix Airways, a C.I.A. operation. While the narrator is describing the dependence of the Biafran army upon outside aid, the camera settles upon an A.I.D. poster on a village wall. Most dramatically of all, the narrator describes for the viewer an arrangement whereby West Germany constructed a poisonous gas factory for the Biafrans. There is no further documentation of the use of this gas, but the mere evocation of poison gas and German technology in this context is enough to stir up dreadful memories of the last World War.

Unlike Frank Capra's Why We Fight series or Newsreel's own We Are the Palestinian People, Nigeria: Nigeria One fails to wield a coherent whole out of its dramatic or its factual material. The goal of mobilizing support for one side of a conflict by contrasting the two sides and arguing that historical justification and moral right lies squarely on one side only is very similar, but Nigeria meanders in its presentation. Its dramatic, emotional moments are strung between sections of far drier and often fuzzy appeals to reason. General Gowan and the policies of the Nigerian government, their actual relationship to the needs of the people, remain ill-defined, as though the filmmakers themselves were uncertain and perhaps opting for what they felt was the lesser of two evils. Hence there is little possibility of arousing a positive emotional identification. To win our support on the basis of negative arguments alone becomes a limited and in many ways self-defeating strategy. Nigeria: Nigeria One provides a starting point for discussion of the civil war in Nigeria, but in the nature of its presentation and in the narrow focus upon the war itself the film is of questionable value and seems to clearly lack the longer range, continuing usefulness of those other films that concentrate more fully upon the positive policies and actions of national liberation movements.

On a more formal level there are some aspects of these films worth discussing in a little more detail. One of the more striking characteristics about almost all of the films is the absence of sync sound. FALN seems to have shot entirely silent with the sound track, primarily the commentary, added later. Some of the others like Revolution in Dhofar have occasional sequences in which we hear as well as see members of the liberation forces. And if sync interviews are excluded, the amount of remaining synchronous material (cinema-verite style indirect address or even simply the presence of synchronous location sounds accompanying a voice-over narration) is virtually nil in each of the films.

The reasons for this absence may be largely economic and/or technical (a question of what kind of equipment was available or could be afforded). And yet to cite such a reason does nothing toward understanding the effect of this absence. In fact, once the effect is understood it may be possible to devise ways of using the same limited equipment that will avoid some of the more problematic implications.

A cornerstone of Bazin's arguments about the cinema's vocation for realism is the desirability of the long take in which temporal and spatial patterns commensurate with those we experience in everyday life can be preserved. By building upon the indexical quality of the image, its existential link with its referent, the long take grounds the cinema in an ontological realism that then forms an adequate base for the manipulations of montage: "It is only an increased realism of the image that can support the abstraction of montage."^{85} Although I do not wish to subscribe to Bazin's metaphysical respect for the real as a treasure-house of ambiguity to be celebrated rather than analyzed, I am impressed by the need to give enough weight to the image to allow it to confront the verbal sound track (especially the voice-over narration of the documentary film) on some kind of par. The valorization of the digital, the notion that information is conveyed through the literal meaning of words, is highly prevalent in our culture and seems to be one reason not only for the prolonged success of voice-over narration as a documentary mode of discourse but also for the extreme difficulty many viewers have in recognizing the full range of possibilities available for establishing other dominant codes in a film where voice-over narration is used. The absence of location sync (by which I mean reproduction of the full range of sounds originating at the time of the pro-filmic event) is one clear method for re-affirming the dominance of a voice-over narration, one perhaps redundant to the dominance we have learned to accord words spoken by an authority in the first place.

The consequence of this absence is thus to deflate further the status of the image, pushing it closer to illustrative accompaniment than a primary source of meaning. As a consistent pattern, since it reduces the amount of information re-presented from the pro-filmic event, it compels us to turn to the filmic codes for guidance, centering around the sound/image relationship. The information provided by the pro-filmic event itself becomes further generalized toward a symbolic function. For example, in Nigeria: Nigeria One and FALN those images of corporate signs and trademarks that are employed to evoke the world of monopoly capitalism strangling the Third World, carry no significance outside of their relationship to the narrator's argument to this effect. This obscures the relationship between surface phenomena and deep structure in its abstraction of the former and the reification of the latter into a product, a thing possessable by the narrator. As Susan Sontag argues, this strategy ultimately seems to undercut the very quality political filmmakers strive to realize--an activation of the spectator's own level of awareness: "The images that mobilize conscience are always specific to a given historical situation. The more general they are, the less likely they are to be effective."[86]

Everyday, experiential reality becomes reduced to a lower ontological status than deep structure instead of being presented as the starting point, the inescapable source of much conceptual understanding (in our awareness of our encounter with the material world). This reliance upon formal codes that make of the image and the pro-filmic event generally an illustrative gloss only results in conjuring up deep structure ex nihil, a deus ex machina accompaniment to a Voice of God narration.

A lesser problem confronting the use of formal codes in these films is the reliance in several of them upon sync interviews with public officials as an integral source of information. The words chosen by any political figure for the benefit of the camera are words whose credibility has been hollowed out for many viewers. Such material can seldom compensate for more direct documentation of points argued. A complicating factor is that many interviews remain unintegrated into a coherent, logical flow. They are inserted en masse as a block of argumentation. Although it may not be desirable to subordinate their own logic to that of the film as thoroughly as Emile de Antinio does in his films, the meandering quality to the presentation seriously affects Nigeria, A Luta Continua and parts of Revolution in Dhofar.

To conclude on a somewhat more affirmative note, it is to the credit of these films that the images of revolutionary struggle in each country are not melded in a revolutionary montage of Third World struggle such as those found in many of Newsreel's own earlier films about the New Left or the movement in general. Each struggle is accorded the dignity of its own geo-political integrity. The commonality of the various efforts is far better conveyed by showing more than one such film than by finding each and every struggle subsumed into an abstract process of world-wide revolution that has no material roots anywhere. While there may be problems with these films, in the kind of discussion context for which Newsreel intended them, they stand as valuable sources of information from the other side of struggles our more official news media seldom cover at all.

FOOTNOTES

Chapter Three

1
Erik Barnouw, Documentary: A History of the Non-Fiction Film (New York: Oxford University Press, 1974), p. 275.

2
These films are all discussed in Nichols, Newsreel.

3
Letter from Allan Siegel, Third World Newsreel, New York, October 25, 1973. Siegel is the only member of the founding group still active in Third World Newsreel.

4
Some of the other principal groups and sources of further information about them are as follows:

New Day Films (a distribution co-operative for six feminist filmmakers. See Carol Emmens, "New Day Films: An Alternative in Distribution," Women & Film, Vol. 2, no. 7 (1975), pp. 72-75.

Pacific Street Film Collective (three radical filmmaker-distributors. See Pacific Street Film Collective, "The Agony and the Ecstasy of Radical Film Production," Cineaste, Vol. 6, no. 2 (1974), pp. 43-45.

Single Spark Films (discussed in Chapter Four). See Csaba Polony and Larry Felson, "Interview with Single Spark Films," Left Curve, no. 4 (Summer, 1975), pp. 28-39.

Cine Manifest (fiction film oriented collective). See Eugene Corr and Peter Gessner, "Cine Manifest: A Self-History," Jump Cut, no. 3 (September-October, 1974), pp. 19-20.

Kartemquin (a loose association of political filmmakers in the Chicago area). See Julia Lesage, "Filming for the City--An Interview with the Kartemquin Collective," Cineaste, Vol. 7, no. 1 (1976), pp. 26-30.

5
Interview with Chris, December, 1974.

6
Gary Wills, "The Human Sewer," review of <u>A Time to Die</u>, by Tom Wicker, in <u>The New York Review of Books</u>, Vol. 22, no. 5 (April 3, 1975), p. 7.

7
<u>Ibid</u>.

8
<u>Ibid</u>., p. 8.

9
Dan Georgakas, "Prison Films," <u>Cineaste</u>, Vol. 6, no. 3 (1974), p. 33.

10
Gary Wills, "Do We Need Prisons? An Exchange," <u>The New York Review of Books</u>, Vol. 22, no. 9 (May 29, 1975), p. 13. Wills' whole solution is a symptomatic discourse: why patrol "homes" when most crime occurs in communities where people are lucky to afford an apartment? Why no mention of organized crime or business crime (price fixing, false advertising, short weighting, etc.). Wills has no solution, only an impulse toward self-protection.

11
"The Intellectuals and Power: A Discussion between Michael Foucault and Gilles Deleuze," <u>Telos</u>, no. 16 (Summer, 1973), p. 105.

12
Interview with Chris, December, 1974.

13
Sorgei Tretyakov et al., "<u>Lef</u> and Film: Notes of Discussion (extracts)," ed. by Ben Brewster, trans. by Diana Matias, <u>Screen</u>, Vol. 12, no. 4 (Winter, 1971-72), p. 76.

14
Dan Georgakas, "We Demand Freedom and Teach Our Children," <u>Cineaste</u>, Vol. 6, no. 1 (1973), p. 47.

15
<u>Ibid</u>.

16
<u>Ibid</u>.

17
Georgakas, "Prison Films," p. 33.

18
Daniel Klughez, "Documentary--Where's the Wonder?" in *The Documentary Tradition: From Nanook to Woodstock*, ed. by Lewis Jacobs (New York: Hopkinson and Blake, 1971), p. 457.

19
Georgakas, "We Demand Freedom," p. 47.

20
Georgakas, "Prison Films," p. 34.

21
Interview with Chris, December, 1974.

22
Ibid.

23
John K. Simon, "Michel Foucault on Attica," *Telos*, no. 19 (Spring, 1974), p. 157.

24
Interview with Chris, December, 1974.

25
Louis Marcorelles with the collaboration of Nicole Rouzet-Albagli, *Living Cinema: New Directions in Contemporary Film-making*, trans. by Isabel Quigly (New York: Praeger, 1973), p. 83.

26
Stephen Mamber, *Cinema-Verite in America: Studies in Uncontrolled Documentary* (Cambridge, Mass.: M.I.T. Press, 1974), pp. 115-140.

27
Carol Wikarska, "Attica," *Women & Film*, Vol. 2, no. 7 (Summer, 1975), p. 62.

28
Interview with Chris, December, 1974.

29
Georgakas, "Prison Films," p. 34.

30
Tretyakov, "*Lef* and Film," p. 74.

31
Quoted in Marcorelles, *Living Cinema*, p. 55.

32
Marcorelles, *Living Cinema*, p. 83.

33
   Interview with Robert, former member Third World Newsreel, New York, June, 1974.

34
   Anthony Wilden, *System and Structure: Essays in Communication and Exchange* (London: Tavistock Publications, 1972), p. xxvii.

35
   David Denby, "Documenting America," in *The Documentary Tradition*, ed. by Lewis Jacobs (New York: Hopkinson and Blake, 1971), p. 481.

36
   Previously discussed in Nichols, *Newsreel*, pp. 129-132 and 84-85, respectively.

37
   See p. 34 above.

38
   The Congress for Afrikan People, for example, concentrates a great deal of its work in the Newark Community and other specific, local areas. The Black Workers Congress has consistently resisted the pressures to form a strong national organization, opting to devote its efforts to local organizing.

39
   "The Intellectuals and Power," p. 104.

40
   Russell Jacoby, "The Politics of Subjectivity: Notes on Marxism, the Movement and Bourgeois Society," *Telos*, no. 9 (Fall, 1971), p. 117.

41
   The other three are *Winter Soldier*, *Only the Beginning*, and *El Pueblo Se Levante (The People Are Rising)*.

42
   Ruth McCormick, "Newsreel Films: Break and Enter and The People Arise," *Cineaste*, Vol. 4, no. 4 (Spring, 1971), p. 24.

43
   Godard's tracking shot flattens the bourgeois world of appearances and denies it the density of deep-focus photography. A thorough discussion of its use and implications is found in Brian Henderson's article, "Toward a Non-Bourgeoise Camera Style," *Film Quarterly*, Vol. 24, no. 2 (Winter, 1970-71), pp. 2-14.

44
   Third World Newsreel (a film catalogue), n.p.

45
   Interview with Ernie, December, 1974.

46
   Ibid.

47
   Jim Pines, "Left Film Distributors," Screen, Vol. 13, no. 4 (Winter, 1972-73), p. 116.

48
   Nichols, Newsreel, p. 58.

49
   Jean-Paul Fargier, "Parenthesis or Indirect Route," trans. by Susan Bennett, Screen, Vol. 12, no. 2 (Summer, 1971), p. 141.

50
   Elizabeth Sussex, "Grierson on Documentary" (an interview), Film Quarterly, Vol. 26, no. 1 (Fall, 1972), p. 24. More recent studies support this view: "What the British formed was in essence a political not an artistic school. There was no consistent aesthetic theory underlying the movement." William Guynn, "Politics of the British Documentary," Jump Cut, no. 6 (March-April, 1975), p. 10.

51
   Henry Breitrose, "Documentary: A History of the Non-Fiction Film," Film Quarterly, Vol. 28, no. 4 (Summer, 1975), p. 38.

52
   Martha Kapos, "The Languages of Realism," Screen, Vol. 13, no. 1 (Spring, 1972), p. 84.

53
   See Nichols, Newsreel, pp. 213-217.

54
   Interview with Larry, Resolution Films, San Francisco, July, 1975.

55
   James Blue, "One Man's Truth--An Interview with Richard Leacock," in The Documentary Tradition, ed. by Lewis Jacobs (New York: Hopkinson and Blake, 1971), pp. 411-412.

56
   Fargier, "Parenthesis or Indirect Route," p. 137.

57
   Third World Newsreel (a film catalogue), n.p.

58
Interview with Robert, June, 1974.

59
Pulliam, "Newsreel," p. 9 (cf. Nichols, Newsreel, pp. 223-231).

60
Dan Georgakas, "Finally Got the News: The Making of a Radical Film," Cineaste, Vol. 5, no. 4 (1973), p. 3.

61
The Editors, Cahiers du Cinema, "John Ford's Young Mr. Lincoln," trans. by Helen Lackner and Diana Matias, Screen, Vol. 13, no. 3 (Autumn, 1972), pp. 5-43.

62
Third World Newsreel (a film catalogue), n.p.

63
James Roy MacBean, Film Quarterly, Vol. 26, no. 1 (Fall, 1972), p. 34.

64
Interview with Allan, July, 1974.

65
Michael and Jill Klein, "Native Land--An Interview with Leo Hurwitz, Cineaste, Vol. 6, no. 3 (1974), p. 7.

66
Walter Benjamin, "A Short History of Photography," trans. by Stanley Mitchell, Screen, Vol. 13, no. 1 (Spring, 1972), p. 24.

67
Interview with Robert, former member, Third World Newsreel and New York Newsreel, New York, March, 1972.

68
Chuck Kleinhans, "Reading and Thinking about the Avant-Garde," Jump Cut, no. 6 (March-April, 1975), p. 25.

69
Diegesis is the level of the fiction, the level at which the events presumed to be observed or simply recorded exist. A narrational voice describing this level is of a higher logical type; it brackets and controls it. As indicated in the concluding chapter, the concept of diegesis in documentary may be fundamentally different from its meaning in fiction films.

70
Jacoby, "The Politics of Subjectivity," p. 118.

71
   Jan Jost, "Afterimages: Notes from Practice," *Jump Cut*, no. 5 (January-February, 1975), p. 7.

72
   Interview with Robert, July, 1974.

73
   "Radical American Film Questionnaire, Part III," *Cineaste*, Vol. 6, no. 1 (1973), p. 20.

74
   Interview with Chris, December, 1974.

75
   The two go together to the degree that Third World struggles involve racial polarization and that the solution to racism in the United States is posed in terms of the right to self-determination for blacks, or other minorities.

76
   McCormick, "Newsreel Films," p. 26.

77
   Ibid.

78
   Ibid.

79
   Lewis Jacobs, "Documentary Becomes Engaged and Verite," in *The Documentary Tradition*, Jacobs, p. 378.

80
   See Nichols, *Newsreel*, p. 198.

81
   Interview with Robert, July, 1974.

82
   Quoted in Marcorelles, *Living Cinema*, p. 40.

83
   Radical Third World Film Catalogue, ed. by Paul Foster (Oxford, England, 1973), n.p.

84
   Interview with Ernie, December, 1974.

⁸⁵ Andre Bazin, *What do Cinema*, Vol. I, essays selected and translated by Hugh Gray (Berkeley and Los Angeles: University of California Press, 1967), p. 39.

⁸⁶ Susan Sontag, "Photography," *The New York Review of Books*, Vol. 20, no. 16 (October 18, 1973), p. 61

Chapter Four

SAN FRANCISCO NEWSREEL

Natoma Street is a narrow alleyway cutting through San Francisco's Mission District. It comes to an early end in the downtown direction where, along with buildings, houses and parking lots, it has been erased in favor of the early signs of what it often called urban renewal: uprooted concrete slabs, intractible foundations, and cyclone fencing. An emblem of successful renewal, a large, squat window-less Crocker National Bank blocks the street's continuation with its bulk, a worthy guardian to the emergent downtown dream of businessmen and civic leaders.

Walking south, further into the Mission District, the street passes the rear of the Herald-Examiner where scores of delivery trucks huddle, waiting the day's ration of news. At the next corner the one-way vein of asphalt sparkles with its downtown jewlery of broken liquor bottles: Red Rocket, Thunderbird, even scab-made Gallo. The sound of breaking glass seldom turns a single head. It is not a place for walking barefoot.

Across the intersection, facing Fourth St., is the Mission District Plasma Center--a shoe box sawn in half with clotted brown walls and tarnished gold lettering that arches across the larger of its two windows. The door is closed. To gain entry visitors must push a button then speak into a rusting intercom box tacked to the wall. Further

down the same block a Black man is maneuvering a large 25" television
set into the back seat of his '64 Pontiac. The uniformed worker from
the Goodwill Industries store helps lethargically.

An auto supply shop, its windows filled with stock car racing
equipment, dominates the next corner. To the east, in the direction of
the bay-side dockyards, another large city block has been bulldozed
clean save for the tenacious stubble of a plastics factory. The low
skyline makes it all the easier to see the Berkeley Hills across the
Bay.

Five or six houses further down Natoma Street is 630, headquarters
of San Francisco Newsreel. A plain white sign used to announce their
presence but now that sign is gone. Thick meshing in a diamond pattern
covers the one window facing the street. It no longer protects glass,
however; beyond the meshing is another layer made of plywood. The only
identifying sign on the door is a smudged card that says, "Press buzzer
hard." The metal mail slot in the door reveals another plywood barrier
beyond the outer door.

The street is almost empty although many of the buildings along
this block are divided into apartments. Next door a Philippino family
of six watches with casual indifference as I wait to be admitted. The
father cradles a young infant of some 8 months while the mother talks
to one of her neighbors. The Newsreel people are well-known to their
neighbors. Had it been common knowledge that several members of the
leadership had been purged, the neighbors would have called the police
when these leaders appeared in the middle of the night to reclaim equipment and films that said belonged to them. Most of the inhabitants of

the area are Third World, many from the Philippines, from Latin America, from Singapore, all crouching here in the Mission District, alert for signs of the American Dream.

Inside, the one-floor offices are divided into a reception-business area where Lawrence, sole survivor of the Newsreel majority which purged four members of the leadership in February, 1973, staffs the telephone and admits visitors. A small magazine rack displays recent issues of leftist periodicals and film magazines devoted to information and practical problems: <u>Filmmakers Newsletter</u>, <u>Cinéma Canada</u>, <u>Cineaste</u> along with flyers and old catalogues describing Newsreel films. An overhead flourescent light replaces the natural sunlight no longer admitted.

Adjoining the office is a storage room for Newsreel's film library. Racks and racks of films fill the room. An individual has recently begun cataloguing all the material that has accumulated alongside the finished films--outtakes, stock shots, television news footage, and so on. Beyond the office worker's desk is another doorway leading to a series of rooms repartitioned by the Newsreel members. One is a small viewing room. The only seat in it now is a second-hand, metal framed couch. In the next room a projector perches atop a tower of milk and orange crates. The projectionist reaches it by climbing onto a small table set behind it. Beyond this small room is a much larger one still cluttered with the paraphenalia of renovation. A portion of it is given over to Resolution Films, a filmmaking group affiliated with Newsreel. The remainder is equipped for graphics work--mainly the production of flyers and posters. Neighborhood groups make frequent use of it. An old but functional automatic film inspection machine has been placed against one wall, the only piece of bulky filmmaking equipment that evokes the aura of large-scale activity. No films are currently in production, nor have there been since the members of the leadership were purged in February, 1973 (with the exception of work carried out by Resolution Films).

In the rear of the building partions have been completed to wall off a 10x10 area as a darkroom for film production and community use. The small end of the L-shaped larger room is intended as an editing area and branching off this portion of the room is the bathroom. Even though much remains to be done elsewhere in the building, a small potted plant decorates the freshly painted bathroom.

Newsreel's Natoma Street office did not always exist in the center of what could almost pass as the landscape for a post-nuclear science-fiction film. A few years ago the now vacant, dehydrated city blocks were brimming with factories, pastel colored dwelling units and the bubbling street-noise of a densely packed, ethnically diverse working-class. Many of the factories are gone now and so are the workers. What appears as an early spring growth of sleek high-rise office buildings pushing through the compost of the wrecking ball predicts what is to come. The new BART station (Bay Area Rapid Transit) is only three blocks from the Newsreel office.

The most recent film by Resolution Films, Redevelopment, elaborates further on what urban renewal has meant in San Francisco.* The

---

*Resolution Films and Redevelopment are discussed further in Chapter Five, pages 242-248.

day after I arrive, the film is scheduled for a screening at The Farm, a community project in the heart of the Mission District. The Farm lies in a cradle of concrete beneath the intersection of two major freeways and their myriad accessways. From the cast iron lawn chairs in front of the white, ivy-covered sides of The Farm I can count fifteen different roads, ramps and major arteries scattered in a multi-tiered series of arcs. I wonder how the concentration of engine exhaust will effect The Farm's crops, once the concrete slabs crusted over their fields have been removed.

The Farm is an old warehouse refitted as a multi-purpose hall. Larry, from Resolution Films, is setting up folding chairs across the tile floor. Near the windows overlooking the scramble of freeways and fading sunlight several picnic tables with blue checkered tableclothes already have a full complement of visitors. Along the other wall are several oversized covers for seed packages: Minature Hyacinth, Azaleas, Sunflowers .... A large hand drawn map indicates what the Farm will look like once the Army Corps of Engineers come to clear away the concrete (that is the hope of The Farm organizers): rich green fields running from the shadow of the freeways to the far end of the vacant block where an elementary school still stands---only in the diagram its flat tar roof is blanketed with a crop of green vegetables.

At the far end of the room, Bonnie, one of the organizers, runs a refreshment bar where coffee, milk, and organic brownies are served. No soda, no liquor, and no foods not homemade. All in all, The Farm is distinctively different from the drab downtown meeting halls where Newsreel and most other political groups could be found a few years ago.

The halls are still there, most of them, and still used, but now there is another series of meeting places that no longer seems a parallel but unrelated phenomenon. Most of the members of the audience are residents of the Mission District, although the ones who have come here are mostly white as well.

Larry introduces the program and begins it with a Mickey Mouse short, an attraction appreciated by the many children and perhaps by the babies who are pointed toward the screen. He follows this with Now, a short film by Santiago Alvarez, which uses lyrics by Lena Horne and a series of images of Civil Rights demonstrations and police brutality to emphasize the point of the unnarrated film: the time is now. Now is an example of what Newsreel calls "turn-on" films which they stopped making or distributing in the early '70s because of their diffuse politics. The film, however, prompts a strong round of cheers at its conclusion.

Redevelopment is sub-titled "A Marxist Analysis," and is specifically used as an organizing tool in the Mission District and other parts of the city where major urban renewal projects have been underway. The general sense of desolation and decline that is apparent to the visitor is a felt reality to the people who live here. They have been trying to do something to prevent it for years and the film chronicles their struggle as well as explaining that renewal has one motive--profit-- and one benefactor---those who make the profit. The benefactor is never identical to the people who try to protect themselves against urban renewal or to the people who have to live with its results.

The film, discussed in further detail later, is a heavy indictment against the forces of redevelopment. Much of its impetus in San Francisco in the last ten years seems to be directly related to the now-functioning BART lines. The years-long scars carved into Market and Mission Streets during its constructions have been healed with transplants of fresh brick and concrete but new scars cut into the surrounding neighborhoods as a scramble to capitalize upon soaring land values got under way remain raw and even festering. Workers may have built the city, and BART, and the redevelopments, but their only memorials are those steel and glass high-rises dedicated to the name of profit.

San Francisco Newsreel, like Third World Newsreel in New York, has had a stormy history since 1971 in which several of the same basic issues have surfaced, primarily the internal relationship between white and Third World members, or the relationship between politically sophisticated individuals in positions of leadership and less articulate, less experienced, new members since this difference very frequently took the shape of a racial distinction. For two years, from 1971 until the early part of 1973, there were very few outward signs of filmmaking activity or internal tension, but in 1973, San Francisco Newsreel released one of their most ambitious films which had been two years in the making, Revolution Until Victory (now known as We the Palestinian People), and four members of group's leadership, people who had primary responsibility for this film, were purged by the remaining members. Prior to this tumultuous period, San Francisco Newsreel worked on completing their Palestine film, planning a film on labor history in the United States, and dealing (in retrospect, inadequately) with the internal tensions that arose as new, mainly Third World individuals came into the group.[1]

Up until the latter part of 1971, San Francisco's economic survival was insured by income from the distribution of films and by their innovative work furlough program.[2] When several fundraising attempts met with success, there was perhaps an inevitable drift toward using this revenue to support individuals in the group as well as film projects. The intense pressures of marginal subsistence, major filmmaking projects, and struggling to build up a distribution system that could make the group self-supporting were great enough without the long hours of low-paying jobs that provided a degree of political contact with Newsreel's intended audience but primarily went toward keeping all the other priorities afloat. Unfortunately, however, the diversion of the newly acquired monies to self-support meant that there were still inadequate funds to carry through quickly on the various projects, so that by late 1972, as the funds began to run out, a new financial crisis struck the group. No one was working, bills were coming in, and stress went to short-range projects such as print sales and more fundraising to the detriment of the filmmaking projects and regular distribution.[3] It was this crisis that precipitated the internal contradictions which had been accumulating since 1971.

The crisis was of major proportions and involved purging four of the most long-standing and politically sophisticated members of the Newsreel collective. These four people were among San Francisco Newsreel's original founders and provided much of the core strength and resilience that resulted in five years of productive work including many of Newsreel's best films (e.g., Richmond Oil Strike, San Francisco

State Strike, Off the Pig, The Woman's Film, People's Park, and Los Siete de la Raza).[4] They were politically experienced and had been studying Marxist-Leninist-Maoist thought for several years. Their political analysis was sophisticated and closely related to the position of the Revolutionary Union (a Bay Area Marxist-Leninist radical group which has since 1973 become national in scope and a major proponent of the idea of creating a new, non-revisionist communist party in the United States).

When New York Newsreel, in the spring of 1971, called for active recruitment of Third World members, San Francisco Newsreel had no reluctance about complying: their films, being about Third World struggles to a large degree, were proof in themselves of the logic of the move. Furthermore, their study with the RU had convinced them that anti-imperialist, multi-national collectives were the best stepping stone to a new communist party in which Marxist propaganda units would play a vital role.

One of the peculiar features of this internal struggle is that neither side succeeded in convincing the other of its correctness in distinction to other Newsreel struggles where a proportion of the membership might split off but where a common understanding of why such a step was necessary and/or desirable would be shared by both sides. The purged members continue to regard the event as "an ideological split" in which they happened to be in the minority, while the purging membership insists that there was none of the principled debate about issues or political line characterizing a split: to them it was a purge straight and simple, removing undesirable, obstructive forces inside the group rather than the formulation of one theoretical position in opposition to another.

The majority, those purging (12 of the 16 members), charged four of the group's leaders with racism (giving only token responsibility to Third World members), elitism (appropriating most decision-making to themselves), opportunism (fundraising to train Third World members in filmmaking then using the funds for other purposes) and authoritarianism (stifling criticism by using theory as a club against the less articulate and well-read--usually but not always Third World members). As the majority stated in their position paper: "Their constant tactic of confusing people in meetings by throwing out theories out of context to hide their bad practices disoriented members and prevented Newsreel's development."[5]

The majority only discovered that these four people were also the legal owners of Newsreel (which had been officially incorporated some years before) after criticism on these points began to take place in the winter of 1972-1973. They concluded that this was a major stumbling block insofar as it encouraged the minority of four to consider the others as interlopers with a less privileged position than their own. Whether this was the case or not, the majority pressed for a transfer of legal ownership which was agreed to but not actually completed until after the purge. For several the delay in effecting a transfer was an example of political blackmail since the minority did not turn over ownership until after they recovered considerable amounts of filmmaking equipment from the majority.[6]

Another important issue was the nature of the internal organization.

The minority favored centralism (in the form of a central committee) over democracy and strongly opposed the formation of a Third Wordl collective apart from the central committee.[7] At this time, in late 1972, how much of this position was attributable to the purged four is somewhat unclear. The central committee consisted of nine members for a total membership of 17![8] This unwieldy arrangement may itself be a sign of a desire to concentrate power into more seasoned hands, or conversely, a distrust of the politics of new members who would have far greater power under an open-ended structure with decisions reached by consensus. As it was, issues were discussed by the central committee and resolutions passed on to the membership. Differences seldom were aired in open meetings which led to a sense of stultification and loss of democracy for many of the majority members.

Near the end of 1972, a "rectification program" was agreed to following the first general discussions of these internal problems. A major portion of this program involved streamlining the central committee to five, three whites and two Third World members. In some ways this served to intensify the conflict since two of the whites elected were also two of the individuals with whom the strongest disagreements had occurred. One of the minority's main points later was to be the application of a "double standard" of criticism in which their practice as members of the central committee was criticized consistently while no criticism was voiced about the role of the Third World and majority members who also had a say in subsequent decisions.[9]

The struggle clearly took on a personal focus for the majority. The differences of political line were a secondary problem for them which further study might well resolve. How to resolve differences at the level of character structure, or personal interaction, seemed far more perplexing and frustrating. Not only did the majority lack the political background and skills to escalate the struggle to a purely political level, they also lacked the ability to articulate the personal conflict in a way so that its crucial political implications would become apparent to the minority. For this "failure of communication" to exist at a political level is not surprising for individuals who were less experienced and new to Newsreel. For it to be so prevalent in terms of the personal conflicts themselves is somewhat more puzzling and an early clue that purges alone would not resolve differences that were still not being clearly articulated and almost certain to recur in one form or another.

An example of the majority's presentation of the situation in personal terms unlinked to any more general understanding is their own position paper in which they flail out at the oppressive tactics of a member of the minority:

> This situation was really bad. Jeff (one of the four purged and on the central committee of five) had consistently tried to prevent Robbie (a Third World member of the majority) from attaining any position of responsibility within the organization simply because he didn't trust him. The third world people brought out that if Robbie had been a pig he could have easily done a great deal of harm to the organization before this. ... Jeffrey was citicized within the Central Committee and the third world members brought this back to the collective.[10]

This and the minority's position paper were used as starting points for a discussion of the events by outside movement people whom both sides agreed to invite in to try to mediate the dispute.[11] The nature of the majority's criticism almost invited outsiders to take sides on the basis of their own personal opinions of the minority. To a large extent this is what happened and outside mediation failed to provide any kind of resolution.[12]

A sign of how murky these issues were for both sides, or at least of their inability to put the issues into words clearly understood by the other side, was the fact that the two position papers were only drawn up following the actual purge. At that point they were also written with a mind to rationalizing past events, a framework within which genuine struggle is bound to suffer. The majority made little or no mention of theoretical or political differences with the minority and instead stressed the contradictions in the minority's practice-- the felt presence of racist acts and so on. When a majority member was given only token responsibility on the We the Palestinian People film, this wasn't discussed in terms of differences over the national question, who should make films, for whom they were intended, etc. It was cited primarily in terms of the felt-experience of humiliation, frustration, and oppressive leadership.[13] The majority's summation of their charges against the minority underscores the personal, subjective feeling that there were sharp differences but without specifying those differences clearly or proposing concrete alternatives (this vagueness was one of the qualities that figured very prominently in the minority's own counter-attack):

> This constant denial of contradictions and heavy resistance to recognize racism, and the lack of struggle by the minority made it necessary for the majority to purge four people from San Francisco Newsreel whom have all been consistent in: 1) evading struggle, 2) perpetuation of the

divisive tactic to pit white and Third World people, 3) their opportunist plot to maintain the status quo by resisting change, 4) their elitist and centralist tactic of keeping political issues and information from the general membership, 5) their lack of practice to engage in mass work and spread of propaganda which is important for the mobilization and organization of the exploited and oppressed working people, for the development of a working class party that will bring about revolution in this country.[14]

Lack of a clear alternative to the minority's political direction suggested that the struggle was perceived as personal only and the current direction might prove acceptable if the group could only resolve these conflicts at a personal level. Inability to resolve them, though, meant that the individuals best equipped to structure the prevailing direction clearly were no longer available. The resultant loss in political clarity may be one of the reasons why many of the majority's members drifted away from the group in the ensuing months.

The position paper prepared by the minority operates on two, seemingly disconnected levels. On the one hand it is remarkably cogent and incisive political analysis; on the other it reveals virtually no awareness of the real nature of the majority's complaints.

The basic response of the minority was to regard the entire course of this internal struggle as an attack on their political line. The absence of a political alternative to their own political analysis convinced them that the personal criticisms were a smokescreen deployed in order to sabotage their politics indirectly rather than openly confront them. As they state in their paper, "It became clear after a while that these charges (attacking the "weaknesses of ... individuals in leadership") were being used as a cover for fundamental differences on the nature of Newsreel work, organization and politics."[15]

To the minority the "real issues" were strictly political questions of strategy:

> Under the guise of criticism of individuals in leadership, there was a basic attack going down against the political direction these individuals stood for and the political direction of Newsreel. But this attack was never opened up for honest struggle in the group. It was always covered up in personal criticism of these individuals. Underneath there was disagreement on 1) who we should be distributing films to; 2) who we should be making films for; 3) what political study should be going on; 4) the points of political unity; 5) and the content of the films .... We believe the primary problem was not the individuals in leadership. The primary problem was to achieve a greater political unity in the group because there was considerable disagreement as to how we should function and who we should serve.[16]

The minority goes on to state, "We began to see that this was all part of a plan to use this flurry of criticism to put forward their political line and kick out those of us who voiced a line opposed to theirs."[17] This is a contradiction that in some ways cannot be resolved. They argue that no clear political line was being presented. They assume that a submerged line nonetheless existed. This leads them to extrapolate from the majority's practice a line which they then assign to the majority even though subsequent events given little indication that there was then or since any clear-cut line at all, revisionist or ultra-leftist, covert or overt. It is as if the minority can only cope with the situation by positing such a line, however, since it is only at the level of political debate that they feel comfortable. For them, the personal is clearly a subordinate aspect of the political line with which the individual associates himself.

The most flagrant example of this peculiar kind of self-denial is the minority's discussion of racism, not in terms of their personal attitudes and practice, but in terms of a "line" on the relationship of racism to the national question. The minority very succinctly summarizes the political line they impute to the majority on the basis of opposition to their own ideas:

1) They (the majority) felt that the struggles of Third World people are merely the fight against racism and not struggles for national liberation.
2) That Third World people in the U.S. do not constitute nations and national minorities but rather they are just "races."
3) That Marxism-Leninism-Mao Tse Tung thought cannot be used as a basis for understanding racism, or to struggle against racism. That the national question has nothing to do with racism.
4) They put forward that all Third World people were in the working class. This had the effect of blurring the class distinctions among Third World people, thereby denying the leading role of Third World workers in the national liberation struggles. [18]
5) They launched attacks on Red Papers #5 by the RU, a work with which we expressed agreement. As an alternative they put forward revisionists and bourgeois sociologists like Chinn, Boggs, and Cox.
6) They believe that point of production organizing is secondary to "community organizing."
7) They opposed the idea of building an anti-imperialist workers movement. They would not agree to make it one of the points of unity of the group.
8) Some people put forward that in the U.S. today Capitalism and Imperialism are two separate things. [19]

The minority goes on to present their own political analysis of racism. Their point of reference, however, is not their actual relationship with new or Third World members of Newsreel but a theoretical position paper they had previously written. They summarize their position by stating, "In fact, the reason that racism is so profitable and key to the entire imperialist system is precisely because it obscures and denies the national and democratic rights of Third World people." [20]

The minority carefully links racism to national oppression and argues that black liberation in the United States means not merely overcoming white racism, but even more means the right to self-determination and that the major force opposing self-determination is imperialism. Hence the logic of anti-imperialist, multi-national collectives. To call someone a racist who is working within a theoretical framework which reflects an understanding of the true nature of racism therefore appears absurd or invidious.

For the minority the movement from theory to practice is so unproblematic that it can be assumed as a natural corollary of a correct line. Hence, when they conclude their position paper with a series of self-criticism they state, "Our major problem was liberalism: liberalism in not promoting active ideological struggle in the group and liberalism in not putting forward Marxism-Leninism-Mao Tse Tung thought more boldly, as a basis of unity in the group."[21] The remedy for the entire crisis is seen as a yet bolder assertion of their political line! There is no suggestion that their line may have weaknesses, that it might benefit from modifications arising out of criticism of their actual practice. There is not even any suggestion that the level of personal practice, of attitudes, habits, and priorities might indeed be a level on which serious struggle should take place.

The minority's retreat into a political line left them in a well-fortified position since the majority was not able to situate the racism they felt personally within an equally elaborate political context, one which might begin by insisting on the unity of the personal and political. This was a major failure on the majority's part. It allowed the minority to brand the rest of the membership as revisionists and opportunists. Revisionists because their political study, lacking direction, included some revisionist authors (Harry Chin) and groups (CPUSA). Opportunist because Lenin's definition, "... vagueness, diffuseness, elusiveness; ... a lack of definite and firm principles"[22] was objectively true. Whether its subjective factor--selfish, self-serving motivation--was also present is not guaranteed by theoretical uncertainty, however.

But the minority refused to recognize subjective factors as valid in their own right. Everything had to be measured against an absolute scale of political correctness: "Subjective rather than true political differences were used to rally the majority of honest people to support this opportunist plan."[23] Subjective factors such as the experience of oppression are simply handles for the unscrupulous, the opportunists, who wish to bypass the capacity for clear political thought inherent in "honest people." It is hard to believe that such sophisticated political activists could have so shallow an understanding of human feelings and emotions.

Subjective experience is ruled out of the minority' legitimate universe entirely. The opposite of political theory is not lived experience, (ideology in Althusser's vocabulary), not the subjective, sensuous encounter with oppression, racism, dominance, alienation, and so on. The opposite of political theory becomes political practice, the application of that theory in the everyday world. By means of this dialectic the minority erect a closed circuit of self-denying abstraction in which the personal and political run as parallel lines destined never to meet. Hence they elaborate on their self-criticism to admit a failure to integrate theory and practice without considering the degree to which their own character, their distinctively personal practice, enters into the picture: "We in the minority faction buried ourselves in the practical work of Newsreel and not enough in the political development of the group."[24]

The minority's refusal to consider the personal in any way comparable to the political, their suspicions regarding a secret political line, their assumption that most of the majority were "honest people" duped by opportunist revisionists--all these qualities convey a sense of moral Puritanism that seems to belie their Marxist sophistication. They present a virtual Manichean concept of social realtionships from which any form of dialectic seems disturbingly absent. Their method of argument is also a chilling reminder of Ernie's warning that the movement struggle must proceed on all fronts if it is to avoid a recapitulation of the methods bourgeois society has of creating repressed individuals.[25] In the 19th century a certain kind of moral puritanism may have been a necessary price for political survival,[26] but its continuation to this day can be nothing less than a grave impediment.

Perhaps one of the most troublesome aspects of the minority's position is what it does to the relationship between the leadership and the masses. There is no qualification in their attribution of opportunism to the majority that would prevent a similar charge from being laid against the majority of working class people for whom a correct political line would be something of an abstraction and in whom various forms of false consciousness are manifest. There is nothing in the course of history to suggest that the importation of such a correct political line would iron out all the kinks in individuals' character armor, that the manifestations of false consciousness on a personal level would be automatically abolished.

By imputing a backward or revisionist political line to the majority, the minority is able to reify a difference of political awareness between leaders and masses into a contradiction between political lines. What role is left for leadership or a vanguard in a movement if the minority brands the less experienced as revisionists because of opposition to their line when that opposition may, in fact, be less to their ideas as such as their personal style of arguing or practicing those ideas?

The minority's counterattack clearly demonstrates their theoretical superiority but at the same time it creates a situation where theory can serve as a smokescreen behind which confrontation and struggle on a personal level is avoided--the precise opposite of what the minority claimed to be the case, ironically enough. A personal critique of racism cannot stand on its own or be directly confronted. For the minority racism must be explained at a political level and one's ability to do so is a measure of one's actual racism. The personal is transformed into the political but not vice versa, and the very authoritarianism which was a major complaint by the majority is symptomatically displayed in the attempts to deal with the complaint. It thus becomes somewhat difficult to believe the minority when they say, "We take the criticisms of ourselves very seriously."[27]

The picture that emerges from the stated positions of each side is paradigmatic of the difficulties within the left as a whole of dealing with personal manifestations of bourgeois ideology (racism, male chauvinism, opportunism, non-dialectical thinking, mind-body splits, etc.). It accurately depicts the difficulty of developing a political analysis that will take these personal manifestations as seriously as deviations from a more abstract political line, or, conversely, of building a coherent theory that can incorporate personal experiences of oppression, racism, and so on into the theoretical position. There are, however, some more specific aspects of the two positions that leave certain issues poorly resolved.

Two considerations that are downplayed are on the one hand the role of the majority members of the reconstituted central committee where they had an opportunity to work out many of the issues that nonetheless persisted and precipitated a crisis. On the other hand, why the situation was allowed to persist for a period of almost two years is not adequately explained by either side. Complaints seem to have been consistently voiced, but either they were voiced with far less urgency at the time or the practice of the minority was not so clearly in error at all points, or both. Otherwise, it is hard to understand why a crisis did not occur much sooner, while the minority was still working to complete We the Palestinian People, for example.

The actions of the majority after the purge are also very puzzling.[28] Within a few months the majority had dwindled down to five or six. All but one of the white members of the majority left. These individuals who left did not remain involved in propaganda work. In terms of sustaining an ongoing commitment to filmmaking as a political practice it is in fact the minority that has proven the greatest continuity before and after the purge, in sharp contrast to the situation in New York where the Third World members continued the Newsreel work and the white members drifted into other activities. The commitment of the majority to the task at hand versus the importance of a personal battle of will to win recognition from the minority is left open to considerable speculation, especially when most of the majority members who left did so without leaving a trace, as if they did not wish to maintain even token alliance with an organization they had helped transport through a major crisis.

The role of women on both sides of the purge is another factor that remains somewhat unclear. From the documents and my interviews it seems clear that women played a far less significant role than they did in New York where the newly constituted Third World Newsreel was dominated by women and where the white members who left also had a large share of articulate women. The bulk of the struggle in fact seems to have revolved around conflicts between males, seen as personal conflicts on one side and political ones on the other. Since it has been the women's movement that has been the leading edge of the drive to integrate the personal and the political, the relative absence of women from the center of the conflictual arena may be one very important reason why both sides constantly talked past one another, or why the struggle was prone to becoming a contests of wills rather than a more open-ended attempt to resolve contradictions in a context of mutual respect for the basic integrity of those on the other side of the conflict. In any case, when women have articulated a personal sense of oppression within a political context, they have been a major force for advancing the struggle beyond subjectivism and dogmatism. Their relative absence here and the intensity of the conflict are certainly suggestive even though no firm conclusions can be drawn.

This unfortunate division, from which no one emerges as a victor, offers some very important lessons for revolutionary workers. If I were to choose sides on the basis of which group is more likely to carry on Newsreel's traditions more strenuously (along with Newsreel's traditional problems), I would choose the minority because of the strength of their political analysis. But the severance of the group dislocates them from a practice in which they had the opportunity and need to struggle with personal weaknesses while also providing political leadership. The majority (which has now dwindled to a single person from the original majority plus several associated individuals)[29] no longer has a context in which their personal awareness of oppression can be linked up to an overall political analysis (or at least this context must be gradually re-established) and the urgency of internal struggle with these questions is relocated within the even greater urgency of sheer survival for both groups.

The division within Newsreel manifests the same schism between leadership and the masses as many find within the left as a whole:

> Our major criticism has to be directed against our own work and our proven inability at a trying time to consolidate our ranks, unify our ideology and advance to a higher level of unity in struggle.[30]

(The Revolutionary Union's formulation does not even take into account the personal/political split and still finds more than enough reason for vigorous criticism!) When this problem of developing and persuasively articulating a "correct line" is coupled to the problem of recognizing and dealing with the markedly different levels of consciousness between leaders and masses, the extent of the crisis on the left becomes more readily apparent. The weakness and incompleteness of the non-leadership's class consciousness and political analysis is understandable; whether this will automatically lead to revisionism or ultraleftism as the minority predicted for the majority in Newsreel remains to be seen. (So ar, after two years, this does not seem to have happened at all.) Certainly, guarding against such tendencies would usually be the task of leadership and to predict flatly such an outcome may itself be indicative of a self-protective reaction: denying the dialectic between leaders and masses in favor of an absolutist psychologism that brands the political novice to perpetual immaturity.

Much of the strength of San Francisco Newsreel over the years seemed to derive from the personal strength of the leadership: tenacity, comradeship, patience, flexibility, openness, and so on. Despite the importance of these qualities to any group interaction, they were consistently downplayed by the leadership itself. When others attempted to account for their success in terms of their personal characteristics or lifestyle, they insisted that it was simply a function of having the right political line.[31] Hence, at the moment of crisis, they assert that the majority is really attacking the "political direction these individuals (those purged) stood for,"[32] (italics mine) or that the minority took "certain political stands attacking the politics the minority represented"[33] (italics mine). The person dissolves into a cardboard simplification, standing in a one-to-one relationship to a political theory as a symbol stands for its referent; only Newsreel's perception does not even ascribe to the individual the multiplicity of meanings or representations that communication systems usually ascribe to the symbol.

This form of self-denial in favor of a generalized abstraction strikes me as one of the most dangerously backward of all tendencies in movement thought. It disavows the individuality of the bourgeois concept of person and yet winds up being its mirror opposite, creating a new person who is nothing but a symbol, a representation of an idealist order (constituted by a link to theory rather than material, real relations) where the ideas so constituting the individual are in contradiction to bourgeois ideology but the process of reflective, representational identity remains the same. People are not only what theory they espouse but also how they act. To refuse to deal with these concrete manifestations of human behavior in favor of an abstract symbolism is a denial of material reality so massive that it casts doubt over the entirely of any political analysis so grounded. Most disturbingly, it prevents Single Spark Films from developing a theory of what are probably the most crucial ideological categories of our time--the subject (the self as ego) and subjectivity. It promotes wandering into the deadly quagmire of subjectivism, escapable only through what the subordination of the personal to the political works to thwart--a <u>theory</u> of subjectivity.

The left can ill-afford these kinds of divisions, these splits between politically advanced but perhaps personally rigid leaders and politically callow but personally sensitive members. The division has haunting echoes of New York Newsreel's early distaste for Communist propaganda in the 1930's which they saw as dogmatic and unrelated to people's real needs and real conditions.[34] There is more than a faint echo of the earlier struggle in New York Newsreel itself where the peripheral members (many of them women and Third World people) held the leadership nucleus accountable for their personal limitations and its political consequences (male chauvinism, elitism, etc.). The ultimate fate of the two sides in the San Francisco Newsreel conflict cannot be foreseen (although subsequent events clarify some of the possibilities and dangers already apparent at the time of the purge), but the nature of the division only seems to fuel the argument that reason, even if based on Marx-Lenin-Mao Tse Tung, cannot provide all the answers. A more personal, intimate and subjective factor must also come into play in order to form a revolutionary movement with radically different patterns of personal relationship and political problem-solving than those of the dominant society.

Since being purged, the minority (joined by two other members of Newsreel) has formed a new filmmaking group called Single Spark Films. They have become even more closely associated with the Revolutionary Union and have completed a film, The Beginning of Our Victory, about the recent, protracted strike against Farah.

This film has taken two years to complete, having been begun in May, 1973 and first shown in May, 1975.[35] During that time the members of Single Spark Films have chosen to work in greater isolation from casual contact with the movement as a whole, in sharp contrast to the traditional practice of Newsreel. One of the distinctive features of

Newsreel, in fact, at least up until the time of the transitions to predominantly Third World membership in New York and San Francisco, was their open-ended relationship to other groups and activities and their relatively open-door policy regarding new members. Single Spark Films, however, has become a collective restricted to these six individuals; its affiliations have been narrowed to the Revolutionary Union primarily, and its contact with those outside this nexus has been slight. In fact, during this period from the purge until the present, it has been impossible to interview or even exchange written communication with the group. Much of what follows is therefore based upon the one interview they have granted, in Left Curve, at a time when they were particularly eager to publicize the recently completed Farah film.

Although the film was completed in May, 1975 and shown in the Bay Area at several high schools and meeting places, by the time I arrived in San Francisco in July, 1975, The Beginning of Our Victory had disappeared from sight. Reviewed in Revolution in May, 1975 (monthly newspaper for the Revolutionary Union), the film is praised for its identification of a major struggle and the role played by the Revolutionary Union itself in that struggle: "It is precisely the strength, unity and growing consciousness of the working-class that the film portrays .... (It is) an inspiring and lesson-filled look at a historic class battle. More it is also a significant contribution to the new proletarian culture developing in the United States."[36] Why would such a film disappear from circulation?

One answer is suggested by San Francisco Newsreel from their own viewing of the film at one of the early screenings: "It's a racist film. It makes the Chicano workers look helpless until the RU (Revolutionary Union) arrived to help them organize."[37] Others suggest that it had a negative reception when shown to Third World workers in the Bay Area. Attempts to reach the members of Single Spark Films for clarification failed, leaving only their Left Curve interview as documentation of their own point of view.

It is a dangerous practice to criticize a film that has not been seen. Instead of attempting to reach any conclusions about the film's merit, I would prefer to use the interview material to posit certain continuities in the thoughts and values of the purged members from the time of the purge until this point two years later. It will become clear that these apparent continuities lend support to the view of Lawrence in San Francisco Newsreel, but I do not wish to endorse that view. Discrepancies between thought and practice and between what is said through art and through one's own life are common enough. The members of Single Spark Films manifest what seems to me a clear, and troubling, "line" in their interview but it is entirely possible that this style of thought does not permeate the film or at least not in the ways we might first expect. The evaluation of the film itself will have to await some future time when it once again becomes available.

There is a definite strategy at work in the interview that would not be apparent without previous knowledge of the history of the members of Single Spark Films. For one thing, they quite consciously minimize their own involvement with Newsreel, even though some of them were in Newsreel from its inception in 1968:

LC: How did your group get together?

SSF: We were with another group at one time, and there was a political split.

LC: Had anybody else made any other films before the Farah film?

SSF: Yeah, we worked on this film which we think was a very good film, We The Palestinian People, about the Middle East.[38]

They say nothing of the view that they were purged, that they were in the leadership, that had participated in making many of San Francisco Newsreel's films, or that they had primary responsibility for the Palestinian film. They sound as though they were a group of people marginally associated with Newsreel who decided to split for political reasons after helping to make one film about the Middle East.

Two further comments suggest where their interests lie at this point in time:

LC: A lot of Newsreel films were almost consciously "bad."

SSF: Yeah, well, things have moved forward.[39]
... There's a Revolutionary Communist Party being formed in this country in the real world, a new one, that's a Revolutionary Communist Party that's going to lead the working-class to make a revolution.[40]

The members of Single Spark Films repeatedly emphasize the importance of the Revolutionary Union as a vanguard organization doing the most to create a new revolutionary communist party. They also maximize the role of the RU in relation to the strike and to their own efforts to film the strike:

LC: How did you come to make The Beginning of Our Victory?

SSF: Well, we knew that the Farah strike existed and we knew that revolutionary people,

particularly the Revolutionary Union was
getting interested in the strike.[41]

It is the example of the RU's interest that they imply was decisive rather than any analysis of their own regarding the strike's importance or any more direct contact with the strikers themselves.

The RU's assistance to their own work was no less crucial. After completing a rough cut which they showed to various individuals they had a mass of criticisms but were not able to bring them together into an effective plan of revision. They could not do the job themselves. At this point the RU once again appears:

> SSF: ... We took it (the film) to communists, to the Revolutionary Union, and asked for their help, and they looked at it and they looked at the stuff we had and they didn't just leave it at loose ends. They summed up what people were trying to tell us. ... The summation was really important. It just made things clear and it was, I feel, completely correct, and the result of that summation is the final film.[42]

The impression the filmmakers give is that they heard the RU was interested in a strike so they decided it was important enough to film. Once they made the film though, they didn't know how to organize it. Therefore they, as political novices, went to an organization with which they had no formal contact then or previously, received a correct analysis of what to do and then went off to carry out these suggestions faithfully. If their interview is a faithful description of the filmmaking process, it may be understandable why others regard the film as propaganda for the RU at the expense of the strikers. (They also note that they received critical suggestions from the strikers but not a "summation.") There is no suggestion in the interview of an interaction

with the RU other than subordination, no hint of any reciprocal or
dialectical relationship with the strikers themselves. To the filmmakers
the crowning moment seems to be when the RU, as a political vanguard,
provides a critical overview that is beyond the reach of anyone outside
this vanguard. (This may also explain why they downplay their own
lengthy affiliation with the RU: if they were associated for so long
there would presumably be far less need for a summation with which they
would already be familiar.) Although a vanguard group may often fill
this role of summing up experiences and offering leadership, it is the
exact nature of the summation that is of greatest interest and that
cannot be determined without access to the film itself.

One final point relates to issues originally raised during the
purge. This is the relative importance of a political analysis or
"line" apart from personal practice. In their interview the Single
Spark Films people stress the absolute importance of such a line:
"Political line is the way forward in the real world, what's going to
move the struggle of the workers--whatever struggle--forward. It's
key--it makes all the difference in the world. So <u>we wanted to put
that in our film</u>, the correct line, the thing that's gonna move the
struggle forward, that's gonna keep pushing things forward."[43] (Italics mine.)

Although the italicized portion of their comment could be meant
metaphorically, the general context in which it occurs suggests that
they mean it quite literally, that they will put this line into the
film where it will remain on permanent display like a crown jewel.
There is no suggestion that any kind of film-viewer relationship is

involved. There is no indication that political awareness involves an active process on the part of the viewer. They assume a passive spectator who absorbs a political line implanted like a seed into the film. This form of treatment for concepts, or for a conceptual relationship between a person and his material existence, seems an extreme form of reification in which the most dialectical of concepts are treated as things which political activists quarry from the world through hard work and then pass on to others by putting them into films.

Such a passive reception of a correct line seems little different from the passive reception of bourgeois ideology itself. Although stress on individual praxis is part of Single Spark Films' understanding of their filmmaking activity, it does not seem to extend to how others are meant to understand their praxis, the line they develop. Once a political vanguard develops a correct line, it can be simply passed along to others passively the way a vitamin supplement can be added to bread. The struggle is enriched, but the materialist method of Marx seems to have become drastically impoverished.

No firm conclusions are possible without access to the film, however. What is disturbing is that the style of commentary and the thematic emphases they give during this interview seem to be extrapolations of attitudes that were near the center of the earlier struggle inside Newsreel. That past seems to have been suppressed and the possibility that significant lessons were learned from it lessened. The defence to the Revolutionary Union as the vanguard rather than themselves, as was the case at the time of the purge (although even then they stated their indebtedness and agreement with the RU's line on racism and the national question), does not seem to represent a shift in style of thinking but only in emphasis. The tendency to dogmatism, to political knowledge apart from personal, more subjective aspects of practice, the identification of practice as the application of a line in which the individual becomes a vehicle for a political idea apart from his own internalizations of bourgeois ideology (a concept of the person strangely similar to that developed by Catholicism in relation to the priest)--all these tendencies were manifest at the time of the purge and they seem to have remained present and perhaps rigidified since then.

Documentary dogmatism is at least as old as the voice-of-God narration as a persistent dominant in films although there have been numerous developments in recent years that suggest more open-ended ways of developing a reciprocal, active relationship between viewer and film. Such open-endedness is a vital priority for political activists in all aspects of their relationships with others and their grasp of politically "correct" concepts. Without such qualities there is a grave danger of political leadership becoming transformed into political stultification. As Anthony Wilden warns:

> As the group (any revolutionary or radical organization) becomes established, the critical faculties of the individual members tend to enter a process of increasing atrophy: the doctrine no longer remains an attack on illusion and resistance, it becomes an illusion and a resistance in itself. There is an increasing tendency to identify positions with words and slogans, and thus to fall into a specular identification with the rhetoric of the group. ... The groups that maintain their original integrity are those which know how to transcend or how to metacommunicate about the facile oppositions they once depended on, and which their own actions necessarily render problematical. Most often, however, the attractiveness and protective pseudo-security of the Imaginary is such that the critical inquiry becomes dogmatism, the

radicals of one generation become the reactionaries of the next.[44]

With the former minority members their continued filmmaking activity is encouraging whereas their development of an integrated understanding of the personal and political is not. With the former majority members, the situation is almost the reverse. A powerful irony, though, is that the one-time majority of 12 or 13 has in the course of two years dwindled to one. Four months after the purge there were only six members left in San Francisco Newsreel. A year later there were five. And a year after that, there was only one.[45] The most puzzling exodus is that which occurred in the four months following the purge. Attempts to locate these individuals failed and the members who remained could offer no clear-cut reasons for their departure.

This rapid reduction in ranks suggests that the majority's commitment to film propaganda was not as strong as the purged minority's. It also suggests that the purge may well have been motivated by personal antagonisms between males that were not effectively mediated by less directly involved individuals and the kinds of integrative understanding of personal conflicts within a political context provided by the women's movement. These points are only speculation, however. What is clear is that without continuity of membership, San Francisco Newsreel was bound to fall upon hard times. This has definitely been the case, and it is only in 1975, two years after the purge, that the group is showing signs of having regained most of its former organizational coherence.

Although there is only one individual remaining from those active at the time of the purge, Lawrence, Newsreel has strengthened itself through alliances with other semi-autonomous groups and individuals. Most significant of these is Resolution Films, a radical filmmaking collective of varying numbers but with a core of three that recently completed the film, Redevelopment which is being distributed in conjunction with Newsreel.[46]

Resolution Films is an offshoot of American Documentary Films (ADF), a political film distributing organization which often funded particular filmmaking projects. The people now in Resolution Films first worked together to make a film on the Pentagon Papers for Jerry Stoll, then head of ADF. They then hastily made a second film based on the same material after Stoll recut their first effort. This was called So the People Should Know. It was acquired for distribution by Third World Newsreel after ADF went bankrupt in 1973.[47] With the demise of ADF, these three filmmakers decided to work together under their current name. They still refer to themselves as Resolution Films although they distribute their films through Newsreel and participate in the day-to-day maintenance of the Newsreel office.[48] A complete merger remains a future possibility.

Since 1973 Newsreel has been preoccupied with rebuilding their inventory of filmmaking equipment, establishing a multi-purpose office, and restoring film distribution to the point where it provides, or approaches providing, self-sufficiency for the group.[49] Equipment has been gradually acquired by donation and second-hand purchase; office space created by volunteer labor; and distribution restored slowly over a sizable period of time. In 1974-1975 San Francisco Newsreel averaged 3 to 10 film rentals per day, with a peak of 5-25 and a low of 0 to 5.

Half of the rentals went to the local Bay Area, the rest to other portions of the western United States. A variable percentage (roughly 50 percent) of the rentals went to colleges and other institutions with the remainder going to political groups and community organizations.[50]

San Francisco Newsreel operates with far greater autonomy from other Newsreel offices than in the past. This is not true only of San Francisco, however, but of Newsreel in general. Like much of the movement, Newsreel has redirected its energies to local organizing and service rather than to the maintenance of a national profile. To the extent that the Newsreel offices still remain in contact this sometimes leads to misunderstanding and even distrust (especially in terms of making copies of films acquired or made by one office available to other offices), but with decreased numbers internally and the lack of clear national organization to the movement at large, this kind of regional emphasis seems virtually inevitable.

This regional emphasis is one of the reasons why Newsreel in San Francisco still seems a long way from disappearing even though only one of the majority members remains active. A wide-range of other groups and individuals share Newsreel's resources making the office a focal point for a number of local struggles and organizing projects. Filmmaking students from nearby colleges sometimes utilize Newsreel's filmmaking equipment and political experience; neighborhood filmmaking groups co-operate with Newsreel, exchanging labor and suggestions on various projects; local community organizations utilize Newsreel's graphic design resources to produce posters and flyers for upcoming events; and the members of Resolution Films assist in general Newsreel

51

distribution while making their own films available through Newsreel. The net impact is to redirect Newsreel's energies from exclusive concern with 16mm film propaganda usually intended for national use to an open-ended receptiveness of all forms of propaganda applicable primarily to local events and struggles.

Although merger with Resolution Films holds promise for a rejuvenation of Newsreel's filmmaking tradition, at the present time Newsreel's role seems more directly centered around community service in a more general sense. Alliance with a national movement, assumptions about playing a leadership role within such a movement, concentration upon films dealing with current events and issues of a broad scope—these older priorities or assumptions in Newsreel seem to be giving way to a new direction that is distinct from Third World Newsreel's but not antagonistic. Third World Newsreel remains strongly committed to a concentration upon making and distributing 16mm films of general relevance with an emphasis upon Third World struggle. San Francisco Newsreel, to the extent that it has regained the equilibrium lost at the time of the purge, is moving toward a more diffuse definition of purpose in terms of its propaganda media and a sharper definition in terms of its relationship to the immediate environment (well exemplified by Resolution Films' Redevelopment). Whether this will lead to propaganda production in a range of media as extensive and revealing of tendencies within the movement as a whole as Newsreel's previous emphasis on film has done will be one of the important questions whose answer lies in the future.

FOOTNOTES

Chapter Four

1
Interview with Chris W., San Francisco Newsreel, San Francisco, June, 1973. (This is not the same individual as the woman interviewed for Third World Newsreel; the initial "W." is arbitrarily used to clarify the difference.)

2
See Nichols, *Newsreel*, pp. 187-189.

3
Interview with Chris W., June, 1973.

4
See Nichols, *Newsreel*, Chapter Seven.

5
Untitled position paper released by the purging majority, San Francisco Newsreel, in Spring, 1973 (photocopied), p. 9. (Hereafter referred to as "The Majority Paper.")

6
Interview with Chris W., June, 1973.

7
The majority states, "The (Third World) collective was seen as breaking democratic centralism. There was in their eyes no need for a collective. This was an idealistic view that everyone was equal. But in actuality racism had set up unequal relationships within the group and therefore the necessity for the formation of a collective. The existence of racism was totally overlooked by leadership." "The Majority Paper," San Francisco Newsreel (Spring, 1973), p. 4.

8
Interview with Chris W., June, 1973.

9
The minority states, "For the last 1½ to 2 years in Newsreel, Third World and white members of the majority faction have been part of the leadership of Newsreel. As leadership and members of Newsreel they have been very much responsible for the practice of Newsreel. Yet as criticism on Newsreel's practice came down, the majority faction

for the most part did NOT accept any responsibility or criticism for what had happened in Newsreel. A double-standard existed." "The Split in San Francisco Newsreel - The Minority Statement," San Francisco, Spring, 1973, p. 4 (photocopied).

10
"The Majority Paper," p. 7.

11
Interview with Chris W., June, 1973.

12
Interview with Lawrence, San Francisco Newsreel, San Francisco, July, 1974.

13
"The Majority Paper," p. 2.

14
Ibid., p. 10.

15
"The Split in San Francisco Newsreel," p. 1.

16
Ibid.

17
Ibid.

18
This point is reminiscent of the problems posed by the film Black Power. The minority does not show much awareness here of the intensity of feelings that lie behind racial solidarity across class lines.

19
"The Split in San Francisco Newsreel," p. 2.

20
Ibid., p. 3.

21
Ibid., p. 7.

22
Ibid., p. 3.

23
Ibid., p. 2.

24
   Ibid., p. 7.

25
   See p. 161 above.

26
   Michel Foucault suggests that the left had to distinguish itself from the criminal population in order to avoid the worst of police repression in the last century. This compelled it to adopt a system of morality which derived from the ruling class: "They were obliged to recreate for themselves a sort of moral puritanism which was for them a necessary condition for survival and a useful instrument in the struggle as well." Simon, "Michel Foucault on Attica," p. 159.

27
   "The Split in San Francisco Newsreel," p. 8.

28
   Interview with Chris W., June, 1973.

29
   Interview with Lawrence, San Francisco Newsreel, San Francisco, July, 1975.

30
   The Red Papers, no. 5 (San Francisco: The Revolutionary Union, n.d.), p. 7.

31
   Interview with Ron, former member of Los Angeles Newsreel, Los Angeles, January, 1971.

32
   "The Split in San Francisco Newsreel," p. 1.

33
   Ibid., p. 2.

34
   See Nichols, Newsreel, pp. 101-105.

35
   Csaba Polony and Larry Felson, "Interview with Single Spark Films," Left Curve, no. 4 (Summer, 1975), p. 30.

36
   "Powerful Film Out on Farah Strike," Revolution: National Newspaper of the Revolutionary Union, Vol. 3, no. 4 (May, 1975), p. 15.

37
Interview with Lawrence, July, 1975.

38
Polony and Felson, "Interview with Single Spark Films," p. 29.

39
Ibid., p. 36.

40
Ibid., p. 38.

41
Ibid., p. 29.

42
Ibid., p. 31.

43
Ibid., p. 35.

44
Wilden, System and Structure, p. 437.

45
Interview with Lawrence, July, 1975.

46
Interview with Larry, Resolution Films, San Francisco, July, 1975.

47
Interview with Larry, July, 1975. So the People Should Know is discussed on pp. 129-132 above.

48
Interview with Larry, July, 1975.

49
After the purge some of the filmmaking equipment and film prints were given to the minority. The minority then broke into the office and took more equipment and prints they claimed as their own. The action was defended, and attacked, in political terms, however, and legal rights to the items were never clearly established.

50
Interview with Lawrence, July, 1975.

51
Ibid.

Chapter Five

SAN FRANCISCO NEWSREEL'S FILMS

Lack of funds and fewer personnel have combined with a growing reluctance to dash out into the street and simply record the violent events with the result that there have been only four films from members of San Francisco Newsreel since the purge in spring, 1973. (38 Families, We The Palestinian People--both of which were initiated prior to the purge but completed by the majority and minority respectively, Redevelopment--by Resolution Films in association with S. F. Newsreel, and The Beginning of Our Victory--by the purged members under the name of Single Spark Films. Of these the two that most directly relate to issues involved in the purge are 38 Families and We the Palestinian People (The Beginning of Our Victory not being available for viewing at all at this time), and these two films will be considered first.

38 Families stands in stark contrast to the technically accomplished, highly ambitious We the Palestinian People, a film that attempts to depict the development of Zionism in the twentieth century in the course of fifty minutes. 38 Families deals with a group of migrant worker families who struggle to obtain housing over the course of a couple of months. It was initially shot on half-inch video tape and then transferred to film.[1] The result is a technically inferior film.

Basically, 38 Families recounts the story of 38 families who were evicted from a trailer court when they joined a strike against the farm company that also owned the trailer court. All the families were Chicano and they banded together, refusing to leave the trailer court. When the company called in the police to evict the families many of them set up a tent camp in an abandoned lot across the street. After a period of placing continual pressure on the city government (in Solinas, Cal.) local officials allowed them to move into an abandoned Army camp where they were told the city will be obligated to relocate them in decent housing within 90 days.

Although this series of events is relatively straightforward, it is actually difficult to reconstruct accurately from the film. There isn't a consistent voice-over narration. Much of the story is told by the participants themselves in interviews (in Spanish, translated voice-over). The film therefore jumps back and forth in time from speakers describing events to more cinema-verite-like coverage of actual events without clarifying at what point in time the speakers are speaking and sometimes alluding to central points such as the onset of the strike in a passing phrase.[2] To some degree the film resembles those of Emile de Antonio, and Firestone's <u>Attica</u>, in its attempt to construct a narrational line from sync interview material. The attempt is less successful, though, partly because the points of view and range of insights are much narrower and partly because the interview material directly addresses the need to construct a narrational argument or account. The first limitation prevents the use of counterpoint and contrast such as Firestone employs when she cuts from the McKay Commission hearings to the inmates' testimony. The second, ironically ties the filmmakers to ordering the accounts of the families into a narration that will cohere at the level of the textual system when that narration was also delivered by each individual speaker as part of a coherent narrative explaining the events from his or her own point of view. This leads to conflicts in levels of awareness, contextual placement, etc. which are difficult to sidestep. Whereas the material de Antonio and Firestone manipulate into a narrational whole seldom is part of a similar whole in the mind of the speaker or character, it is almost always so in 38 Families. This ties the filmmakers into duplicating the omissions, repetitions, emphases, and contextual understanding of the participants rather than formulating their own at the level of the formal codes. The result is a high degree of confusion rather than clarity in the narrational development.

Another aspect of this problem is that the film makes little effort to extract lessons or points of more general application from this particular incident. This problem extends beyond the structure of the interviews, however, and also indicates a choice involving other codes —editing, voice-over commentary, etc. It stands in contrast to the emphasis of a film like El Pueblo Se Levante or Break and Enter. It may well be a function of the political inexperience of the majority members who made the film with little assistance from the members of leadership who were purged, especially considering that Newsreel's movement away from following events without providing a broader, more critical perspective only emerged gradually as a result of practice and reflection on that practice. In any case, it is a drawback which limits the film far more severely than those from New York which also deal with specific, local events but place them within a larger context.

The film's greatest value lies in its explicit treatment of a people and their struggle on levels that are consistently neglected by the mass media. The utilization of interview material yields a strong sense of "being there" through the direct address of the people carrying out the struggle themselves. These qualities of the extratextual codes that communicate something about the feel of the situation from the participants' point of view represent an appreciable achievement. Writing about ethnographic film, David MacDougall argues for the central role of film in providing information only inadequately presented by verbal or written description: "(film conveys) the relation of people to their environment--their knowledge of it, use of it, movement within it; ... the rhythms of the society, and its sense of geography and time."[3] Although the detached and considered tone of the ethnographer may not be what Newsreel seeks, especially when they are presenting their own culture and not a foreign one, these qualities are precisely the ones most in evidence in 38 Families. In this regard, the film fulfills a need that other forms of communication are generally less well-equipped to deal with. The equally crucial set of questions clustered around the locus of context--this event in relation to other political struggles, these people at this point in time in relation to earlier and later points, and so forth--are clearly accessible to the film medium, but in the case of 38 Families elude the textual strategies that inform the film.

The makers of the film are aware of most of these short-comings and argue that they are symptomatic of their relationship to the minority that was later purged. Little guidance was provided, an overall strategy was not worked out in advance, the political questions relevant to the Chicano movement as a whole were not raised and debated. The Third World members undertook the project in order to do something, to feel useful, and because they thought their own Third World heritage would afford them some measure of rapport with the people they filmed.

This form of impulse recurs in the group's subsequent history. Sentiment or feelings, subjective or personal impressions led to a sense of solidarity in relation to the minority that seemed to evaporate with remarkable speed once the purge was completed. Both internally and externally, in their group structure and their filmmaking practice, the majority seemed ready to settle for gestures of support and rapport that may have masked a vague or unanchored notion of purpose--both in terms of filmmaking and of the group's direction. There is strong evidence in this film of a need to integrate this kind of impulse with a more conceptual approach: at the level of filmmaking, the need for tighter control of the formal codes and more deliberate shaping of the textual system; at the level of group structure, the need for political analysis of the group's purpose and the relationship of specific filmmaking projects to this larger context of political struggle and group organization. Whether these needs are a critique more of the leadership at the time of 38 Families than of the people making the film is difficult to determine, but the result in either case is a film, and a political drift, that raises serious questions about the future of Newsreel, questions which subsequent events have not entirely eradicated.

In contrast to 38 Families, We the Palestinian People is one of Newsreel's most ambitious and provocative films. Designed as a compil-

ation film in the tradition of the Why We Fight series overseen by
Frank Capra, We the Palestinian People has received appreciable attention and considerable use, especially by Arab student groups.[4] It is
also the last effort by the purged members of San Francisco Newsreel,
terminating a line of filmmaking continuity that extended back to the
group's first film, Off the Pig (retitled Black Panther).

We the Palestinian People sets out to provide an historical account
of the origins and goals of Zionism and to present the alternative
claims of the Palestinian refugees for access to their homeland and
their rights to self-determination. This objective is one which quickly
unravels into great complexity: there is the relationship between a
drive to re-establish a nation and the drive toward a socialist nation;
there is the tension between the Palestinian liberation movement and
the Arab governments which are often feudalistic and conservative;
there are the conflicting claims and strategies of different Palestinian
organizations; there is the diversity of organizational functions of
which military operations are but one (as the films on national liberation struggles previously discussed make clear); and there is the need
to draw a clear distinction between anti-semitism and anti-Zionism, a
distinction which Lenny Rubenstein argues in his review, "may be impossible to make without political rebellion in Israel."[5]

The most distinctive feature of the film is undoubtedly its historical orientation. This is a rarity in Newsreel's history where films
have generally centered on contemporary events or processes with minimal attention to historical background. Even in The Woman's Film, on
which some of the same people participated, historical background is

tucked into a brief montage sequence in the middle of the film with the bulk of the attention going to interview material with working-class women discussing their present situation. This concern seems to have been carried over into <u>The Beginning of Our Victory</u> (on the Farah strike), and represents an invaluable addition to Newsreel's range of activity. Seeds of this approach can be found in <u>We Demand Freedom</u>, <u>Teach Our Children</u>, and <u>El Peublo Se Levante</u>, but it only emerges as the dominant concern of the overall film with <u>We the Palestinian People</u>.

The film begins by introducing us to Palestinian refugees living in tents. Yassar Arafat is introduced as a spokesman for the Palestinian liberation movement, a position he occupies exclusively in the film which has led to criticism among Arab viewers who would prefer a broader spectrum of Palestinian leadership.[6] After illustrating the present plight of the Arab refugees the film backs up and begins its historical analysis of the Zionist movement which finally concludes with additional material detailing the present-day lives and policies of the Palestinian guerrillas.

In broad outline the film argues that Zionism has been preoccupied with the creation of a Jewish homeland over and above any other question with the result that it has played into the hands of other nation's imperialistic or counter-revolutionary interests without scruple. Zionist activity, it is argued, therefore involved collaboration with the Nazi regime rather than resistance and aided a relatively small number of German Jews who immigrated to Palestine at the expense of larger numbers without the means of such escape. Earlier it involved appeals for British support which played into British desires to control indir-

ectly this strategic area and displace Turkish domination. More recently
it involves dependence upon the United States which helps maintain an
American middle-eastern presence and provides American investment with
an lucrative internal market.

These points are made by means of a voice-over narration which is
divided among several different narrators, male and female, an effective
device for undercutting the omnisience of the voice-of-God narrator and
giving the impression that a number of more ordinary people have all
arrived at the same conclusions. The image track is primarily archival
footage arranged to illustrate the narrational argument. As the summary
above of this narration's main points might suggest, one of the most
persistent problems confronting the viewer of We the Palestinian People
is separating historical analysis from historical judgment. In fact,
a strong undertow of moral value judgments runs throughout the film,
compelling the viewer to choose sides when the viewer is also aware
that she is not being told the whole story. This approach recalls some
of Single Spark Films' comments regarding the correct line for there
seems to be an impulse to insist on correctness of historical interpretation by its extension into a judgment upon those considered to be in
the wrong (the Zionists in this case).

The number of examples of this tension between analysis and judgment (in a strongly Manichaen manner) are too numerous even to summarize. There are, however, three general areas of judgment that are of
considerable importance. First, there is the use of Jewish accents on
the part of narrators interpreting or reading the words of Zionist
leaders. This seems to be the single most obvious failure of the film

to maintain its own distinction between Zionism and Judaism, especially since the accents drift toward a German accent thereby compounding the problem with inaccuracy plus the spectre of Naziism (once again incorrectly identified with Germans generally). At one point, however, the use of accents works extremely effectively. Individuals describe, voice-over with Jewish accents, how the Zionists collaborated with the Nazi government whereas other Jews joined the resistance. The use of Jewish accents here stresses the fact that not all Jews are Zionists and that Zionism followed policies detrimental to many Jews such as those represented in the voice-over commentary.

Second, the narration and supporting image track make frequent reference to Zionist military atrocities associated with the creation of the Israeli state and its subsequent expansion. Massacres at Deir Yassin (254 civilians killed), Kfar Kassim (43 men, women, and children killed) are cited. A narrator tells us that an Israeli court fined the Army 1¢ for the latter massacre. At that point the only sound is the ringing clink of a penny falling onto a table. These incidents seem to be meant to imply that Zionists have no regard for Arab lives. Other sequences reinforce this point by likening Israeli tactics to American tactics in Vietnam. In this context a remark by Moshe Dayan is made to mean only one thing: "A solution should be found so as not to leave too big an Arab minority within our frontiers." (The remark is delivered by a narrator and attributed to Dayan whose is shown in non-sync images.)

These points, assigning moral guilt to one side, are an inadequate justification for the Arab cause in any case. One would not cease to support the side correct in the long view because of atrocities committed in its name (especially if they are not systematic; part of the implication here is that they are). And since in the minds of many the most blatant atrocities, or at least senseless acts of violence, have been committed in the name of the Palestinian liberation movement, the film seems to make a disingenuous argument when it does not once refer to these acts of Arab terror or offer any explanation for their place within a larger strategy, or of why the mass media pay so much more attention to them than Zionist acts of a similar nature. With this particular approach the film almost invites disbelief in its own credibility.

Finally there is a strong tendency to associate the Palestinian liberation movement with its guerrilla wing and to valorize militarism as the most emblematic aspect of the liberation struggle. This approach is one that persists throughout much of the left in America and that surfaces in many of the early Newsreels such as those on the Black Panthers. It is in distinct contrast to the relative de-emphasis given to militaristic values in the films on national liberation struggles discussed earlier. These films were, for the most part, not made by members of the New Left, and do not reflect much of the general tendency toward a celebration of violent revolution in the abstract where specific struggles and situations are of primarily metaphoric interest. Although Newsreel avoids the worst of these dangers in this film, the stress on armed struggle remains a peculiarity of the American New Left that has outlived the New Left itself.

A corrolary problem is that Palestinian culture is demoted in emphasis and treated in somewhat stereotypic fashion. This is most evident when an Arab woman tells us that the guerrilla movement has kept the Arab culture alive. This portion of the narration is accompanied by images showing children performing a dance. This illustration of culture equates it with its more formal, occasional, and traditional forms. The everyday fabric of cultural interaction is overlooked in favor of picturesque. Patterns of relationship, roles and institutions, the structure of the family, concepts of authority and responsibility-- these concerns are not expressed by the film. It is an unfortunate failure for it tends to make foreign cultures appear artificial, undynamic and detached from normal, non-ceremonial relationships. And although the film gives considerable attention in its concluding section to the guerrilla's efforts to support a complete culture with schools, hospitals, governmental structures, and so on, the stress falls upon the guerrilla training carried out by schoolchildren and the most easily identifiable differences in cultural patterns. This approach is certainly not without appeal, especially to male members of what was the New Left who share these priorities, but perhaps also to those who share the "I regret that I have but one life to give" attitude that percolates through much of American culture. The history of countries where socialism has been won by military victory, though, raises more serious questions about the ongoing value of a military infrastructure than this film attempts to deal with.[7]

Many of the problems at this level of the film's organization are well criticized by Lenny Rubenstein in his review when he states that We the Palestinian People fails to question the components of their (Palestinian liberation movement's) radicalism beyond military cadres and an occasional showpiece workshop; the extent of activity beyond military attacks; the rationale behind apparently suicidal terrorist attacks; their relationship to the demands of the Soviet Union's foreign policy, and their following among the Palestinians who cannot quit their jobs to devote themselves full time to the PLO.[8]

In the midst of the uncertainty that seems to surround the exact nature of the Palestinian movement it appears as if Newsreel chose to reserve its most forthright certitude for the evils of Zionism. This lapse toward moral absolutism makes a curious application of the purged members' concern with presenting a correct line. In this case it is not so much a clear political analysis as a series of moral judgments accompanying that analysis, judgments which at times such as in the use of accents by voice-over commentators runs the risk of condemning all Jews. Even so the treatment of the development of Zionism is presented with more clarity than the nature of the liberation movement. The intentions and motivations of Zionist leaders are systematically identified, and criticized, whereas the statements of Palestinians are allowed to stand unclarified. This can lead to discrepant explanations of the movement's goals as these two statements indicate:

> (An Arab boy says) We must liberate Palestine and make it possible for all people to live in peace--Jews, Arabs, or Christians. Our war is a war of liberation, it's not a war against the Jews. We do not want to push them into the sea .... We also don't want them to push us into the desert, that is why we must fight.

> (An Arab male adult says) The giant U.S. corporations and banks have billions of dollars invested in the Arab countries. They want to continue exploiting the Arab people. That is why they are trying to suppress the revolution. As Palestinians we are asking people to fight against imperialism and its partners ... the reactionary Arab regimes.

The film refuses to make judgments about differences in Palestinian strategy, preferring instead to give a blanket, emotional endorsement to guerrilla organization and an equally sweeping condemnation to Zionist policies. In the midst of a highly dynamic, panoramic film this approach leaves a peculiarly stable and even rigid core.

Newsreel's assumption seems to have been that if the political issues were somewhat unclear at least the emotional issue was not. Revolutionaries clearly ought to identify with the Palestinian liberation movement. Revolutionaries should feel revulsion at the Zionist policies that have displaced millions, encouraged imperialist infiltration of the Middle East, and adopted tactics of suppression akin to those of the U.S. in Vietnam. Hence a great deal of the film's power lies in its ability, like the Why We Fight series, to arouse strong feelings for the Palestinians and against the Zionists. This approach requires a certain amount of flattening of historical complexity in order to stress the emotional constants--Zionist scheming and Palestinian resistance--that serve as the viewer's points of identification. Information must be asserted to support emotional and moral interpretations. The original multiplicity of meanings is narrowed to support a line of moral argument that is sustained primarily by the films textual codes (editing, narration, music). The viewer is not given the data that would allow her to diverge very far from the film's own conclusions. Knowledge is placed in the service of a leftist morality that seems dangerously close to a latter-day Puritanism. Hence the film is organized most carefully, and successfully, to win our moral assent, and knowledge is exploited as a tool in this battle for the emotions of the viewer. This leads to a non-dialectical understanding and evaluation. In this regard the film seems a very typical product of a pattern of thought common within the New Left in earlier years:

> If information is "deposited" into people's heads, or if "knowledge" is <u>given</u> to them in such a way as to prevent them from acquiring it for themselves, then it may happen that they will grow intellectually, but there is no imperative--no reliable causal mechanism--which can <u>make this intelligence flow into action</u>. The strong emphasis on information apart from praxis was one of the major shortcomings of the Left in the 1960's.9

<u>We the Palestinian People</u> not only deposits information but subordinates it to emotional response; in this way it doubles the barriers to praxis while halving the distance to Puritanism.

The most consistent dominant in <u>We the Palestinian People</u> is the verbal band: a ribbon of verbal analysis and evaluation presented by an array of narrators and voice-over characters for the most part. This approximates the organizational role of music in <u>We Demand Freedom</u> but escapes the indeterminacy arising from a musical dominant. The film's structure thus most closely approximates an essay, again like the structure of the <u>Why We Fight</u> series which seems to have been a consciously chosen model. The argument as such is carried by the verbal band to which images and other aspects of the sound track are joined as illustration or emotional overtone. The argument does not derive from the combination of sequences which retain their own internal image-sound relationships but form a new pattern of relationships as a result of being compiled into the same film (as in the case of de Antonio who allows shot fragments to retain local autonomy). The argument is <u>applied</u> to the images which in most cases have been stripped of their original sound accompaniment (or were originally shot silent). This allows for an overall conceptual utilization of the narrational element unlike its more local use in We Demand Freedom as well as the possibility, largely excluded in de Antonio from the outset, of contrapunctal interaction between the narrational dominant and other potential dominants.

The presence of such a narrational code seems inescapable once the decision is made to pursue a subject from an historical point of view. A non-narrational, cinema-verite style of organization (most purely represented perhaps by the films of Fred Wiseman) would seem to lack the capacity for bridging time gaps with a sense of historical determinacy (whereas it is well suited for more synchronic examinations of processes or events). Only by resorting to a careful orchestration of the pro-filmic event in the manner of Rossellini's The Rise to Power of Louis XIV could a non-narrational style expose the lynchpins of historical movement, but with such a decision the filmmaker has moved very clearly into the world of fiction.

The question remains of how well such a strategy can represent historical processes. And although the choice by Newsreel to apply a narrational code to a basically subordinate image track[10] allows them potentially to escape the uni-dimensional conception of history found in de Antonio, their actual exploitation of this potential is limited. The greatest dangers seem to lie in the directions of moralism and determinism: compelling the viewer to subordinate herself to the moral judgments of the film--or to reject the film outright, and implying a one-to-one transfer between a narrational code's singular point of view, omniscience, the causal overtones of narrational, verbal logic and iamge juxtapositions and the actual mechanism of historical change.

Two general tactics exemplify the problems with the film's moralism best. The first is the problem of utilizing accents for voice-over characters which has already been discussed. The second is one of attribution: many quotes are presented as the authentic words of individuals, often historically important figures, in a voice-over mode. The use of accents only complicates the problem of determining whether the voice-over voice is truly that of the figure to which it is attributed. The choice of voice-over attributions also increases questions about accuracy or authenticity. This question is again compounded by the question of context: to what degree is the quotation being placed in a context such as to alter its meaning or to stress certain possible meanings. (The quote attributed to Moshe Dayan on p. 232 is a good example of this problem.)

The most glaring example of the use of attribution for moralistic ends occurs during a description of the Jordanian government's military attacks against refugee camps in 1970. Much of the sequence is developed by means of what appears to be a network news report in which an American reporter whom we see standing near the site of an attack describes the action and the huge casualities inflicted. His final sentence, though, "This is the real Rogers Peace Plan," is so clearly a critical comment alien to the so-called objective style of television newscasting that it raises retroactive doubts about the credibility of the entire sequence. Once Newsreel attributes their own interpretation to a seemingly unaltered television newscast that was in fact fabricated,[11] questions of historical accuracy and credibility begin to spiral almost out of control.

Determinism surfaces in the attempt to thread history through the eye of the narrator who is himself above and beyond history. It is as if there were a teleological principle at work in the historical moment which corresponds precisely to the retrospective analysis of the narrator. The function of the "correct line" then is to lay this teleology bare. Since it was originally _in_ the historical moment and can be recovered precisely it would seem that moral power accrues to the narrator. The moralism of the narration can be excused as the judgmental privilege of he-who-knows, the narrator.

Narration seems to be indispensable to the film attempting to trace historical development. The danger lies in identifying the direction of that development with the organization of the narration so that to unfold a narrational argument is to unfold the workings of history. Not only does this limit the function of other non-narrational codes in the textual system to a subordinate or illustrative role, it assumes a uni-dimensionality, a linearity, a teleology to historical development that seemingly can only be overcome by overcoming the dominance of the narrational code itself. Once its dominance is loosened, a less deterministic presentation of history seems to become possible.

Some indication of this possibility is evident in We the Palestinian People in those sections dealing with the most recent events. Historical direction is admittedly most difficult to find in events that are still unfolding, but Newsreel seems at this point to be willing to allow for a multiplicity of meanings, an array of voices with the authority of a narrator, from which a sense of a goal-seeking process emerges without the determinism that marks the more clearly historical discussion. In dealing with the present, Newsreel utilizes the voices of Palestinian refugees, liberation movement leaders (principally Arafat), and voice-over narration. Conflicting or contrasting views are allowed to stand on the nature of the liberation movement and Zionism (as an archetypal form of aggression based on inherent, morally superior rights vs. an outgrowth of imperialist aims and motives). This open-endedness may have seemed unavoidable to Newsreel (and the comments by the people responsible for the film in their subsequent interview in Left Curve indicates a preference at that later point at least for the more deterministic, "correct line" approach of the historical sections), but it also offers a sense of balance to the overall film that seems highly beneficial. Even if there is a "line" to past events, at least the present is an arena where struggle takes place without the benefit of such clarity.

We the Palestinian People is one of Newsreel's most distinctive films, especially in the sense of attempting to reach an audience of unconvinced rather than reconfirming the already convinced. As such it is one of the few Newsreel films that develops an overall analysis and argument about a major struggle and one of the very few that attempts such an analysis from an historical perspective. Insofar as this marks a new direction for Newsreel (one unlikely to be pursued with any great continuity given the history of division within San Francisco Newsreel since the time this film was first conceived), it also calls out for new aesthetic and theoretical levels of understanding. This is a challenge which the film only partially meets, leaving serious gaps along the lines I have indicated above. It is a challenge which it does meet more successfully in other ways, perhaps most of all in its conciseness, its fusion of rational argument with emotional appeal (when this appeal is not coupled to moral judgment or a call to celebrate violence as a liberating act in its own right, as in their selections of Palestinian songs and the use of dynamic visual rhythms), and its fragmentation of the narrational code into many voices. All of these achievements need qualification for none of them is sufficient to overcome the film's limitations, and yet they indicate a continuing potential for growth and change in Newsreel's development. We the Palestinian People is a long way from Newsreel #1 in 1968 ("Draft Resistance: An Interview with Noam Chomsky"). Unfortunately, as with many other groups on the left today, the political divisions which have taken place inside Newsreel virtually guarantee that further progress will also involve repeating the errors of the past.

Whereas We the Palestinian People took the filmmakers far from their own backyard (an excursion they were to repeat in The Beginning of Our Victory), the only film to be associated with the remnant of the majority side in the purge of 1973 deals very specifically with a problem centering in San Francisco--urban renewal. Redevelopment, although made by Resolution Films, therefore seems to reflect the same kind of concern with local problems and community organizing that have characterized the majority. Its overall structure is less tight than We the Palestinian People and there is a stronger tendency to linger over specific events or situations rather than constantly move toward a more general overview, but this approach reveals both advantages and disadvantages that make the film of particular interest.

The greatest strength of Redevelopment perhaps lies in the vast range of material it covers (usually in the words of actual participants) although it is the problem of integrating this material into a cogent whole that may also be the greatest problem. Like We Demand Freedom, one of the strongest impressions at the end of the film is a sense of confusion, of having been overwhelmed, that seems to be a direct function of the amount of material covered and the way in which it is related. A brief summary of what seem to be the main sections of the film may help indicate both the strength of the film and its problems:

1. the current problem of redevelopment (from the point of view of a developer and a displaced resident).

2. how redevelopment of an area takes place over time in S.F.

   a) use of media to imply that the area is deteriorating and unsafe, followed by redevelopment plans and actions.

   b) reactions of residents to whom the area remains viable even though redevelopment cuts off its life blood--loss of street life, social gathering places, etc.

3. the context for redevelopment at a non-local level

   a) the role of government is co-ordinating large scale reorganizations in land use as economic needs change.

   b) San Francisco's envisioned role as hub of Pacific Rim business, a finance capital center.

4. local resistance to the local effects of this strategy TOOR (Tenants and Owners in Opposition to Redevelopment): protest marches, non-response of city government. composition of TOOR and most other resistance groups is largely immigrant, low-income, many former Longshoremen and seamen in particular.

5. more general traditions of class struggle in the Bay Area

   a) 1934 general strike over union recognition.

   b) union struggles against lettuce growers in Salinas.

6. the issue of community control

   a) pitfalls exemplified by local redevelopment agencies that strengthen local pockets of wealth and power at people's expense (investments of community churches, e.g., managed by high-paid, outside advisors).

   b. the necessary overview: Engel's argument that redevelopment helps rationalize and maximize profits; victory requires abolition of capitalist production.

7. problems of urban transit

   a) functions of urban transit: shuttle workers from a distance and increase land values along the transit route. (example of high rises clustered near exits of Toronto's subway system, related to increased values in Mission District near BART exits--Bay Area Rapid Transit).

   b) community response: businessmen see resistance as attempt to discredit city, resist progress. residents see transit as betrayal, unresponsive to their needs.

8. class structure in community organizing: petty-bourgeois organizing tactics (reforms that do not prevent redevelopment) and the dissipation of energy from basic issues. citation of concrete examples in San Francisco.

9. overview of urban core renewal

   a) will BART aid the worker, the average person? official answer: yes, relieve congestion and pollution, attract new industry. narrational, unofficial answer: no, will rationalize profits and relations of production in finance center but will not provide jobs. To the contrary, will squeeze even more workers out.

   b) the international economic picture from which to view mass transit. companies relocate overseas not because of lack of adequate mass transit, but because of cheaper

>   labor, political "stability, and minimal worker
>   organization. (examples with quotes by officials
>   of Hewitt/Packard).
>
> 10. the present dilemma
>   live coverage of a meeting between residents of
>   Daly City and the local government, ending with
>   the frustrated outcry of a woman protesting the
>   lack of community control: "What is the recourse
>   for an oppressed majority?"

Some of the difficulties in integrating these sections into a single, coherent argument may be apparent from the differences in scope and level of argument between sections and the jumpy quality of their sequential arrangement (the similarity between sections #4 and 6a or between #7 and 9, for example, with intervening material on other, parallel aspects of the problem). These difficulties do not undercut the integrity of the individual sections, however, most of which are internally organized in a crisp, efficient manner. Within sections the voices of participants--men and women, old and young, white and Third World, activists and less prominent residents, businessmen, government officials and local residents--figure prominantly. It is their perceptions that structure the internal organization and infuse it with credibility and everyday understanding. The temptation to draw a common thread from these perceptions that could be summarized by a voice-over narrator(s) is resisted and the dangers of moralism and determinism that surface in We the Palestinian People are avoided.

The function of the narration in this film is more conceptual than in We Demand Freedom but less overwhelmingly dominant than in We the Palestinian People. There is little sense of a predetermined narration divided up between various commentators as there is in We the Palestinian

People. A great deal of the narrational code is derived from the comments of the various participants and their juxtaposition. These comments, though, relate most strongly to other material within a given section; they do not provide the thread for an overall narrational argument as they do in de Antonio's films. This strength of local reference, the rootedness of commentary in specific situations, gives a very strong sense of how issues "feel" to the participants and how they are dealt with. The choice to give priority to the local context, the situation within a given section of the film, need not lead to overall diffuseness; de Antonio's solution is not the necessary corrective. What seems to make the overall structure somewhat murky has more to do with the arrangement of sections in relation to each other. The film simply seems to attempt to cover too much ground via a pattern that shifts levels and topics far more often than is necessary. (The introduction of a discussion of run-away corporations in section 9b is a good example: the point is valid and well-made, but its link to urban transit does not seem to be its most distinctive feature. If anything it seems to relate better with 3a and 6b, sections dealing with the general conditions of capitalist production that relate to urban redevelopment.)

Redevelopment does not evidence a singular point of view mediated by a single textual code as We the Palestinian People does in its historical sections (via a narrational code). The exact vantage point from which redevelopment is observed seems to shift as though the film were trying to examine all its many facets without making any assumptions about which facet is most important or determining. This may well be indicative of the relative lack of leftist commitment to issues like redevelopment during the period of the New Left. Redevelopment, like prison issue so heavily treated by Third World Newsreel, manifests itself most forcefully in terms of oppression rather than exploitation, and in the community rather than at the point of production.[12] Issues like these have not been given the same degree of importance as exploitation and point of production organizing by those leftist groups that are most rigorous in developing a theoretical rationale for their priorities (groups like the Revolutionary Union with whom Single Spark Films is associated, the October League, the New American Movement, and the Revolutionary Workers Congress). Consequently, filmmakers may have less theoretical reference to rely upon and a degree of confusion about the overall placement of the issue may be the result. Redevelopment fluctuates between an historical and a current event point of view, between a contextual overview and in-depth examination of specific confrontations or contradictions. The facets so exposed are all important and well worth examining. In the context of the film, however, their integration into an overarching point of view is less successful than the individual examinations.

Redevelopment's greatest strength is in the analysis of specific aspects of a crucial problem with immediate revelance for San Francisco Newsreel's local constituency. Its greatest weakness is in the overall integration of the aspects the film examines into a structured pattern at the level of the whole film. Once again this seems to point toward the relative weakness of theoretical work among leftist filmmakers in terms of film structure, in terms of how specific codes, or elements, can be combined to make the whole greater than the sum of the parts. The parts tend to move in different directions, with different emphases; without the structuring intervention of an overall strategy the film will convey a greater sense of confusion than is necessary or desirable. Redevelopment like We Demand Freedom is of considerable value and usefulness. The problems that arise in the midst of its successful use as an organizing tool limit more than negate its value: they point to problems of film theory and practice still unresolved by Newsreel and other leftist documentary filmmakers.

FOOTNOTES

Chapter Five

1
Interview with Chris W., June, 1973.

2
In fact, the strike began accidentally when the workers thought a strike being called against another company (Fresh Pick) also applied to their employer (Pick 'n Save). The film doesn't explain the exact nature of their own grievances with Pick 'n Save, thus making the Chicano families appear somewhat foolish and rash.

3
David MacDougall, "Prospects of the Ethnographic Film," Film Quarterly, Vol. 23, no. 2 (Winter, 1969-70), p. 28.

4
In both New York and San Francisco the film was one of the most widely distributed in 1974. Critical reception has ranged from high praise ("The most commendably skilled long film to come out of the New Left Newsreel collective ...." Program Note, Pacific Film Archive (Berkeley, August, 1974), n.p.) to disappointment. A review in Cineaste concludes, "Relying on the simplistic slogan of 'Third World struggle' is no longer enough to win an audience's support." Lenny Rubenstein, "We Are the Palestinian People)" (sic), Cineaste, Vol. 6, no. 3 (1974), p. 36.

5
Rubenstein, "We Are the Palestinian People," p. 36.

6
Interviews with Chris, July, 1974 and Lawrence, July, 1975.

7
Cf., John M. Swomley, Jr., Liberation Ethics (New York: MacMillan Co., 1972) in which the argument is advanced that violent revolution requires militaristic values and patterns of organization that spell disaster if allowed to persist after the establishment of a new form of society.

8
Rubenstein, "We Are the Palestinian People," p. 36.

9
 David Gross, "On Writing Cultural Criticism," Telos, no. 16 (Summer, 1973), p. 49.

10
 Henderson cogently proposes a model of image or sound dominance similar to the one I am advancing here: "... intensive visual organization and intensive sound organization are probably not possible within the same film. That is, one or the other must be the dominant formal principle; one will tend to organize and dominate not only itself but the other also." "Towards a Non-Bourgeoise Camera Style," Film Quarterly, Vol. 24, no. 2 (Winter, 1970-71), p. 7. The area Henderson fails to explore is the relationship between an overall dominant and more local shifts in the dominant for sequences or sections.

11
 I have no concrete evidence that the sequence was actually fabricated or done especially for Newsreel. My assumption is based on a comparison of this sequence to the normal style of television newsreportage. If I am in error, Newsreel could have easily avoided encouraging false inferences by identifying the original source of the news report with a printed title.

12
 Redevelopment facilitates exploitation in a diffuse manner, rationalizing the city core's land use in accordance with a larger plan, in the case of San Francisco, the strategy of creating a finance capital administrative center for the entire Pacific Rim. Oppression, though, is direct. It is felt by local residents who are uprooted and displaced, but not necessarily exploited. The structural principle at work has a diffuse impact; the surface effect is direct and immediate. Hence, resistance is in response to oppression, and need not involve the workers whose exploitation is most explicitly facilitated. Hence the form of resistance is community organizing and not point of production organizing and the dangers of petty-bourgeoise ideology are perhaps proportionally greater. As with prisons there is a displacement of resistance from those whose exploitation is rationalized and/or facilitated by the process or institution to those most directly oppressed.

Chapter Six

CONCLUSIONS

In 1962 Students for a Democratic Society offered the Port Huron Statement as their analysis of the contemporary American society. It celebrated a revival of participatory democracy and saw the university as a logical meeting ground for the forces of social change. A concise summary of the spirit in which this statement was made exists in the modified preamble to the SDS constitution:

> (SDS) maintains a <u>vision</u> of a democratic society, where at all levels the people have control of the decisions which affect them and the resources on which they are dependent. It seeks a <u>relevance</u> through the continual focus on realities and on the programs necessary to effect change at the most basic levels of economic, political and social organization. It feels the <u>urgency</u> to put forth a radical, democratic program counterposed to authoritarian movements both of communism and the domestic right.[1]

Much could be said about the humanism, the lingering anti-communism (presumed to be a "foreign body" in distinction to the "domestic right") and the vague expression of a need for immediate and direct action rather than polite and quasi-detached suggestion or advice. These are qualities that characterized much of the New Left for a considerable time. They help establish the originating parameter from which the New Left developed toward a more Marxist-minded, but still confrontational and polarizing expression of white, middle-class, student discontent.

Thirteen years later most agree that the New Left is dead, and for all practical purposes it is. Nonetheless, one of its last remnants, the Weather Underground, has recently surfaced long enough to re-articulate some of the principles of the New Left in the form of a pamphlet and a film being made by Emile de Antonio.[2] In a <u>Rolling Stone</u> article discussing this filmmaking effort the Weather Underground's view of the Sixties is summarized. They see the media and the government as attempting to discredit the left's achievements during this period by arguing that it all ended in failure. This they regard as part of an attempt to promote acquiescence in the face of a declining standard of living as we enter the "terminal crisis of American capitalism."[3] The authors continue their summation:

> The Weather Underground sees the Sixties as a watershed in the American political experience. Racism was exposed and fought; women, youth, blacks, Indians and Latinos recovered their own identities and struggle to free themselves from the economic, political and psychic snares of male-dominated melting-pot liberalism; young women and men rejected the dominant values of conformity, materialism and security; white middle-class youth discovered that imperialism was not just a term in history books but that it could be used without quotation marks to describe the political realities of mid-century America.
>
> Moreover, all these revelations hung together. As <u>Prairie Fire</u> put it: "We also came to recognize that issues which once seemed separate had a relationship to one another. Imperialism was 'discovered' as a whole, one system. This was a tremendous breakthrough--it made sense of the world and our own experience. The same school which tracked students by sex, race and class into the appropriate niche, turned out to own slums in the black community and to develop anti-personnel weapons and strategies against revolution--to be in fact a tool of the corporations and the military."
>
> At the same time that it became apparent that imperialism was woven out of whole cloth, the cloth itself began to fray. Vietnam, according to <u>Prairie Fire</u>, taught us that "the U.S. imperial system is not permanently superior, not invulnerable even at the height of its power, not loved by

the people of the world, not satisfying the needs of the
great majority of the U.S. people."[4]

Although there are very obvious differences in these statements, what strikes me most about them is their similarity. Other comparisons of early and late statements and events point toward a similar congruence: throughout its history the New Left as a movement primarily composed of white, middle-class youth who came from <u>inside</u> the milieu of affluence (or in what still seems a somewhat euphoric term, a "post-scarcity society") has placed its main emphasis upon qualitative, consciousness-associated struggle. Quantitative, economic or material struggle--the core of the old left--was demoted as inadequate. The revolution could not stop with the stomach, or even begin there: any change that did not reach or begin with the heart and mind was no change at all.

This emphasis has led to a stress upon oppression more than exploitation, a stress which Newsreel's films clearly share. And for the most part it is an emphasis which has avoided lapsing into the stability that centers around the extremes to which it might lead: consciousness-raising apart from political or economic struggle altogether (represented in books like <u>The Greening of America</u> or <u>Earthwalk</u> and in actions like the development of rural communes) or political and economic struggle with minimal attention to consciousness-raising or the personal experience of oppression (represented in Newsreel by the direction taken by the members of Single Spark Films and in the New Left by the Progressive Labor Party in the Sixties and by groups like the Revolutionary Union in the Seventies)[5]. This fusion of the personal and the political, this stress upon a response to the experience of oppression more than the fact of exploitation is perhaps what, more than anything else, made the New Left the cutting edge of a movement of consumer revolt that has redefined the consumer as far more than simply the purchaser of products.

Consumption was perceived in its global aspects and was refused: the New Left did not "buy" the rationale for America's involvement in Vietnam, did not buy the Cold War, did not buy the dominant ideology of success, status, and conformity-in-individuality. Nor did it buy the oppressive function of racism and sexism, nor that of their controlling master, imperialism. It was a thoroughgoing rejection of the values, attitudes and roles which capitalism offered for psychic investment. It was a rejection more violent, more impatient, and more radical than that of a Ralph Nader but it was similar in kind: the arena of struggle was not primarily the point of production but the point of consumption. Revolutionary affinity was not based upon a common work experience but a common consumption experience. It was this ideological nexus which the New Left sought to confront at first within the rest of the American social fabric, but later within itself as well.

The greatest asset of this neo-Marxist movement lay, it seems to me, in the truth of its critique (most glaringly obvious perhaps in regards to Vietnam) and in its emergence as the first sustained revolt against monopoly capitalism from within the mother country since the Depression. And in its insistence upon the personal, upon questions of quality, upon the struggle against the ideological grasp on consciousness the New Left seems to articulate well the shifts in revolutionary strategy that correspond to advanced industrial society. The effects of these shifts upon the kind of social organization that would follow a revolutionary victory, its contrast with socialist societies that have emerged in less developed countries, is a matter that only the future can determine. The fact that a different path has already been manifest would almost certainly affect the nature of a new American revolution is clear, however, even if its specific impact remains a matter of speculation.

The greatest weaknesses of this movement seem to lie in its inability to secure a working-class base and its failure to provide for its own perpetuation through an institutional framework of footholds within the existing institutions or the creation of alternative ones. (I personally favor the first path, but in the mass media, schools, colleges, factories, unions, and social services, to name a few key institutions, there are virtually no strongholds of radical activity. Many current college students, in fact, have little or no knowledge of the radical activity on their own campuses in the last decade let alone of the general shape of New Left activity. Alternative institutions have persisted, marginally, but serve more as a meeting place for the already committed than a mechanism for providing a transition between generations.) The stress upon qualitative change has been of extreme importance but it has also meant a general lack of base-building and has posed the danger of calling forth a movement unable to perpetuate itself.

The history of Newsreel clearly fits within this general shape. Its painful transition to a predominantly Third World organization also locates it within the continuing movement of the left in America. It is a movement which has not foresaken the New Left's general emphasis upon the personal and a consciousness of oppression. A film like Black Power clearly indicates that such concerns were given articulation within the

Third World movement at the same time as they were formulated by the New Left (with a distinctive inflection, however). More recent films like Redevelopment, G.I. Jose, We Demand Freedom and most of Newsreel's films of national liberation struggles emphasize the continuing importance of this point of view. The sense of racial and national identity defined from the interior rather than in opposition to white and imperialist standards, the articulation of an immediate perception of the effects of oppression and the resolve to overcome them, the stress upon struggle at an ideological as well as an economic level all indicate something of the legacy bequeathed by the Movement through the Sixties, a legacy whose dynamic of change is still visible in the barometric relationship of Newsreel to the left as a whole.

In one regard at least, Newsreel's relationship has been less barometric than exemplary: its persistence from 1968 to the present. This feat of survival is matched by very few groups (the Black Panthers, SDS, Progressive Labor, the Yippies--all have disappeared or lost most of their credibility). It is an important sign of the left's potential to form organizational units that can perpetuate left values over a period of time and, ideally, between generations. It is a potential that has been poorly realized in general, partly because of the anti-institutional, anti-authoritarian aspects of those values. But Newsreel's exemplary status has not been without a price.

In speaking of Newsreel's difficulty in eliminating racist elements from their work when the group was predominantly white but dealing with issues centered around Third World people, I wrote, "(Racism) is a problem within Newsreel itself and is another reason why Movement propaganda work may require more abrupt reorientation than the present organization can withstand."[6] And although the name of Newsreel persists along with a continually revised selection of earlier films, the group has changed to such a radical extent that its potential function of providing institutional continuity is seriously undercut. Newsreel no longer provides a point of entry for white, middle-class youth into the arena of political activism. Newsreel has become a media propaganda arm for a movement among Third World peoples who have long lacked direct access to the means of production in the areas of film and video. The take-over of the filmmaking process in Finally Got the News (1970) from a white Newsreel crew by members of the League of Revolutionary Black Workers seems retrospectively to have been a harbinger of the kind of reorientation that took place both within New York and San Francisco Newsreel between 1971 and 1973.[7] Newsreel has become a channel for media access to a movement that is clearly centered around Third World struggle rather than an arm of the predominantly white New Left. At the broadest level it has succeeded in providing film material for the cutting edge of a larger movement, but the shape of that edge has so radically altered that much of the continuity we might have expected Newsreel to exhibit has been seriously broken.

Just how massive this break actually is, however, depends upon our reading of the history of the past fifteen years. Most accounts of the left during this period have centered upon the New Left, a focus which places Third World struggles on the periphery of the mainstream. At this point, I would simply like to repeat my suggestion that the main line of movement struggle on the left in America may well have its axis in Third World struggle, running from the Civil Rights movement through the Black Panthers, Young Lords, and United Farm Workers to the Congress of Afrikan Peoples and the Revolutionary Workers Congress. Such a revision may also be premature if this line of development fades away as suddenly and completely as did the New Left, but at this point in time the emergence of Third World struggle both within the United States and in the Third World itself seems to be a movement with far greater potential for effecting fundamental change than the relatively shortlived phenomenon of the New Left. At the very least, it seems safe to say that the main line of continuity within the political left in America in the mid-seventies is centered within Third World struggles and that the organizational transition, or upheaval, within Newsreel is indicative of this centering.

In any event, as a facet of Third World struggle more than the New Left, Newsreel's character has shifted noticeably. This is perhaps most evident in the films' movement away from metaphorical identification of and with revolutionary process. Various struggles throughout the world are not linked together in a blinding montage as they were in earlier Newsreels; the center of struggle in the United States (being shifted from the New Left to the Third World) is not treated metaphorically, as a witness against a decadent social system whose greatest damage is done elsewhere; the individual's involvement is not regarded as symbolic protest against the quality of life. With few exceptions the films made or acquired by Newsreel since 1971 do not see the primary contradictions being made manifest somewhere else. The struggle's full force is situated within the frame, within the film, within the personal experience of the individuals it presents. There is no need for a metaphorical construction at the base; that can be reserved for a more secondary level of yet-to-be-realized unity among diverse struggles.[8]

At the level of structure and political orientation Newsreel's character has also changed considerably. It is basically a closed organization at this point in time rather than a relatively amorphous, open-ended conduit for radical energies. Priority for selection definitely goes to members of the Third World, but both in New York and San Francisco recruitment has not been actively undertaken or even encouraged for several years. Initially, this was a function of the need to re-orient the organization and establish priorities without the confusing welter of voices and interests more common to an open-membership.[9] More recently, it seems to be a reflection of the practical advantages of developing a close-knit group which can then combine to various degrees with other groups or individuals on the basis of specific projects rather than constantly altering its own membership and with it its policies and goals. As a result Newsreel no longer serves as one of the possible rites of passage for a larger movement and its members tend to have a long range commitment to the task of creating agitational and/or educational material for political struggle.

A relatively closed membership has been an important means for resolving some of the organizational problems that confronted Newsreel in its early years, but also of considerable importance has been the decline in numbers. Creating a non-authoritarian, non-patriarchal structure for 60 or 70 individuals (as in New York Newsreel's early days) is far more difficult than doing so for 7 or 8 people. This has always been a bigger problem in New York than San Francisco where the numbers never did reach the same scale, but in both cases a reduction in total membership helped smooth the path toward non-hierarchical decision-making within the group. The problem of achieving similar results with larger numbers remains unresolved, however, and still requires serious attention since Newsreel's decline in numbers corresponds to a decline in left activism more than any hard and fast decision to turn away possible members. In less quiescent times, however, it may well be that many smaller filmmaking units will prove more viable than large umbrella organizations such as New York Newsreel during its first few years of existence.

Already Newsreel's role within the left seems to have shifted towards this kind of alignment. In distinction to its status in 1968-1969 as <u>the</u> movement filmmaking group Newsreel is now one of many filmmaking organizations associated with the left. Other groups vary from the relatively traditional like Tri-Continental Films through more politically motivated but less collectively organized groups like New Day Films to strikingly similar groups like the Pacific Street Film Collective or Cine-Manifest. (Cine-Manifest, in fact, describes an income sharing plan similar to Newsreel's work furlough plan. Subsistence salaries are based on the need and the program has been successfully at work for over two years. Cine-Manifest's goal, however, is different: the production of feature fiction films aimed largely at the white working-class but with a definitely Marxist point of view.)[10] Within this range of groups Newsreel retains a distinctive position, however, primarily through its Third World membership and orientation but also through its relative longevity. Newsreel also continues to combine collective organization,

filmmaking activity and film distribution (especially outside the usual
16mm outlets, among community and political groups) in a pattern that
makes them particularly effective within a context of political organizing and struggle.

Newsreel's recent work also suggests a broadened perspective within
this political context. Marvin Karmitz argues that there are two types
of political film: "the militant film and what I call the democratic
front film. Militant films are in the form of a tract and are designed
to attract an activist audience. The democratic front film is designed
to unify all those who can be unified politically, whether they are militant or not."[11] Most of Newsreel's early films, including all of the
first ten films, were militant films in this sense. This may have been
indicative of the New Left's confidence in its own strength, the scope
of its power, as well as a simpler, less time-consuming brand of filmmaking. In any case, by the early seventies Newsreel had moved noticeably toward the democratic front film while the coherence of the New
Left itself began to crumble. Early works like Los Siete de la Raza
(1969), Richmond Oil Strike (1969), and The Woman's Film (1971) pointed
toward this less strident, more analytical direction. (In fact, these
were the only films identifiable as "democratic-front" films when I
wrote Newsreel: Film and Revolution in the fall of 1971.)

Virtually all of the films acquired or made by Newsreel since 1971
extend this less polemical and more persuasive tendency with those films
dealing with national liberation struggles being perhaps the most exemplary of this general shift. It is another one of the changes that iden-
tifies Newsreel more closely with other left oriented filmmaking or dis-

tributing groups and less specifically as the filmmaking arm of a political movement chronicling each event on the road to imminent revolution.

Karmitz's distinction is adequate to describe the transition in Newsreel toward films like We the Palestinian People and Teach Our Children that seek to persuade those who may not yet be militant or on the side of the Palestinians or prisoners. The transition has been a useful way of keeping alive a struggle to improve filmmaking techniques and broaden Newsreel's audience base. The distinction, however, does not exhaust the possible forms of political filmmaking; there is at least one more type of film which Karmitz omits and Newsreel has so far left unexplored. Peter Wollen's three-way division of political film points this out:

> I think you have to distinguish between three levels of political film, which is a classical distinction: films of agitation, propaganda and theory. All have different purposes and different audiences. Agitation is for a specific conjuncture and for a specific limited audience. Propaganda is aimed at a mass and presents a general kind of political line and broad ideas, and the theoretical film again is for a limited audience and a specific conjuncture but a theoretical conjuncture rather than an immediately political one. Theoretical films are for so to speak a 'cadre' audience. Obviously, most political films are either agitational or propagandist. To my mind, all three levels are necessary, although the problem of political film is often posed in terms of one as against the other.[12]

This theoretical level of filmmaking has not only remained outside Newsreel's filmmaking practice; it has also been more or less excluded from the group's ongoing collective study which has tended to center around economic and political theory. This seems to leave Newsreel prone to such strategies as adopting the techniques of Capra's Why We Fight series to a context less well served by moral exhortation (the Palestinian situation in We the Palestinian People) and to the kinds of problems of organization within the textual codes discussed in terms of the prison films. Although a preoccupation with theoretical filmmaking may seem academic, not immediate enough, the consequences of the omission of its consideration stand out as a significant trace in the agitational and propaganda films which Newsreel has produced.

The schism between theoretical and propaganda films in Wollen's sense has only been sharpened by practitioners and critics who boast one side of the dialectic at the expense of the other. Newsreel's own pragmatic, down-to-earth outlook has often led to a disparagement of theoretical filmmaking, a point of view even more prevalent in the late sixties than now. Film critics who prefer the sanctuary of intellectual rumination often enclose theoretical filmmaking within the confines of analytic purity rather than foster its dissemination among groups not primarily concerned with formal strategy. A distinction gets transformed into an opposition and apologists then defend their half of the equation as if it were more primary, more adequate, more necessary. James Roy MacBean's articles (referred to in Chapter Three) on the work of the Dziga Vertov group fall into this trap, defending Godard and Gorin's approach as "better" than Newsreel's propagandistic one because it does not emphasize "the 'you are there' immediacy quality of events at the expense of a thorough analysis of the causes, effects, relations and contradictions of events."[13] This kind of antagonism from either side of the real but unproductive theory/practice split only breeds further opposition where there should be collaboration. It is one of the areas of struggle that Newsreel has not taken very seriously during its existence. The continuing development of the group and its ability to deepen existing filmmaking skills would seem to depend heavily upon a serious effort in this direction, especially at this point in time when many of the urgent and critical questions of political organization and priorities seem to have been at least temporarily resolved.

One possible means by which this need to develop a more complete theoretical model for political filmmaking might be avoided would be Newsreel's active involvement in the question of party building. Such a choice could exhaust the group's allocation of time for study and debate very easily and might also lead to subordinating their theoretical work to the guidance of a party should they join one. (This seems to in fact be the case with the purged members of San Francisco Newsreel, now known as Single Spark Films, whose film on the Farah strike, The Beginning of our Victory, was organized according to the advice of the Revolutionary Union who have since become the Revolutionary Communist Party.) But the inclination of both Third World Newsreel and San Francisco Newsreel has been to steer clear of the debate about party building in favor of a more immediate involvement with local issues and community organizing. This choice to remain outside the arena of the most intense theoretical and organization debate on the left these days may well be a sound one, allowing Newsreel to evade the dangers of sectarianism and dogmatism which have often been more characteristic of other aspects of the movement than of Newsreel itself. On the other hand, it means that Newsreel is indeed largely on its own in developing a theoretical analysis either of the existing political situation and the possible courses of action or of the existing state of propaganda filmmaking and the ways in which it can be informed by theoretical inquiry.

These two needs are not unrelated. At the conclusion of <u>Newsreel</u>: <u>Film and Revolution</u> I spoke of the need for Newsreel to develop a "reality-transcending dimension" in their films in order to overcome too close an adherence to the here and now. Otherwise, a negation of existing conditions is prone to lead to cyncism or spiritualism, entrapment within the oscillating polarities of that which can only be surpassed through a negation of the negation, through what Marcuse calls a reality-transcending dimension or Adorno "negative dialectics."[14] This need remains a crucial one although the terms in which it is discussed can perhaps be shifted to reveal better the interconnection between political analysis and film theory.

It is Newsreel's movement toward propaganda or democratic-front films that makes the need for this interconnection all the more pressing. Propaganda films in this sense are often very directly concerned with questions of consciousness-raising, with persuasion, with education in order to win assent, with stating the truth so that it will be believed.[15] This means running squarely up against the question of ideology in Louis Althusser's sense of the term: "Ideology represents the imaginary relationship of individuals to their real conditions of existence."[16] Propaganda seeks to pry people loose from these imaginary relationships in order to re-establish the primacy of symbolic relationships, a vantage point from which the negation of the negation becomes possible. But if imaginary relationships are the <u>modus operandi</u> of ideology as Althusser, extrapolating from the work of the French psychoanalyst Jacques Lacan, asserts, and if ideology is what anchors people to a system of exploitation and oppression, then a theoretical analysis of ideology would be a necessary precondition for effective propaganda, propaganda which could indeed promote a radicalizing process. As Adorno argues:

> The critique of ideology is thus not something peripheral and intra-scientific, not something limited to the objective mind and to the products of the subjective mind. Philosophically, it is central: it is a critique of the constitutive consciousness itself.[17]

And yet in Newsreel's films consciousness-raising, the radicalizing process, and the functioning of ideology in constituting this consciousness has been generally overlooked. Consciousness has been seen as outside of ideology, as the pathway to radical awareness. (In Homefront, for example, Lisa's consciousness is admitted to have flaws but it nonetheless posed as higher than her neighboring tenants' rather than being seen as a central aspect of the problem--ideology's foothold in our day-to-day lives.) Althusser states this paradoxical misrecognition of ideology's everyday mechanism quite well:

> What really takes place in ideology seems therefore to take place outside it. That is why those who are in ideology believe themselves by definition outside ideology: one of the effects of ideology is the practical denegation of the ideological character of ideology by ideology: ideology never says, "I am ideological."[18]

This invisibility is a result of constituting individual consciousness as an apparently autonomous mechanism when it is in fact bound up in those imaginary relationships through which it acquires recognition and hence identity. (Identity is an interesting word since bourgeois individualism assumes it to mean unique, distinctive; but the mechanism of ideology assures that it means identical, identity between self and those others who constitute it through imaginary relationships.) As Althusser dissects it, the brilliance of the ideological function rests in the fact that "... the individual is interpellated as a (free) subject in order that he shall submit freely to the commandments of the Subject, i.e. in order that he shall (freely) accept his subjection .... <u>There are no subjects except by and for their subjection</u>. That is why they 'work all by themselves'."[19]

Newsreel has not yet shown a concern for the intricacies of this dynamic and in fact their movement away from the metaphorical treatment of revolutionary struggle which characterized earlier Newsreel films (where the "real" struggle always seemed to be taking place somewhere else) has tended to reinforce this neglect. A radicalizing process and a revolutionary consciousness are taken for granted when we see a detailed treatment of the principles and practice of a national liberation movement or when we see the everyday reminders of oppressive domination that surround the largely Third World subjects of Newsreel's more recent films. It seems natural and obvious that tenants in New York City would occupy abandoned buildings given the totally inadequate conditions in which they must live; it seems equally obvious that the Attica inmates and other prisoners would show contempt for a prison system that brutalizes and dehumanizes them. What is at issue is not the process by which one becomes radicalized but the tactics by which one confronts exploitation and oppression.

This is in sharp contrast to the largely white, middle-class New Left and Newsreel from 1968 to 1971 in which some kind of radicalizing process that would effect a positive identification with the pressure points of revolutionary struggle was necessary if revolt was not to degenerate into mere discontent with affluence and hypocrisy. Hence the subject matter of Robert Kramer's feature fiction film, Ice, was basically an examination of the questions of false consciousness and a formal attempt to perhaps get beyond it, an attempt which Kramer seemed to be saying was not being very successfully carried out by his characters who, in turn, embodied many of the common assumptions of the New Left in 1967-68.[20]

Unfortunately, success seems no more assured today than in 1968. Newsreel's focus upon Third World oppression and the struggle against it poses the question in a different light to be sure. A radical consciousness often does spring up out of an awareness of the nature of everyday encounters, day-to-day oppression and many of Newsreel's films vividly portray the articulation of this consciousness as well as show it mobilized in action. There is far less need to trail after someone else's rebellion hoping to gain emotional support for one's own discontent, vicarious identification for a struggle that in being seen through a metaphorical perspective becomes no struggle at all, only the pale reflection of its actual shape (a paleness that sometimes only exacerbates a fiery insistence on immediacy, confrontation, Manichean polarization). And yet this more direct immersion in the most intense contradictions may also obscure the still powerful forces that localize, contain and limit these struggles, the ideological patterns that work to prevent radicalization, that make of consciousness a locus for resistance to revolution. For even among the Third World and other minorities ideology and false consciousness are not without their effect.

Hence the mechanism of constituting the subject clearly seems central, for example, in terms of the degree to which the oppressed identify with (recognize themselves in) the oppressor (who collectively represents the Subject). This mechanism goes beyond matters of self or class interest which imply that the problem is one of choice, accessible to rational arguments in which the irreconcilability of the interests of the oppressed and oppressors are made clear. The notion of our own subject-ness, our consciousness as autonomous egos (in fact the reflection of an Other) is taken for granted, it is an unquestioned premise to our entire epistemology and is itself sunk down, by force of habit, into the unconscious, outside the arena of reasoned persuasion. "The ego regresses into unconsciousness; it becomes automatic."[21] Or as Marcuse puts it, "The conscious processes of confrontation are replaced to an increasing degree by immediate, almost physical reactions in which comprehending consciousness, thought, and even one's own feelings play a very small role." It is a matter of the reification and automatization of the ego."[22]

Accessibility to these premises is thus not a matter of simple argument. Revolution is not imminent, simply awaiting a convincing, rational articulation of its validity and value. The problems of consciousness-raising and radicalization arise in the borderland between Marx and Freud. Ideology supports an economic infrastructure ultimately, but it is rooted, internalized in the individual by psychological means. Gilles Deleuze summarizes this point well:

> ... it is clear who exploits, profits and governs. But authority is something much more diffuse. I would make the following hypothesis: in most cases Marxism poses the problem in terms of interest (power and authority are held by a dominating class defined by its interests). Immediately one runs against the question: how is it that people who don't really have a vested interest follow, and even strongly espouse authority, in begging for a small portion? Could it be that, in terms of investment, both economic and unconscious, interest

> is not the last word? There are investments of desire which
> explain how in certain cases one can desire ... in a broader
> and deeper way than according to one's interest.23

If desire is, as Hegel put it, fundamentally desire for recognition and if recognition comes from imaginary identity with the Other, the Subject who subjects, then it will only be breaking through this specular relationship of identity and opposition that consciousness can be truly mobilized for revolutionary action.

There is then a great need for an understanding of the processes by which consciousness can be "raised," and of the mechanisms which safeguard investments resistant to this necessary <u>aufhebung</u>. This is a task and challenge to the entire left; it is surely not one which Newsreel alone can resolve or perhaps even spearhead. But is certainly one in which Newsreel will need to be involved if it is to continue to function in a propaganda or democratic-front format and function effectively.

The area in which Newsreel's own confrontation with this problem might best focus is an examination of the ways in which film communication works to support or confirm an imaginary relationship to the real conditions of existence. Ironically, although the New Left had qualities of a consumer revolt, the spill-over into filmmaking, at least in early Newsreel, was relatively simplistic and crude. It is these characteristics to which Tom Brom was referring in his epigraph to Chapter Three. In fact, the film as hand-grenade or can-opener, the battle-footage look that was deliberatly defended, was little more than an extension of characteristics built into the bourgeois cimena: they did little to raise questions about or expose the workings of imaginary relationships between viewer and screen and instead supported a process of ideological recognition (if the viewer <u>already</u> had identified with the other represented on the screen, the Movement). And those for whom there did not already exist an investment of desire that would provide an acceptance of this kind of recognition might well agree with Richard Leacock's complaint against the general tactic which Newsreel so often reverted to:

> When I become intrigued by ... film, it is when I am not being <u>told</u> something, and I start to find out for myself. This is when it gets exciting for me. When I have <u>a basis for speculation</u>. The moment I sense I'm being <u>told</u> the answer, I tend to start rejecting it.[24]

Leacock's objection does not penetrate to the heart of the problem since imaginary relationships in cinema are sustained by far more crucial mechanism than "being told" things, but it nonetheless points to one of the most obvious shortcomings of early Newsreels in terms of any attempt to deconstruct these relationships at a formal level.[25] It might be therefore appropriate to review Newsreel's more recent work at the level of film form now that we have seen how Newsreel's political direction leads to an interface with Newsreel's filmmaking direction at theoretical as well as practical levels.

* * *

Summation of Newsreel's work at a formal level should logically belong within the context of a theory of the form they use, the documentary film. Such a theory does not yet exist, and most current theory is directed toward the fiction or narrative film. For that reason this conclusion will be both fragmentary, highlighting problematic areas related to Newsreel's own practice rather than documentary as a whole, and inaugural, insofar as it marks a series of questions which a full-fledged theory would need to amplify.

The status of the subject is raised at least at two points: the point of production--the process of constructing the textual system, and the point of consumption--the process of deconstructing the textual system. The first corresponds to filmmaking, the second to film viewing. The two, however, are not so neatly divided. Consumption also marks a point of production in which the viewer makes sense of the film; this production of meaning, or ideology, makes of consumption an active process. It designates an arena of potential struggle between the consumption of ideology (in content, but also in terms of imaginary, viewer-screen relationships calling forth the subject) and the production of meaning, or theory.

Questions about the formal implications of the film arise insofar as Newsreel seeks to establish a certain relationship between the film and the events or processes to which it refers. They once again arise insofar as the film proposes a certain relationship between itself and the viewer. Newsreel often seems to assume a kind of mechanical duplication function between these two questions. The relationship between the film and its referents, particularly its "line" or analysis, will be automatically transferred to the viewer in his/her relationship to the film. The same line Newsreel holds toward an event will be transferred from the film to the viewer and the needs of education or propaganda will have been served.

This assumption seems to operate within the bounds of a mimetic aesthetic, i.e., that if real needs, conditions, perceptions are reproduced via the codes of realism, then these referents will be experienced by the viewer in the same manner as they were by the filmmaker. This assumption though collapses the film-viewer interaction into a point of uniplanar consumption, a transfer station of less importance than the point of production (also deflated in complexity) and the context of consumption. These other locii are clearly vital ones, and without denying their importance, I want to focus here upon the film-viewer interaction in Newsreel films in order to open up some of the considerations squeezed aside when the construction of the textual system as a whole is undervalued as a theoretical project both in terms of filmmaking and filmviewing. Before we can discuss how a film proposes we make sense of the real world we must discuss how it proposes we make sense of itself.

What kind of models then does Newsreel propose at the level of the whole; what part-whole relationships come to the fore as nodal points or zones indicating particular difficulties in the construction of the whole?

The very choice of the documentary form centers Newsreel's work on terrain that is theoretically ill-defined. The contemporary writer often regarded as the cinema's leading semiotician, Christian Metz, has done littel to resolve this problem. His own view of cinema's history, in fact, excludes documentary from theoretical priority. He writes,

> It is by no means certain that an independent semiotics of the various non-narrative genres is possible other than in the form of a series of discontinuous remarks on the points of difference between these films and "ordinary" films.[26]

Metz goes to state,

> Now, it was precisely to the extent that the cinema confronted the problem of narration that ... it came to produce a body of specific signifying procedures.[27]

Since documentary, by his definition is a non-narrative genre, and cinema devised specific signifying procedures only through its encounter with

273

narrative (which is clearly the sense in which he means the word "narration"), documentary could not possibly devise specific signifying procedures of its own. It is my belief that the contrary is the case, that there are specific signifying procedures in documentary and that they are not related to documentary's occasional utilization of narrative techniques (i.e., they are not sporadic but systematic). Focus on Newsreel precludes exhaustive development of this point but some indication of the possible lines of development will, I hope, become clear. In other words, although the documentary form has been traditionally neglected by theoreticians this neglect does not seem to correlate to a lack of structure, an absence that would justify neglect. The elaboration of a theory of documentary cannot help but strengthen the context within which political filmmaking groups like Newsreel have chosen to work.

The imprecision of theoretical models for documentary is well indicated in this brief definition by William Sloan, "The term documentary is used in its broadest sense to refer to films that possess truth and project reality, and are intended primarily for non-theatrical use."[28] Truth as reified possession, reality as something that can be mechanically reproduced upon a silver screen, and a non-commercial intentionality: one lame stab at intentions and two gross errors of epistemology scarcely constitute an adequate model. Yet NonFiction Film, a book devoting an entire chapter to definitions, only repeats these concepts at greater length, compounding them with a quantitative absurdity: "its (documentary's) typical running time is thirty minutes."[29] If nothing more could be said, Metz's contention would seem beyond dispute.

A more adequate definition of documentary would seem to require placing it within the context of genre (or specifying in what regards genre proves inadequate as a tool of definition), and alongside the context of narrative (by showing in what ways it merges with and departs from this parameter). Both these concepts are under close scrutiny at the present time, narrative perhaps in a more rigorous manner, especially in regard to those elements of narrative that can be considered cinematic, unique to filmic discourse. Both, however, remain somewhat imprecise in their exact outline, making a clear definition of documentary all the more difficult. For the time being let me simply suggest that documentary may be profitably examined as a genre with its own conventions (iconography, e.g.) and audience expectations as other genres, and that documentary does not form a simple opposition to the term narrative. Some documentary incorporates narrative concepts into its formal structure (especially clear perhaps in the cinema-verite work of Leacock-Pennebaker with its "crisis structure") and some non-narrative film is not documentary (certain forms of experimental film such as flicker films). And some documentaries, although utilizing some of the codes of narrative, seem to have their formal structure organized around a locus that might be called the codes of exposition. This seems to be where most of the films by Newsreel could be located.

Development of a model for the codes of exposition would require accounting for its multiplicity of forms (essay, speech, documentary) and distinguishing those expository codes that are unique to film, or cinematic rather than filmic in Metz's terminology. The notion of rhetoric would certainly loom large but on its own, in its historical trace, would seem no more adequate as a model for the textual system of specific documentaries than notions of theatre or the novel do for the fiction film. The whole film can only be accounted for theoretically by models of the cinematic whole. This statement, though, serves more to demarcate the terrain for a theoretical project scarcely begun than to introduce a model that actually fulfills that need.

That Newsreel's documentaries utilize an expository model for the most part is perhaps best indicated by their reliance upon narration, not just in the form of narrators but in all its manifestations. This undoubtedly correlates with their desire to address the viewer with their analysis of the real conditions of existence. In practice this leads to the danger of easing aside the distinction between the deep structure of the argument (the textual system) and the deep structure of the referent (the real conditions of existence). This seems to be based on the assumption that the viewer's relationship to the screen will be identical to his relationship to real conditions if he subscribes to the argument, or expository model. This assumption, however, fails to take into account the fact that the codes and systems of codes are different in each case. Hence, Newsreel's weakness at the level of the textual system and the need to point out some of the primary weaknesses and their consequences.

Of the two modes of address available to the filmmaker, Newsreel almost invariably has chosen the mode of direct address, which is another way of saying that they have placed heavy reliance upon narration. Although indirect address is also available to the documentary filmmaker, Newsreel seems to regard this method as riddled with risks of empiricism (as much cinema-verite indeed is). The alternative risk, which Newsreel has been more willing to accept but also increasingly eager to avoid, is dogmatism.

The prime advantage of direct address is its precision, an advantage based on its reliance upon digital communication in the form of verbal discourse. The greatest disadvantage is the loss of an evocative texture, a disadvantage based on its subordination of analogical communication (including the analogical aspects of digital communication) to a discourse that is, strictly speaking, of a lower logical type (but greater order of complexity).[30] Films like We Demand Freedom and Redevelopment, the first in its utilization of music, the second in its imprecise arrangement of internally precise sequences, give some indication of Newsreel's more recent effort to avoid dogmatism by altering the structure of the whole. They also indicate the inadequacy of the solutions thus far attempted.

Indirect address is the principal mode of narrative and is a prime contributor to the creation of the diegesis, the fictional plane of reality, insofar as it is a mode that is self-enclosed, that does not rupture its internal plane of reality by directly addressing the viewer. As previously indicated it is also a mode at the disposal of the documentary filmmaker but one which Newsreel has eschewed, at least as a dominant mode. When it is utilized, therefore, its usage is within the context of direct address. This alters its function considerably since the diegesis which it normally serves to maintain is not present. Consequently it very seldom serves to advance a narrative, the temporal development of the diegesis, but rather serves to support an exposition.

Extending this point, we might say that the diegesis is no longer a spatio-temporal universe plausibly maintained in its autonomy but a conceptual universe, the domain of the exposition. This however, removes diegesis from its close association, in Metz among others, with the image track and the projection of an illusionistic universe; it makes diegesis a notion more closely linked with the sound track, with verbal discourse primarily, and the logical universe of its order. Such a radical shift in meaning, however, may more properly call for a different word than an upheaval in the meaning of diegesis where it could easily lend itself to continuing the erroneous definition of documentary as somehow projecting or catching reality. The principal role of indirect address in Newsreel is to serve a descriptive function.

Indirect address thus normally is found as a portion of a sequence and usually follows a verbal statement to which it is related. In The Woman's Film after Vonda describes in direct address how she finally rejected her husband's demands that she remain at home we see her leave the kitchen and walk down the street with her bowling bag in indirect address. In Homefront after we have heard Lisa explain the difficulties of tenant organizing for a rent strike we see a tenant meeting in indirect address where these very problems are made manifest rather than stated. Such examples are relatively limited but are more common in Newsreel's recent work. Usage, though, seldom departs from this general pattern of illustrative or evocative support for the exposition and so it is to the larger question of the techniques of exposition to which we should now turn.

Direct address occurs in two forms or through two vehicles, narrators and characters, which we will take up in turn. These very terms, however, may seem problematic, especially in upholding the distinction between narrative where characters figure and exposition where it might seem they would be excluded. The narrator, first of all, stands in direct relation to the exposition, seldom causing any confusion with narrative modes. Characters, though, stand in an indirect relation to the exposition and are presumed to enjoy a certain autonomy from it (they begin as real people who contribute to an exposition rather than as a function of the exposition embodied by a real person, the narrator). They thus enjoy an extra-textual autonomy as characters that the narrator does not enjoy _as a narrator_. The establishment of this autonomy within the film, however, may recall the notion of diegesis in fiction. Two distinctions should be pointed out. Firstly, that as a spatio-temporal continuum, the "diegesis"* is intermittent in the documentary of direct address rather than continuous as in fiction. Secondly, the diegetic plane is located externally to the film, (it is in fact equated with reality itself in most instances in Newsreel at least). Such a location proposes less the notion of fictional closure than the notion of open access to the real. In this respect documentary intersects the fictional project in its illusionistic strategies. The temporal dimension, however, remains differentiated insofar as direct address organizes an exposition rather than a narrative.

Another general point about direct address and exposition in relation to narrative involves the question of the sequence, a major building

---

*At this point, I prefer to retain the word "diegesis" in reference to documentary although its meaning must be altered in the manner indicated on pp. 277-78. A more complete theory of documentary may well coin a new word.

block in any discussion of the function of narrators or characters. The sequence is part of the problem of an overall theory of part/whole relations within the textual system. Insofar as the whole is different when we speak of exposition than when we speak of narrative, it would seem to follow that the sequence too might need to be differently constructed.

In inaugurating any kind of distinction the first point to make would be that the sequence has long remained ill-defined in the theory and criticism of the narrative film itself. As Henderson has indicated,[31] both Eisenstein and Bazin constructed theories of the sequence as though the sequence were identical to or at least need not be distinguished clearly from the whole film. No clear-cut definition of the sequence can be found in either theorist. Christian Metz, in attempting to specify part/whole relations within the narrative film, principally through the construction of his grande syntagmatique, does offer a definition of the sequence as syntagma, or units of narrative autonomy: a sequence is "A coherent syntagma within which the "shots" react (semantically) to each other."[32] He also likens the sequence to the classical rhetorical requirements of dispositio, the principle of how elements whose internal structure is unspecified (like sequences) are related to each other. But for Metz the controlling force of dispositio in film is narrative and his grande syntagmatique is a catalog of sequences constituting a paradigm of narrative choices.

The general notion of a coherent syntagma might well be retained, but if the sequence is an element within an expository whole, the narrative framework that Metz employs will have to be replaced. Perhaps most significantly the sequences (and any syntagmatique of them) can no longer be thought of primarily as categories of the image track as they are for Metz. This corresponds to the shift in meaning of diegesis and requires locating the sequence primarily in relation to the verbal sound track. Such a shift, in fact, corresponds with Metz's own evolution; his comment about sequences in <u>Language</u> <u>and</u> <u>Cinema</u>[33] needs only slight modification to apply to expository sequences as well:

> the distinctive element in such a code (that of the <u>grande</u> <u>syntagmatique</u>) is not the sequence itself, ... but only <u>the</u> <u>logical</u> <u>principle</u> <u>of</u> <u>ordering</u> (italics mine) which animates it and which assures it cohesion, permitting the images (a term which we must change to "sound/image relationships, at least--BN) to form a sequence instead of remaining isolated views.[34]

A categorizing of expository sequences cannot even be attemtpted here, but one further distinction between exposition and narrative may be made in relation to sequences. Whereas the appearance of a narrator speaking in direct address almost invariably ruptures the diegesis of fictional narrative, it can <u>constitute</u> the diegesis of documentary exposition. Hence the diegesis cannot be ruptured by its presence, although it sometimes can be by its absence. (Primarily by the eruption of incoherence, as in the fragmentary confusion of <u>38</u> <u>Families</u> or the diffuseness of <u>We</u> <u>Demand</u> <u>Freedom</u>, the lack of a logical principle of ordering to the whole which the narrator usually makes manifest.) If narration stands outside the narrative sequence and intrudes upon it or marks it off, narration can found the expository sequence and with it, the principles of organizing such parts into a whole different in its structure from a narrative whole but no less complete or complex, contrary to Metz's original assertion.

Newsreel's usage of direct address has been innovative, particularly at the level of tactical deployment rather than in organizing strategies for the whole which remains underdeveloped. These innovations mostly involve forms of dispersion: more than one narrator, women as narrators, narrators and characters choreographed into a singular line of exposition. We the Palestinian People, We Demand Freedom, Teach Our Children, In the Event Anyone Disappears, Rompiendo Puertas--these and other films typify this tendency with varying degrees of success. As a more prismatic, less fully assertive or dogmatic means of argumentation, this innovation represents one of Newsreel's continuing strengths at the tactical level. It correlates well with their concern to have people speak for themselves, to film rank-and-file individuals rather than more rhetorically accomplished leaders and can be expected to remain an area to which Newsreel will give priority.

The narrator in direct address can often serve to bridge sequences: to make manifest the logical principle that orders the sequences into segments and a textual whole. The bulk of the national liberation struggle films acquired by Newsreel are structured in this manner. In general, this function, though, has been neglected by Newsreel in their own filmmaking, perhaps indicating the lack of a firm grip on the overall strategy ordering a film or suggesting a misplaced desire to avoid rigidified coherence in favor of a more evocative flow. Redevelopment seems indicative of the first possibility whereas We Demand Freedom, with its reliance on music, tends toward the second. In El Pueblo Se Levante (The People Are Rising) this bridging function is performed by intertitles specifying the four major divisions of education, health, food and housing, but this device has not been systematized.

The narrator can also be localized within a sequence in which case his/her function is usually restricted to either the statement or elaboration on a particular point, and sometimes both. This is the predominant function of the narrators in all three of Newsreel's prison films, for example, where intertitles also serve to pinpoint specific aspects of the argument. The risk of systematic localization within sequences is fragmentation, the loss of overall coherence. It is a risk multiplied even further by the organizing principles of Emile de Antonio where narrators are eliminated in favor of interviews and compilation footage. Great care seems necessary if the logical bridging that a narrator could provide is to arise from other sources. Newsreel seems to be most successful in achieving this bridging in those films organized around characters which are discussed below.

When the line of reasoning of the narrator bridges sequences, threading its way through the entire film (often as a narrator-pretext, a physical marker for the filmmaker's point of view), it usually promotes the verbal sound track to a position of dominance. It organizes the remaining tracks (location sound, music, image, and graphics) and provides the viewer's point of entry to the expository whole. To a large degree then, criteria of logical argumentation developed elsewhere (in formal logic, in rhetoric) can be applied as tests of the narration's coherence. Conversely, the actual form of the argument (like the actual form of narrative in fiction films) may be, in part, specifically cinematic. To what degree this fact calls for new criteria of assessment must await a more complete elaboration of the cinematic codes of exposition (perhaps especially those involving sound/image relationships: verbal statements followed by image and music couplings as illustration, verbal statement with visual contradiction or ironic shading, etc.).

A few general points, however, can nonetheless be made. Although the verbal sound track may be the primary organizing component, it may itself be subordinated to its own graded, or analogical, aspects. For example, a lackluster, monotonous narration utilized to explain the strategy and tactics of a national liberation movement may do more to stymie understanding or support than its denotative aspect, however brilliant, can overcome. On the other hand, this lackluster quality to the narration served as a perfect dominant to the factual recitation in U.S. Techniques and Genocide in Vietnam. It is not the absolute priority of the analogical codes that is in question but their contextual effect. Newsreel's own domestic films, rich with the tonal inflections and rhythms of characters in direct address seem far more exemplary in this regard than the national liberation films they distribute where character speech is overshadowed by interpretative narrators.

The relation of the narration to the image track also calls up a number of problems. All too often images seem to function as visual filler, purporting to play an illustrative or contrapunctal role, but lacking any clear association with the narrational dominant. A distinct exception to this is Newsreel's repeated use of lateral tracking shots as accompaniment to a narrational presentation. From its first appearance in Black Panther (formally Off the Pig) to El Pueblo Se Levante (the tracking shot of Puerto Rican slums with high rise luxury buildings in the background) this kind of sound/image relationship has been highly appropriate to Newsreel's goals.[35] Another recurring form of sound/image relationship is that of metaphor, one which has frequently been problematic; it is taken up in more detail under the discussion of characters in direct address.

A final relationship to consider is that of the verbal sound track to the other sound tracks under conditions of a narrational dominance. (Absence of this dominance leads to different problems as in the abstract closure of We Demand Freedom where music and images both lack expository specificity.) The greatest danger, discussed mostly in relation to the films of national liberation, seems to occur when location sound is totally absent. Insofar as the narrator(s) serve to constitute the expository diegesis, the lack of location sound in conjunction with the image track works to heighten the sense of discrepant levels, of an argument operating on an abstract plane to which images, operating on another abstract plane, are appended. Their appendage is usually meant to add specificity, to make concrete--factually, or historically rooted--the narrational commentary. The absence of location sound often leaves the images freefloating, unspecified, and unable to fulfill the function for which the film recruits them.

This critique, however, does not seek to revive the ontological status of the image, ala Bazin, with the addition of the sounds of physical reality "mechanically reproduced" to offset the meta-physical quality of the narration--the hazards of the illustrated lecture syndrome-- by recourse to any essentialism. The critique is at the level of pragmatics, not ontology, and makes no claims for the film medium's "inherent tendencies," or the ontological status of its sounds and images. Given a film's own structure in which such a neo-Bazinian formulation is implicit, the utilization of location sound seems to be a prerequisite for overall integration of the sound and image tracks. Its lack of <u>inherent</u> necessity is perhaps made clear by the films of the Dziga-Vertov group such as <u>Letter to Jane</u> in which the narration, by also functioning as a meta-commentary, a commentary upon itself, locates a specificity at the level of the textual codes rather than in the extra-textual referent, the "real world" with which the Newsreel films propose a transparency or fidelity.

Characters in direct address seem to figure more predominantly in Newsreel's films than narrators. <u>The Woman's Film</u>, <u>38 Families</u>, <u>El Pueblo Se Levante</u>, <u>Rompiendo-Puertas</u>, <u>G.I. Jose</u>, <u>Black Power</u>, <u>Redevelopment</u>, <u>Homefront</u>, and <u>A Space to Be Me</u> are among those films where the exposition is organized principally or even exclusively by characters while <u>We the Palestinian People</u> manifests a distinctive tension between the historical quality (and moral judgments) of its narrators and the contemporary, open-ended quality of its characters (a distinction further complicated by fictitious characters inserted into the historical exposition). Like the dispersion of the narrator, the predominance of direct address characters seems motivated by Newsreel's desire to document contemporary struggle as it is articulated by the participants themselves.

Organization of the verbal sound track in relation to sequences can once again be of two kinds: characters can serve a bridging function or their commentary can be localized within the sequence.[36] The first case needs clarification since it can easily lead to a confusion of characters and narrators. Characters cannot themselves serve a bridging function deliberately without foreknowledge of the film's overall structure in which case they do in fact occupy an in-between status of character-narrator. (John Watson's commentary in Finally Got the News would be an excellent example. Watson participated in the film's planning but also appears as himself, as a worker-organizer. He is not only the embodiment of an argument whose integrity resides strictly within the film; he also extends integrity by reference to his extra-textual autonomy as a real person in the midst of the struggle to which he refers.)[37]

As a result characters strictly as characters only serve an extra-sequential, bridging function through the manipulation of textual codes. In this case their bridging function for the film is implicit, not part of the original design of their commentary. Bridging, via characters, then becomes a function of the editing process, the manipulation of textual codes by the filmmaker. The purest example of this is the work of de Antionio, but G.I. Jose also builds to a coherent whole by the patterning given to character-sequences without the intervention of a narrator. More common in Newsreel is the occasional use of narrators to perform such bridging although this remains an area in need of additional development. In either case, the question of tone, of the graded, analogical qualities to which the denotative line of reasoning is subordinated tends to be less problematical than with narrators. The characters do not seek or choose a tone appropriate to the film's overall design so much as reveal their natural ones, bringing with them the inflectional, rhythmic richness of everyday speech, particularly noticeable when minority group characters speak for themselves in films like El Pueblo Se Levante, Rompiendo Puertas or G.I. Jose.

In most cases then characters in direct address function within sequences rather than between them. If a film stresses the development of such sequences with comparatively slight attention to their overall connection, the result need not be a garbled whole. This occurs most often when exposition is directed toward advancing a specific argument or line of reasoning and consequently suffers from the weakness of the connective tissue. A less problematic course is to aim the exposition toward elucidation or description rather than argumentation. The overall argument may then be flattened into simple assertion (the U.S. Army is an agent of imperialistic, racist policies, e.g.) and the emphasis laid upon the descriptive or elaborative aspects of this assertion at a personal level, at the level of testimony by character witnesses as in Only the Beginning, Winter Soldier, or G.I. Jose.

At this point it would be profitable to develop a typology of character-sequences and their possible relationships, but this must await elaboration of the codes of exposition. In its stead, some general impressions can be offered. Characters in direct address (classically, the interview format) can speak through a wide range of forms: from describing events or situations that were intensely personal experiences to those that are seen calmly with impersonal detachment or perhaps indirectly experienced--the difference between witnesses and authorities. They can describe events or situations as they occurred or they can analyze such phenomena after the fact. They can speak about the effect of events or situations upon themselves or about their own level of awareness, their articulative beliefs at the time of the event or situation. Alternatively, this level can be completely suppressed or ignored, depending on the particular circumstances. All of these alternatives are combinatory among themselves and their formal combination in the film, along with other choices (multiplicity, e.g. where each character develops a different point or several characters elaborate on the same one--a difference between We the Palestinian People and A Space To Be Me), works to realize the textual system in its distinctiveness.

No hard and fast aesthetic rules can be pinned to this array of possibilities. More intensely personal testimony is not necessarily better than detached testimony, for example. Whether testimony serves the character's self-interests or not is not an absolute criterion. Self-interest is served directly in A Space To Be Me and only indirectly if at all in Winter Soldier, but A Space To Be Me's weakness does not derive from this fact, but from how these interests are met (the childcare center's deus ex machina appearance). There is not less self-interest in the testimony of the women in Childcare but the film's value is less a function of this fact than the stress upon the women's collective initiative in fulfilling their own interests.

In general, though, it can be said that interviews have worked particularly well in Newsreel films when they have been concerned specifically with the articulative value patterns of characters, especially insofar as these have been altered by the experience of an event, process or situation. This focus figures heavily in Oil Strike (workers describe changes in their attitudes about the company, the police, and the law as a result of their strike), In the Event Anyone Disappears (prisoners describe their changing attitudes toward prison on the basis of concrete experiences), G.I. Jose (Puerto Rican ex-G.I.'s describe changes in attitude toward machismo, the military and Vietnam after a "tour" of service), as well as in parts of Homefront, Childcare, The Woman's Film, Redevelopment, and Rompiendo Puertas. Its effectiveness is related to the congruence between the character's goal (of describing or explaining a change in values or beliefs that she/he can articulate) and the kind of discourse faciliated by direct address (explicit statements) with characters instead of narrators (an element of personal involvement or witness). But it also correlates with one of Newsreel's larger political goals: providing a focus on and forum for the changes of consciousness that constitute a radicalizing process. For this reason interviews of this kind often fit well within the structure of a textual system which may be directed thematically toward questions of education, consciousness raising, or radicalization.

Sound/image relationships involving characters in direct address appear to break down into four categories. Most common is synchronous sound accompanying images of the character. This relationship seems virtually indispensable: to hear and never see a character would be quite unusual; to hear and never see a narrator is quite common. Sync sound/image shots or sequences serve to anchor characters within their milieu and realize (make real) the surface manifestations of their extra-textual identity (dress, physique, gestures, etc.). In a film like Rompiendo Puertas these sequences are a valuable means of specifying the hazardous physical condition of the apartments and buildings lived in by the tenants who address us.

Three relationships are possible within the general class of non-sync sound/image combinations. The first involves images of illustration, also referred to as "cutaways" or "inserts" that serve to clarify or specify a speaker's point. Often the cutaway is presumed to maintain the space-time continuum established by a sync interview but whether spatio-temporal continuity is maintained or not, the structuring principle remains that of illustration.[38] Extension or circumscription of the argument are different and, in fact, constitute the two remaining cases.

Circumscription, counterpoint, or contradiction of the verbal sound track by the image track is the least common relationship in Newsreel. The simplest reason is that Newsreel seldom interviews characters with whom they profoundly disagree and whose integrity or logic they wish to subvert. This marks one of the principal differences between Newsreel's use of characters in direct address and Emile de Antonio's. De Antonio frequently organizes whole sequences or even films around patterns of circumscription, Milhouse: A White Comedy being the purest example.

Extension of a character's commentary is most often seen in Newsreel's utilization of metaphor. Problems with this method have been indicated earlier, particularly its tendency to deny historical specificity to particular events (e.g., the numerous montage sequences of Third World revolution, here, there, and everywhere) and its symptomatic indication of the New Left's general inability to merge the personal and the political, the continual search for a real revolution somewhere else to identify with (Vietnam, most often) without a concomitant trust in the reality beneath one's own feet (the New Left student base, which eroded, or the ideological side of one's own character and ego, which women's liberation brought to light most forcefully). Teach Our Children's metaphorical identification of prisoners, slaves, and workers in terms of oppression, for example, establishes one bond of commonality at the expense of distinctions between stages of historical development and forms of exploitation peculiar to each stage. In fact, by metaphorically likening prisoners to workers, the film overlooks the distinction between exploitation and oppression altogether. In this regard, however, it is significant to note the absence of metaphorical relationships that override historical specificity or logical distinctions in Newsreel's films on national liberation struggles along with the tendency, accompanying Newsreel's transformation to a Third World organization, to treat the personal as a valid and crucial arena for political struggle.[39] The possible uses of metaphor in relation to characters in direct address, however, is difficult to determine from Newsreel's work given the narrow and problematic range within most usage has fallen.

A final large area to be touched upon involves the question of dominants, dominance, and viewer-screen dynamics. The utilization of the notion of a dominant as a structuring principle can be traced back at least to Eisenstein.[40] For Eisenstein the dominant was the "characteristic emotional sound of a piece," or the principle "conflict between colliding shots."[41] It was, then, a formal category that served to guide film construction or montage. Eisenstein's usage ultimately fell back upon a psychological base--how do we recognize a structural element at all and how do we recognize one among many as dominant--but this level is left undeveloped. Eisenstein simply assumes the dominant can be recognized within frames or shots and that our attention to the whole can be organized by dialectic manipulation (via montage) of these dominants and those new ones arising from combination. At this point Eisenstein veers toward Pavlovian reflexology in assuming that a formally defined dominant (stimulus) will produce a specific emotional effect (response) at all levels from the single shot to the whole film.

My own utilization of this concept turns more toward dominance than dominants, i.e., the presence within communication of an hierarchical arrangement of systems of codes such that the system of the higher logical type will establish a context controlling the nature of the communication. Dominance is then a function of defining the context which controls a given communication. Analog messages, for example, define a context for digital ones. They are of a higher logical type. Although this relationship is true in general, it is sometimes reversed insofar as we learn to valorize digital messages over and above analog ones: the controlling power of voice-over narration frequently testifies to this effect. No absolute rules of hierarchical relationship can be established. They must be redefined at each moment of analysis. In fact, the work done by Gregory Bateson and others has provided a model for understanding how all communication is tiered and our own place within a relationship is keyed to those messages of the highest logical type. It is dominance as a function of logical typing (and systems theory) more than dominants as a function of formal analysis (aesthetic theory) which seems the more useful model. The former is defined precisely as those messages establishing or controlling the context within which communication occurs; the latter may or may not be related to the question of context and control depending upon the level at which a dominant is located.

There are two large areas to which the principles of logical typing and dominance can be applied. The first is in terms of the extra-textual system (i.e., the textual system or film as a structured whole plus the extra-textual codes coincident upon its screening). This is the question of distribution or screening context and Newsreel's priorities in this regard--to promote discussion, to break down passive reception of a "message" or entertainment--have been commented upon elsewhere.[42] More precise scrutiny of this area in terms of contextual typology, though, would require data of a more sociological kind than is presently available and will have to be deferred.

The other large area is at the level of the textual system itself (the combination of textual and extra-textual codes, or cinematic and extra-cinematic codes in Metz's terminology, into an ideolect, a stylistic pattern involving a formal structure built up from series and levels of choices). It is at this level that the preceding analysis of Newsreel's films lends itself most readily to some concluding remarks.

It has been argued that in narrative fiction films our relationship to the narrative is established by a tutor-code at the level of the narrative work (i.e., the level at which narrative is constituted by principles applicable across the range of narrative cinema rather than the level of the individual narratives so constituted).[43] This tutor-code is the principal means of sustaining the apparent autonomy of the diegesis which is accomplished at our expense--via a specular, imaginary relationship that tyrannizes the viewer by robbing him of his present and constituting him as a subject.

Inasmuch as documentary film is not organized around narrative principles and diegesis takes on a radically different meaning, we should not expect the same tutor-code to be at work. And just as criticism has been levelled at the notion of a tutor-code always generating the same, tyrannical relationship in narrative cinema, we should be cautious to assert an omnipresent tutor-code of uniform effect in expository cinema. In fact, I would propose that such a singular code does not exist, that the textual system as a whole reciprocally interacts with the codes comprising it in a distinctive manner precluding one-to-one correlations of code and effect. At this point I suspect that the principle code of documentary would involve those sound/image relationships that establish the expository diegesis rather than this so-called tutor-code of the image track--point of view shots or shot/countershot.

But only two points can be made at this level for now. There is not, even within only Newsreel's work, a single sound/image relationship (a corresponding tutor-code for exposition) but a multiplicity of relationships and two distinct modes (direct and indirect address); and, secondly, that Newsreel's work operates within such a circumscribed portion of the total universe of documentary film that I am very reluctant to venture any further speculation at this level. Statements about documentary film should be applicable to all films utilizing the same expository model, but to generalize from Newsreel to all similar films seems a leap overburdened with risks at this point.

At the level of the text, of any particular exposition, a few additional points can be made. First, is that the exposition as a whole, like the narrative as a whole, itself dominates or controls its parts. The exposition establishes a context, to a large degree retroactively but also in an anticipatory mode, within which our own relationship to the film is determined. It is at this level that questions about the tone of a narration might arise, the predominance of a narrator in direct address, the use of narrational linkage between sequences, the logical organization of sequences temporally, or the effect of different forms of interview sequence. This is generally a level to which Newsreel has not addressed itself very rigorously.

Second, at a local level the locus of dominance is only partially (though profoundly) determined by larger levels--the expository segment, or codes governing the whole. In its particularity a given sequence may establish a communicational typology at variance with that of the larger levels. Sequences devoted primarily to elaboration whose own context is established by images of illustration (as in parts of El Pueblo Se Levante) may be controlled by codes of the image track while the whole is organized around codes of the verbal sound track.[45] It is possibilities of this kind that make it important to develop part/whole theories that distinguish levels like the shot, sequence, segment and whole. In documentary theory, and practice, this work has scarcely begun. In Newsreel, at least, there is also a strong tendency for sequences to be controlled by extra-textual codes (dress, gesture, inflection, architecture) rather than textual codes (montage, sound/image relationships in general) which is sometimes symptomatic of a weak textual whole (Childcare) and sometimes part of a strategy to exploit a realist mode of presentation (The Woman's Film) which attempts to minimize or efface the intervention of textual codes upon extra-textual ones.

The predominance of extra-textual codes that control context at the local level is also related to the manner in which the whole is constituted generally. The whole or textual system only exists ex post facto, at the completion of a film's duration (for the naive viewer, one watching for the first time). Assuming knowledge of the whole before it has been constituted promotes a suppression of the very discrepancies that can be at work between part and whole. At the level of critical methodology, Cahiers du Cinéma's collective text of Young Mr. Lincoln elaborates on this distinction: "The first method (of a simultaneous reading) has the drawback of turning the film into a text which is <u>readable a priori</u>; the second (of taking up scenes chronologically, discussing their different determining moments) has the advantage of making the text itself participate in the <u>film's process of becoming-a-text</u> ... the work will involve breaking down the closures of the individual scenes by setting them in action with each other and <u>in</u> each other."[46] That a documentary might address us at the local level predominantly through extra-textual codes is not surprising; it would be in accord with a general consensus that documentaries capture the real, or contain truth, a consensus that encourages a realist transparency at least at the local level. What retroactive and/or interactive relationship is established between this local operation and the film as a whole only seems analyzable by the kind of approach Cahiers du Cinéma's editors propose.

One of the interactions that may be most common in Newsreel, and perhaps in expository films generally, is the establishment of an anticipatory relationship by exposition itself (in a manner akin to but distinct from narrative). Exposition's appearance is usually in the form of a tacit proposal: the invocation and proposed gratification of a desire to know. Its beginning therefore proposes an ending, inauguration stands as the marker of closure; a desire is invoked (to know, to understand, to be the possessor of or possessed by truth) which the film's temporal trace promises to gratify. If the succession of sequences and segments, if the reflux of whole upon part, if meta-communicative or self-reflexive bracketing devices fail to provide what has been promised, the film may collapse into being no more than the sum of its parts. Something close to this seems to occur in <u>Redevelopment</u> or, even more, in <u>America</u> where what is initially proposed is only weakly or partially delivered.

Two aspects of this particular and decisive interaction require elaboration. The desire to know that is invoked does not have the kind of continuous, filmic referent that the inculcation of desire by narrative does. There is no diegesis in the sense meant by narrative diegesis. The diegesis, insofar as it can be identified with the plane of the exposition has no continuous physical marker unlike the narrative plane which has the image track (where Metz situates the narrative syntagms constituting the narrative whole). This only serves to shorten the already slight distance between sign and referent in the cinema: the desire to know called up also encounters the apparent proposal that it will be fulfilled in terms of the referent, the real conditions of existence, the pro-filmic event apart from the mediation of the system of textual codes. The uncritical adoption and regular deployment of realist techniques in Newsreel's documentaries only serves to further this slippage between sign and referent, textual system and real conditions, our relation to the expository diegesis and our relation to the real conditions of existence.

The second significant aspect of this part/whole interaction--the invocation of a desire to know--involves the characteristics of direct address itself, the mode most often used by Newsreel. This mode explicitly invokes the viewer as subject. It is an appeal to reason and a proposal to satisfy reason. It presumes a center for its own discourse, the locus of He-Who-Knows, which reciprocally calls the viewer into being as a comparable center, or locus, distinguished by a lack, the lack of knowledge, which is promised him. The mode of direct address as used by Newsreel seems to fall inside the problematic of the ideology of the subject as discussed earlier in this chapter. The verbal sound track, or language, is utilized in a manner that preserves, at the level of the desire to know, the implications of the ideology of the subject that are being challenged in much contemporary writing.[47] The kind of proposition that argues that "language and metalanguage determine as much as reflect the relations of self and others, and, ultimately are constitutive of the formation of the self insofar as forms of communication are not merely part of the superstructure or the economic base but are themselves the substance of the institutions in which individuals are located and legitimate their activity"[48] has not been seriously entertained by Newsreel at this point.

Godard, in his Dziga-Vertov group films, has explored ways of interrogating this invocation of viewer-as-subject within the structure of his films. Other documentaries in indirect address (notably those of Fred Wiseman) may possibly work to de-center the viewer from his own subject-ness. What is clear, however, is that the manner in which the viewer is addressed, the precise way in which the gratification of the desire to know is proposed by the exposition is a matter of political importance.

It is a site of ideology within the text whose parameters and implications need much closer examination (to avoid the risk of over-generalization about its tyranny, like the over-inflated charges laid against narrative's "tutor-code," and to specify precisely at what levels ideological operations are in greatest force and how they might be overcome).

What is involved, basically, seems to be a repetition of the question of psychic investments which is a basic component of our relations to the real conditions of existence. Here investments figure into our relationship to the film experience; how we are interpellated, what promises or propositions are established by the exposition (or narrative), how they are fulfilled, and what investment of self we make to achieve that fulfillment. For the investment made is the reciprocal of the self so constituted. It is a structured investment, promoted by a textual system grounded in style, and dedicated to propositions whose ideology we must carefully consider.

These considerations provide a broad context of formal, theoretical and ideological questions within which Newsreel's work can be placed. Newsreel's own involvement in such questions is presently slight; in that regard Newsreel remains issue and event oriented. If these times are characterized by relative quiescence on the political left,[49] this would seem to allow space for reflection, consolidation and theoretical work in general by groups, like Newsreel, not directly struggling to form a revolutionary vanguard themselves. Once such a period of quiescence comes to an end, either through neo-fascist repression or mass movement on the left with clearly defined revolutionary party leadership, the space for theoretical struggle would narrow. The need for immediate action would intensify actions guided by ongoing theoretical struggle wedded to practice as well as that guidance afforded by lessons learned during periods of quiescence, outside the heat of battle. It would seem that Newsreel's ongoing vitality and centrality will depend heavily upon the advances made at this point in its history when there is time and space to raise questions of the ideology of film's formal structure, technology and the viewer-screen relationship.

Newsreel has continued to occupy a barometric relationship to the movement at large and the nature of its primary task (making educational or propaganda films about and for the movement) would seem to assure the retention of such a position as long as it can remain economically and politically viable. In this regard Newsreel's engagement with theoretical and formal issues may depend upon a shift in the American left's traditionally pragmatic tone with its aversion to struggle within a theoretical arena outside the context of producing immediate results. This tradition has impeded reflection on questions at one or more remove from direct action (the kind of questions raised here, for example, about textual systems or the status of the subject). In this regard it would seem that the growth and development of the left and Newsreel are bound together and that the question of the unity of theory and practice will have both general importance to the left and specific relevance to the work of Newsreel. Only further historical development can tell us how this question will be dealt with and how Newsreel's own struggle will correlate to struggle within the left and between the left and the economic system that continues to prevail, however desperately.

FOOTNOTES

Chapter Six

1
Quoted in Sale, SDS, p. 56.

2
The pamphlet is *Prairie Fire*, first printed in July, 1974 and reprinted in Spring, 1975. De Antonio's film was scheduled for completion at the end of 1975.

3
Peter Biskind and Marc A. Weiss, "The Weather Underground," *Rolling Stone*, no. 199 (November 6, 1975), p. 43.

4
Ibid.

5
In Fall, 1975 the Revolutionary Union dissolved and became the Revolutionary Communist Party, fulfilling its own call for a new communist party which it had begun in the early seventies. The backbone of this new organization appears to be essentially the same as that of the former Revolutionary Union.

6
Nichols, *Newsreel*, p. 280.

7
A useful summary of the background of this film's making can be found in Dan Georgakas' article, "Finally Got the News: The Making of a Radical Film," *Cineaste*, Vol. 5, no. 4 (1973), pp. 2-6.

8
El Pueblo Se Levante seems particularly exemplary in this regard, linking the struggle of Puerto Ricans in New York to the situation in Puerto Rico not in order to make one a metaphor for the other but to link up struggle in the mother country and the colonies through a material analysis. Solidarity is thus structurally derived rather than the result of a metaphorical construction. In general, the shift is best represented by Newsreel's selection of films on national liberation struggles which deal with all aspects of a liberation movement rather than emphasize guerrilla insurgency in the context of a more generalized notion of violent revolution.

9
Interview with Robert, June, 1974.

10
Corr and Gessner, "Cine-Manifest: A Self-History," pp. 19-20.

11
Gary Crowdus and Irwin Silber, "Towards a Proletarian Cinema: An Interview with Marin Karmitz," Cineaste, Vol. 4, no. 2 (1970), p. 21.

12
Claire Johnston and Paul Willemen, "Penthesilea, Queen of the Amazons: An Interview with Laura Mulvey and Peter Wollen," Screen, Vol. 15, no. 3 (Autumn, 1974), p. 131.

13
MacBean, "Godard and the Dziga-Vertov Group," p. 34.

14
See Theodore W. Adorno, Negative Dialectics, trans. by E.B. Ashton (New York: The Seabury Press, 1973) and Herbert Marcuse, One-Dimensional Man (Boston: Beacon Press, 1964).

15
Some of the Newsreel films for which this is true would include We Demand Freedom, Teach Our Children, Attica, In the Event Anyone Disappears, G.I. Jose, Only the Beginning, Winter Soldier, Homefront, Rompiendo Puertas (Break and Enter), Childcare, Black Power, and We The Palestinian People.

16
Louis Althusser, Lenin and Philosophy and Other Essays, trans. by Ben Brewster (New York and London: Monthly Review Press, 1971), p. 162.

17
Adlrno, Negative Dialectics, p. 148.

18
Althusser, Lenin and Philosophy, p. 175.

19
Ibid., p. 182. The subject is the unique, absolute other that solidifies the specific others of day-to-day encounter. The notion is similar to that of God or of "the generalized other" in distinction to significant others in Peter Berger and Thomas Luckmann's discussion of the internalization of reality in The Social Construction of Reality (New York: Doubleday and Co., 1966), pp. 132-134.

20
A full discussion of the film occurs in Nichols, Newsreel, pp. 110-118.

21
 Russell Jacoby, *Social Amnesia: A Critique of Conformist Psychology from Adler to Laing* (Boston: Beacon Press, 1975), p. 88.

22
 Herbert Marcuse, *Five Lectures*, trans. by Jeremy J. Shapiro and Shierry M. Weber (Boston: Beacon Press, 1970), pp. 13-14.

23
 "The Intellectuals and Power," p. 108.

24
 Blue, "One Man's Truth," in *The Documentary Tradition*, p. 406.

25
 Some recent articles that develop in more detail mechanisms whereby imaginary relationships between viewer and screen are called in being include: Daniel Dayan, "The Tutor-Code of Classical Cinema," *Film Quarterly*, Vol. 28, no. 1 (Fall, 1974), pp. 22-31; Jean-Louis Baudry, "Ideological Effects of the Basic Cinematographic Apparatus," trans. by Alan Williams, *Film Quarterly*, Vol. 28, no. 2 (Winter, 1974-75), pp. 39-47; The Editors of *Cahiers du Cinema*, "John Ford's *Young Mr. Lincoln*, trans. by Helen Lackner and Deana Matias, *Screen*, Vol. 13, no. 3 (Autumn, 1972), pp. 5-43; *Screen*, Vol. 15, no. 2 (Summer, 1974), (a special number on "Brecht and a Revolutionary Cinema"); Stephan Heath, "Touch of Evil," *Screen*, Vol. 16, nos. 1 and 2 (Spring and Summer, 1975), pp. 7-77 and 91-113 respectively; Christian Metz, "The Imaginary Signifier," *Screen*, Vol. 16, no. 2 (Summer, 1975), pp. 14-76; Jackie Rose, "The Imaginary - The Insufficient Signifier," a B.F.I. Seminar Paper (London: British Film Institute, 1975); Laura Mulvey, "Visual Pleasure and Narrative Cinema," *Screen*, Vol. 16, no. 3 (Autumn, 1975), pp. 6-18.

26
 Christian Metz, *Film Language: A Semiotics of the Cinema*, trans. by Michael Taylor (New York: Oxford University Press, 1974), p. 94.

27
 Ibid., p. 95.

28
 William J. Sloan, "The Documentary Film and the Negro," in *The Documentary Tradition*, p. 425.

29
 Richard Meran Barsam, *NonFiction Film* (New York: E.P. Dutton & Co., 1973), p. 4.

30
 The relationship between logical typing and order of complexity is discussed in Wilden, *System and Structure*, pp. 170-172.

31
Brian Henderson, "Two Types of Film Theory," *Film Quarterly*, Vol. 24, no. 3 (Spring, 1971), pp. 33-42.

32
Metz, *Film Language*, p. 115.

33
Language and Cinema (The Hague and Paris: Mouton, 1974) is a translation of *Langage et Cinema* (Paris: Larousse, 1971), published after *Essais sur la signification au cinema*, Vol. I (Paris: Klincksieck, 1968) which became *Film Language*. Still untranslated is *Essais sur la signification au cinema*, Vol. II (Paris: Klincksieck, 1972).

34
Christian Metz, *Language and Cinema*, trans. by Donna Jean Umiker-Sebeok (The Hague and Paris: Mouton, 1974), p. 201.

35
See Nichols, *Newsreel*, pp. 193-194, 198-199 for additional discussion of this sound/image relationship's usage.

36
Sequence localized commentary by characters in *Attica* supports the need to redefine diegesis in documentary. Sequences are intercut or alternate, but rather than proposing any kind of temporal matching (in fact, a temporal disparity is made evident by various cues)--as such cross-cutting does in Metz's *grande syntagmatique*--the editing establishes a continuity of logical argument. The editing relationship between sequences replaces narrational bridging devices, which are lacking, but serves the same purpose.

37
For additional discussion of this film see Georgakas, "Finally Got the News," pp. 2-6.

38
Unless the shift is made within the shot (by panning or zooming away from the speaker as she/he continues to speak), the assumption that spatio-temporal continuity is being maintained seems to depend upon the steady flow of the diegesis through the image track; but if spatial continuity is broken (by a cutaway to another location) the diegesis does not need careful protection against disintegration as in narrative films where such breaks are signalled by a change of sequence, point of view shots, flashbacks, etc. This again suggests that although the diegesis in documentary may sometimes be considered as a function of the *visual* depiction of the pro-filmic event, this level operates more intermittently than in narrative, with the integrity of the diegesis through time being secured by the codes of exposition.

39
    The lack of such a transformation in the work that can be attributed to those members of San Francisco Newsreel's white leadership purged because of their failure to integrate the personal and political in their own practice (within Newsreel and perhaps as Single Spark Films also), suggests how significant the shift to a Third World membership has been in furthering this kind of development.

40
    Cf., Sergei Eisenstein, Film Form and The Film Sense, ed. and trans. by Jay Leyda (Cleveland and New York: World Publishing Co., 1957), pp. 54-55, 75-78.

41
    Eisenstein, Film Form, pp. 75 and 54, respectively.

42
    Nichols, Newsreel, pp. 266-269.

43
    Daniel Dayan, "The Tutor-Code of Classical Cinema," Film Quarterly, Vol. 28, no. 1 (Fall, 1974), pp. 22-31.

44
    William Rothman, "Against 'The System of the Suture'," Film Quarterly, Vol. 24, no. 1 (Fall, 1975), pp. 45-50.

45
    In John Berger's Ways of Seeing series for the BBC, it is precisely this shifting of the controlling, contextual codes between sequences that makes the overall exposition on the one hand compelling and on the other difficult to analyze formally: assertions, proofs, illustrations are often a function of local contextual control by selective panning across an image, image juxtaposition, verbal sound/image and music/image relationships to name a few. The overall texture of the exposition becomes exceedingly dense and yet remarkably coherent.

46
    The Editors of Cahiers du Cinéma, "John Ford's Young Mr. Lincoln," p. 14.

47
    In addition to the film references cited in footnote 25 to this chapter, the following more general works also pursue this point: Theodore W. Adorno, Negative Dialectics, trans. by E.B. Ashton (New York: The Seabury Press, 1973); Louis Althusser, For Marx, trans. by Ben Brewster (New York: Vintage Books of Random House, 1969); Louis Althusser, Lenin and Philosophy and Other Essays, trans. by Ben Brewster (New York and London: Monthly Review Press, 1971); Gregory Bateson, Steps to an Ecology of Mind (New York: Ballantine Books, 1972); Bruce Brown, Marx, Freud, and the Critique of Everyday Life (New York and London: Monthly Review Press, 1973); Jurgen Habermas, "Moral Development and Ego Identity,"

trans. by George Ellard, Telos, no. 24 (Summer, 1975), pp. 41-55; Max Horkheimer and Theodor W. Adorno, Dialectic of Enlightenment, trans. by John Cumming (New York: Herder and Herder, 1972); Russell Jacoby, **Social Amensia: A Critique of Conformist Psychology** from Adler to Laing (Boston: Beacon Press, 1975); Jacques Lacan, "The Mirror Phase as Formative of the Function of the I," trans. by Jean Roussel, New Left Review, no. 51 (September-October, 1968), pp. 71-77; Jacques Lacan, The Language of the Self: The Function of Language in Psycho-analysis, trans. with notes and commentary by Anthony Wilden (Baltimore and London: The Johns Hopkins Press, 1968); Anthony Wilden, System and Structure: Essays in Communication and Exchange (London: Tavistock Publications, 1972).

48
Stanley Aronowitz, "Marx, Freud, and the Critique of Everyday Life by Bruce Brown," Telos, no. 18 (Winter, 1973-74), p. 179.

49
There is clearly appreciable activity with growing Marxist-Leninist and Third World organizations. This activity cannot be slighted or ignored. It can serve as the necessary foundation for large-scale, mass movements at a later date. At this point, however, leftist activity remains primarily geographically localized and often cadre-oriented. (The formation and development of new communist party organizations are a good example of the latter point. These parties at this point, are not umbrella organizations but a new mantle for the cadre of their principal founding organizations. I am thinking mainly of the Revolutionary Communist Party which has failed to induce any other major leftist group to join ranks with its principal founder, the Revolutionary Union.) This is real and indispensable work, but it is not yet at a point of mass organization and mobilization where, presumably, a single, united communist party would assume leadership and provide direction for a large-scale, national movement.

SOURCES CONSULTED

Books

Barnouw, Erik. Documentary: A History of the Non-Fiction Film. New York: Oxford University Press, 1974.

Barsam, Richard Meran. NonFiction Film: A Critical History. New York: E.P. Dutton & Co., 1973.

Barthes, Roland. Elements of Semiology. Translated by Annette Lavers and Colin Smith. London: Jonathan Cape, 1967.

Bazin, Andre. What Is Cinema, Vol. I. Essays selected and translated by Hugh Gray. Berkeley and Los Angeles: University of California Press, 1967.

Burch, Noël. Theory of Film Practice. Translated by Helen R. Lane. New York: Praeger Publishers, 1973.

Eisenstein, Sergie. Film Form and The Film Sense. Edited and translated by Jay Leyda. Cleveland and New York: World Publishing Co., 1957.

Fielding, Raymond. The American Newsreel 1911-1967. Norman, Oklahoma: University of Oklahoma Press, 1972.

Furhammer, Leif and Isaksson, Folke. Politics and Film. Translated by Kersti French. New York and Washington: Praeger Publishers, 1971.

Jacobs, Lewis, ed. The Documentary Tradition: From Nanook to Woodstock. New York: Hopkinson and Blake, 1971.

Levin, G. Roy. Documentary Explorations: Interviews with Film-makers. Anchor Press. Garden City, New York: Doubleday and Co., 1971.

Mamber, Stephen. Cinema-Verite in America: Studies in Uncontrolled Documentary. Cambridge, Mass.: M.I.T. Press, 1974.

Marcorelles, Louis with the collaboration of Nicole Rouzet-Albagli. Living Cinema: New Directions in Contemporary Film-making. Translated by Isabel Quigley. New York: Praeger Publishers, 1973.

Metz, Christian. Film Language: A Semiotics of the Cinema. Translated by Michael Taylor. New York: Oxford University Press, 1974.

Metz, Christian. Language and Cinema. Translated by Donna Jean Umiker-Sebcok. The Hague and Paris: Mouton, 1974.

Reisz, Karel and Gavin Millar. The Technique of Film Editing. London and New York: Focal Press, 1968.

Rosenthal, Alan. The New Documentary in Action: A Casebook in Film Making. Berkeley, Los Angeles and London: University of California Press, 1971.

Wilden, Anthony. System and Structure: Essays in Communication and Exchange. London: Tavistock Publications, 1972.

Periodicals and Documents

Alexander, William. "Frontier Films, 1936-1941: The Aesthetics of Impact." Cinema Journal, Vol. 15, no. 1 (Fall, 1975), 16-28.

Aronowitz, Stanley. "Marx, Freud and the Critique of Everyday Life." Telos, no. 18 (Winter, 1973-74), 178-182.

Baraka, Amiri. "Sectarianism, Undermining, Secret Agents and Struggle." Unity and Struggle (Newark, New Jersey). December, 1974.

Benjamin, Walter. "A Short History of Photography." Translated by Stanley Mitchell. Screen, Vol. 13, no. 1 (Spring, 1972), 5-26.

Beskind, Peter and Weiss, Marc N. "The Weather Underground." Rolling Stone, no. 199 (November 6, 1975).

Brom, Tom. "Towards the Socially Conscious Entertainment Film - An Interview with Cine Manifest." Cineaste, Vol. 6, no. 3 (1974), 12-17.

Corr, Eugene and Gessner, Peter. "Cine Manifest: A Self-History." Jump Cut, no. 3 (September-October, 1974), 19-20.

Crowdus, Gary. "The Murder of Fred Hampton." Cineaste, Vol. 5, no. 4 (1973), 50-51.

_____ and Silber, Irwin. "Towards a Proletarian Cinema: An Interview with Marin Karmitz." Cineaste, Vol. 4, no. 2 (1970), 21-25.

Dayan, Daniel. "The Tutor-Code of Classical Cinema." Film Quarterly, Vol. 28, no. 1 (Fall, 1974), 22-31.

The Editors of <u>Cahiers du Cinéma</u>. "John Ford's Young Mr. Lincoln."
   Translated by Helen Lackner and Diana Matias. Screen, Vol. 13, no.
   3 (Autumn, 1972), 5-43.

Fargier, Jean-Paul. "Parenthesis or Indirect Route." Translated by
   Susan Bennett. Screen, Vol. 12, no. 2 (Summer, 1971), 131-144.

Foster, Paul, ed. Radical Third World Film Catalogue. Oxford, England
   (1973).

Garnham, Nicholas. "Reply to Thierry Kuntzel's 'The Treatment of Ideology in the Textual Analysis of Film'." Screen, Vol. 14, no. 3
   (Autumn, 1973), 55-58.

Georgakas, Dan. "Finally Got the News: The Making of a Radical Film."
   Cineaste, Vol. 5, no. 4 (1973), 2-6.

_____. "Prison Films." Cineaste, Vol. 6, no. 3 (1974), 33-34.

_____. "Revolutionary Cinema - Italian Style." Cineaste, Vol. 4,
   no. 3 (1970), 33-34.

_____. "We Demand Freedom and Teach Our Children." Cineaste, Vol. 6,
   no. 1 (1973), 47-48.

Gross, David. "On Writing Cultural Criticism." Telos, no. 16 (Summer,
   1973), 38-60.

Guynn, William. "Politics of the British Documentary." Jump Cut, no. 6
   (March-April, 1975), 10-12, 27.

Henderson, Brian. "Towards a Non-Bourgeoise Camera Style." Film Quarterly, Vol. 24, no. 2 (Winter, 1970-71), 2-14.

_____. "Two Types of Film Theory." Film Quarterly, Vol. 24, no. 3
   (Spring, 1971), 33-42.

Henny, Leonard M. "Film Technology and Revolutionary Social Change."
   Paper delivered at the International Conference on Alternative
   Media, Montreal, June, 1974.

"The Intellectuals and Power: A Discussion between Michel Foucault and
   Gilles Deleuze." Telos, no. 16 (Summer, 1973), 103-109.

Johnston, Claire and Willemen, Paul. "Penthesilea, Queen of the Amazons:
   An Interview with Laura Mulvey and Peter Wollen." Screen, Vol. 15,
   no. 3 (Autumn, 1974), 120-134.

Jost, Jan. "Afterimages: Notes from Practice." Jump Cut, no. 5 (January-February, 1975), 4-7.

Kuntzel, Thierry. "The Treatment of Ideology in the Textual Analysis of Film." Screen, Vol. 14, no. 3 (Autumn, 1973), 44-54.

Klein, Michael. "Native Land: Praised then Forgotten." The Velvet Light Trap, no. 14 (Winter, 1975), 12.

Klein, Michael and Jill. "Native Land - An Interview with Leo Hurwitz." Cineaste, Vol. 6, no. 3 (1974), 2-11.

Kleinhans, Chuck. "Reading and Thinking about the Avant-Garde." Jump Cut, no. 6 (March-April, 1975), 21-25.

Letter. Allen Siegel, Third World Newsreel to Bill Nichols. October 25, 1973.

Lesage, Julia. "Filming for the City - An Interview with the Kartemquin collective." Cineaste, Vol. 7, no. 1 (1976), 26-30.

Lyons, Sherry. "Third World Newsreel." The Paper (student newspaper for the City College of New York), December 12, 1974).

MacBean, James Roy. "Godard and the Dziga-Vertov Group: Film and Dialectics." Film Quarterly, Vol. 26, no. 1 (Fall, 1972), 30-44.

MacCabe, Colin. "Realism and the Cineam: Notes on Some Brechtian Theses." Screen, Vol. 15, no. 2 (Summer, 1974), 7-27.

McCormick, Ruth. "My Country Occupied." Cineaste, Vol. 5, no. 1 (1971) 22.

_____. "Newsreel Films: Break and Enter and the People Arise." Cineaste, Vol. 4, no. 4 (1971), 24-26.

_____. "Women's Liberation Cinema." Cineaste, Vol. 5, no. 2 (1972), 1-7.

MacDougall, David. "Prospects of the Ethnographic Film." Film Quarterly, Vol. 23, no. 2 (Winter, 1969-1970), 16-30.

McGarry, Eileen. "Documentary Realism and Women's Cinema." Women & Film, Vol. 2, no. 7 (1975), 50-59.

Nichols, William J. Newsreel: Film and Revolution. Unpublished M.A. Thesis, U.C.L.A., 1972. This study's bibliography contains reference to additional, relevant material.

Pines, Jim. "Left Film Distributors." Screen, Vol. 13, no. 4 (Winter, 1972-73), 116-126.

Polony, Csaba and Felson, Larry. "Interview with Single Spark Films." Left Curve, no. 4 (Summer, 1975), 28-39.

"Powerful Film Out on Farah Strike." Revolution (National newspaper of the Revolutionary Union), Vol. 3, no. 4 (May, 1975).

Pulliam, Rebecca. "Newsreel." The Velvet Light Trap, no. 4 (Spring, 1972), 8-9.

Rothman, William. "Against 'The System of The Suture'." Film Quarterly, Vol. 24, no. 1 (Fall, 1975), 45-50.

Rubenstein, Lenny. "Radical American Film: A Tactless Tirade." Cineaste, Vol. 5, no. 4 (1973), 35-36.

_____. "We Are the Palestinian People." Cineaste, Vol. 6, no. 3 (1974), 35-36.

San Francisco Newsreel. Untitled Position Paper, herein referred to as "The Majority Paper." San Francisco, Spring, 1973. (Photocopied.)

Simon, John K. "Michael Foucault on Attica: An Interview." Telos, no. 19 (Spring, 1974), 154-161.

"The Split in San Francisco Newsreel - The Minority Statement." San Francisco, Spring, 1973. (photocopied.)

Third World Newsreel. (A film catalogue.) New York, (Fall, 1974).

Tretyakov, Sergei et al. "Lef and Film: Notes of Discussion (extracts)." Edited by Ben Brewster. Translated by Diana Matias. Screen, Vol. 12, no. 4 (Winter, 1971-72), 74-80.

Weiner, Bernard. "Radical Scavaging: An Interview with Emile de Antonio." Film Quarterly, Vol. 25, no. 1 (Fall, 1971), 3-15.

Wikarska, Carol. "Attica." Women & Film, Vol. 2, no. 7 (1975), 60-67.

Wills, Gary. "Do We Need Prisons? An Exchange." The New York Review of Books, Vol. 22, no. 9 (May 29, 1975), 13.

_____. "The Human Sewer." Review of A Time to Die by Tom Wicker. The New York Review of Books, Vol. 22, no. 5 (April 3, 1975), 3-8.

Zavattini, Cesare. "The New Free Newsreels." Cineaste, Vol. 3, no. 2 (Fall, 1969), 17.

Interviews

Los Angeles, California. Interview with Richard, former member of New York Newsreel (April, 1974).

Los Angeles, California. Interview with Ron, former member of Los Angeles Newsreel (January, 1971).

New York, New York. Interview with Allen, member of Third World Newsreel (July, 1974).

———. Interview with Allen, member of Third World Newsreel (December, 1974).

———. Interview with Chris, member of Third World Newsreel (July, 1974).

———. Interview with Chris, member of Third World Newsreel (December, 1974).

———. Interview with Ernie, member of Third World Newsreel (December, 1974).

———. Interview with Robert, former member of Third World Newsreel (March, 1972).

———. Interview with Robert, former member of Third World Newsreel (June, 1974).

———. Interview with Robert, former member of Third World Newsreel (July, 1974).

San Francisco, California. Interview with Chris W., member of San Francisco Newsreel (June, 1973).

———. Interview with Larry, member of Resolution Films (July, 1975).

———. Interview with Lawrence, member of San Francisco Newsreel (July, 1974).

———. Interview with Lawrence, member of San Francisco Newsreel (July, 1975).

DISSERTATIONS ON FILM 1980

An Arno Press Collection

Allen, Robert C. **Vaudeville and Film 1895-1915: A Study in Media Interaction** (Doctoral Dissertation, The University of Iowa, 1977). 1980

Bordwell, David. **French Impressionist Cinema: Film Culture, Film Theory, and Film Style** (Doctoral Dissertation, The University of Iowa, 1974). 1980

Brown, Kent R. **The Screenwriter as Collaborator: The Career of Stewart Stern** (Doctoral Dissertation, The University of Iowa, 1972). 1980

Cozyris, George Agis. **Christian Metz and the Reality of Film** (Doctoral Dissertation, The University of Southern California, 1979). 1980

Curran, Trisha. **A New Note on the Film: A Theory of Film Criticism Derived from Susanne K. Langer's Philosophy of Art** (Doctoral Dissertation, Ohio State University, 1978). 1980

Daly, David Anthony. **A Comparison of Exhibition and Distribution Patterns in Three Recent Feature Motion Pictures** (Doctoral Dissertation, Southern Illinois University, 1978). 1980

Diakité, Madubuko. **Film, Culture, and the Black Filmmaker: A Study of Functional Relationships and Parallel Developments** (Doctoral Dissertation, Stockholm University, 1978). 1980

Editors of *Look*. **Movie Lot to Beachhead: The Motion Picture Goes to War and Prepares for the Future.** 1945

Ellis, Reed. **A Journey Into Darkness: The Art of James Whale's Horror Films** (Doctoral Dissertation, The University of Florida, 1979). 1980

Fleener-Marzec, Nickieann. **D.W. Griffith's** *The Birth of a Nation*: **Controversy, Suppression, and the First Amendment as it Applies to Filmic Expression, 1915-1973** (Doctoral Dissertation, The University of Wisconsin, 1977). 1980

Garton, Joseph W. **The Film Acting of John Barrymore** (Doctoral Dissertation, New York University, 1977). 1980

Gehring, Wes D. **Leo McCarey and the Comic Anti-Hero in American Film** (Doctoral Dissertation, The University of Iowa, 1977). 1980

Kindem, Gorham Anders. **Toward a Semiotic Theory of Visual Communication in the Cinema: A Reappraisal of Semiotic Theories from a Cinematic Perspective and a Semiotic Analysis of Color Signs and Communication in the Color Films of Alfred Hitchcock** (Doctoral Dissertation, Northwestern University, 1977). 1980

Manvell, Roger. **Ingmar Bergman: An Appreciation**. 1980

Moore, Barry Walter. **Aesthetic Aspects of Recent Experimental Film** (Doctoral Dissertation, The University of Michigan, 1977). 1980

Nichols, William James. **Newsreel: Documentary Filmmaking on the American Left** (Doctoral Dissertation, The University of California, Los Angeles, 1975). 1980

Rose, Brian Geoffrey. **An Examination of Narrative Structure in Four Films of Frank Capra** (Doctoral Dissertation, The University of Wisconsin, 1976). 1980

Salvaggio, Jerry Lee. **A Theory of Film Language** (Doctoral Dissertation, The University of Michigan, 1978). 1980

Simonet, Thomas Solon. **Regression Analysis of Prior Experiences of Key Production Personnel as Predictors of Revenues from High-Grossing Motion Pictures in American Release** (Doctoral Dissertation, Temple University, 1977). 1980

Siska, William Charles. **Modernism in the Narrative Cinema: The Art Film as a Genre** (Doctoral Dissertation, Northwestern University, 1976). 1980

Stewart, Lucy Ann Liggett. **Ida Lupino as Film Director, 1949-1953: An Auteur Approach** (Doctoral Dissertation, The University of Michigan, 1979). 1980

Strebel, Elizabeth Grottle. **French Social Cinema of the Nineteen Thirties: A Cinematographic Expression of Popular Front Consciousness** (Doctoral Dissertation, Princeton University, 1973). 1980

Veeder, Gerry K. **The Influence of Subliminal Suggestion on the Response to Two Films** (Doctoral Dissertation, Wayne State University, 1975). 1980

Vincent, Richard C. **Financial Characteristics of Selected 'B' Film Productions of Albert J. Cohen, 1951-1957** (Masters Thesis, Temple University, 1977). 1980

Williams, Alan Larson. **Max Ophuls and the Cinema of Desire** (Doctoral Dissertation, The State University of New York, Buffalo, 1977). 1980